F. Edward (Frederick Edward) Hulme

Natural History

Lore and Legend

F. Edward (Frederick Edward) Hulme

Natural History
Lore and Legend

ISBN/EAN: 9783337151171

Printed in Europe, USA, Canada, Australia, Japan

Cover: Foto ©ninafisch / pixelio.de

More available books at **www.hansebooks.com**

NATURAL HISTORY LORE AND LEGEND

NATURAL HISTORY
LORE AND LEGEND

--->•◆•<---

BEING SOME FEW EXAMPLES OF QUAINT AND BY-GONE BELIEFS
GATHERED IN FROM DIVERS AUTHORITIES, ANCIENT AND
MEDIÆVAL, OF VARYING DEGREES OF RELIABILITY

BY

F. EDWARD HULME, F.L.S., F.S.A.

AUTHOR OF

"WAYSIDE SKETCHES," "SUGGESTIONS IN FLORAL DESIGN," "FAMILIAR
WILD FLOWERS," AND DIVERS OTHER BOOKS THAT NEED NOT
HERE BE SET FORTH

"As some delighte moste to beholde
Eche newe devyse and guyse,
So some in workes of fathers olde
Their studies exercise."
"*Historicall Expostulation*" *of John Halle,
Chyrurgeon,* A.D. 1565

BERNARD QUARITCH
15 PICCADILLY, LONDON
1895

LONDON:
G. NORMAN AND SON, PRINTERS, FLORAL STREET,
COVENT GARDEN.

CONTENTS.

CHAPTER I.

PAGES

Mediæval naturalists honest searchers after truth—Sir Emerson Tennant thereupon—Recent discoveries confirm many statements once contested—"Travellers' tales"—Mediæval natural history largely based upon ancient—Difference of aim between modern and ancient and mediæval nature-study—The moral treatment—Illustrations from the "Speculum Mundi"—Falsification of natural facts justified by the ecclesiastics—Ready credulity a mediæval characteristic—Two examples thereof—The love of the marvellous—Astrological influences—The mental equipment of a mediæval surgeon—Quaint book titles—The unchanging East—Suttee, Juggernaut, &c. in the pages of mediæval writers—The "Mirabilia descripta" of Bishop Jordanus—The "Voiage and Travaile" of Maundevile—The coca plant—Burton's "Miracles of Art and Nature"—The "Historia Mundi" of Pliny—English editions of it—Herodotus—The writings of Aristotle—The sources of information in the Middle Ages—The praise of books—Books of travel—Munster's "Cosmography"—The interest and beauty of old title-pages—Elephants in lieu of towns in the old maps—A tale of a tub—Herbert's "Some Yeares Travels into Africa and Asia the Great"—The travels of Marco Polo—Geography of Peter Heylyn—Raleigh's, Hakluyt's, Purchas', Struys', Acosta's books of travels—Medical books—Potter's "Booke of Physicke"—Cogan's "Haven of Health"—Indifference to animal suffering—"Bestiare Divin" of Guillaume—The "Bestiary" of Philip de Thaun—The Armories of Guillim, Legh, and Bossewell 1-53

CHAPTER II.

The pygmies—Ancient and modern writers thereon—Conflicts with the cranes—Counterfeits—Modern travel, confirming the statements of the ancient geographers—Pygmy races now existing—The "Monstrorum Historia" of Aldrovandus—Crane-headed men—Men with tails—The Gorilloi—The dog-headed people—The canine king—The many-eyed men—The giants of Dondum—The snake-eaters—The Ipotayne—Mermaids—Syren myth—Storm-raisers—The mermaids of artists and poets—Shakespeare thereupon—As heraldic device—The mermaids of voyagers—The seal and walrus theory—Mermaids in captivity—Mermaids as food—Counterfeit mermaids—Mermaid in Chancery—The "Pseudodoxia Epidemica" of Browne—Oannes or Dagon—Mermaids and Matrimony—Lycanthropy—The "Metamorphoses" of Ovid—The fate of Lykaon—Nine years of wolfdom—Wehr-wolves—Mewing nuns—Olaus Magnus—The doctrine of metempsychosis—Influence of enchantment—The dragon maiden—The power of a kiss—Witchcraft—Scot and Glanvil, for and against it—The good old times.   54-114

CHAPTER III.

The lion, king of beasts—Unbelievers in him—Aldrovandus on the lion—The lion of the heralds—The "Blazon of Gentrie"—Guillim as an authority—The lion's medicine—The lion's antipathies—Why some lions are maneless—De Thaun's symbolic lion—Lion's cubs born dead—The theory of Creation held during the Middle Ages—Degenerate lions of Barbary—The Leontophonos—Hostility between lion and unicorn—Literary references to the unicorn—Martin's "Philosophical Grammar"—How to capture the unicorn—The value of the horn—The elephant—The capture thereof—Feud between elephant and dragon—Use of elephant in war—Performing elephants—Moon-worshippers—Knowledge of the value of their tusks—The first elephant seen in England—Sagacity of the elephant—Kindliness to lost travellers—Ethiopian huntresses—Difference between the creations of Fancy and of Nature—Elephants cold-blooded—Hippopotamus prescribing himself blood-letting—The river-horse of Munster—The panther—Powers of fascination—Beauty of coat—Fragrance—Red panthers of Cathay—Aromatic spices as diet—Antipathies between various animals—Antipathetic medicines—Porta's " Natural Magick "—The hyæna—Counterfeiting human speech—The wolf—Producing speechlessness—The dragon's parentage—Enmity between wolf and sheep—Value of wolf-skin garments—The stag-wolf—The bear—Licking cubs into shape—Bees and honey—The hare—Cruelty of many mediæval remedies—The hedgehog—The deer—Stories with morals—The boar—Swine-stone—The ermine—The goat—The malevolent shrew-mouse—The horse—Why oxen should drink before horses—The donkey—The sparrow's aversion—The dog—The cat—Rats and mice. . . 115-199

CHAPTER IV.

The phœnix—Various ancient and mediæval writers thereon—The Bird of Paradise—The Museum of Tradescant—The roc—The barnacle goose—The eagle—Its power of gazing upon the sun—Its keenness of vision—The pelican—The swan and its death song—A favourite idea with the poets—Hostility between the swan and the eagle—The ostrich—Its digestive powers—How its eggs are hatched—The cock—Antipathy between lion and cock—Cock-broth and cock-ale for invalids—Incorporation in man of various valued animal characteristics—The stone alectorius—Animals haled before the judges for offence against man—The deadly cockatrice—Cock-crow—The " Armonye of Byrdes "—The raven—How it became black—The ravenstone—The owl—The swallow—Sight to the blind—Oil of swallows as a remedy—The robin and the wren—

Their pious care of the dead—The nightingale—The doctrine of signatures—Thorn-pierced breast—Philomela—The **cuckoo—His** voice-restorer—The peacock—Its pride and its shame—The kingfisher—As a weathercock—Sir **Thomas Browne** thereon—Halcyone—Halcyone **days**—The filial stork—The cautious cranes 200-263

CHAPTER V.

Forms reptilian and piscine—The basilisk—Shakespeare and Spenser thereupon—**King** of serpents—The dragon—Aldrovandus thereon—The dragon-stone—The griffin—The scorpion—The " **Newe Jewell** of Healthe "—Toads—Antipathy **between toad** and spider—The toadstone—How to procure it—The weeping crocodile—Cockeram's Dictionary—The treacherous seal—The salamander—Its potent venom—Its home in fire—Prester John and his kingdom—Pyragones—The chamæleon—Its changing colour—Serpents from air—The gift of invisibility—The serpent-stone—Theriaca—Viper-Broth —Antidotal herbs—The soil of Malta—The deaf adder—The two-headed Amphisbæna—Aldrovandus on serpents—Hairy serpents—The deadly asp—Monstrous snails—Snail and spider **remedies**—Bees—Virgil on their production—Glowworm ink—Marine forms the counterparts of those on land—The sea-monk—The sea-bishop—The sus marinus —The brewers of the storm—The hog-fish—The sea-elephant—The sea-horse—The sea-unicorn—The remora—The dolphin, its special fondness for man—Its love of music—Its changeful colouring—The acipenser—The loving ray—The sargon—The friendship between the oyster and the prawn—The voracious swam-fish—Leviathan—Cause of the crooked mouth of the flounder—The healing tench—Fish medicaments—The vain cuttle-fish—The fish that came to be eaten—Conclusion . . 264-339

INDEX 341-350

NATURAL HISTORY
LORE AND LEGEND

CHAPTER I.

MEDIÆVAL naturalists honest searchers after truth — Sir Emerson Tennant thereupon—Recent discoveries confirm many statements once contested—" Travellers' tales "— Mediæval natural history largely based upon ancient— Difference of aim between modern and ancient and mediæval nature-study—The moral treatment—Illustrations from the " Speculum Mundi "—Falsification of natural facts justified by the ecclesiastics—Ready credulity a mediæval characteristic—Two examples thereof—The love of the marvellous—Astrological influences—The mental equipment of a mediæval surgeon—Quaint book titles — The unchanging East — Suttee, Juggernaut, &c. in the pages of mediæval writers—The " Mirabilia descripta " of Bishop Jordanus—The "Voiage and Travaile " of Maundevile—The coca plant—Burton's " Miracles of Art and Nature "—The " Historia Mundi " of Pliny— English editions of it — Herodotus — The writings of Aristotle—The sources of information in the Middle Ages —The praise of books—Books of travel—Munster's " Cosmography "—The interest and beauty of old titlepages—Elephants in lieu of towns in the old maps—A tale of a tub—Herbert's " Some Yeares Travels into Africa and Asia the Great"—The travels of Marco Polo—Geography of Peter Heylyn—Raleigh's, Hakluyt's, Purchas', Struys', Acosta's books of travels—Medical books— Potter's " Booke of Physicke " — Cogan's " Haven of Health " — Indifference to animal suffering—" Bestiare Divin " of Guillaume—The "Bestiary" of Philip de Thaun —The Armories of Guillim, Legh, and Bossewell.

In the following pages we propose to consider at some little length the state of zoological knowledge in the Middle Ages, and in so doing we shall, we doubt not, discover much of interest. While we shall undoubtedly find from time to time strange errors that greater opportunity of observation has in these latter days rectified, and encounter many things that may provoke a smile, we must in the forefront of our remarks very definitely assert that much of the literary work of our ancestors in this branch of study is worthy of high commendation, and that anything approaching scorn or sneer is entirely out of place. Strange, indeed, would it be if the modern man of science, with all the advantages of travel now so freely available, with the microscope, with the great facilities for the interchange of ideas or of specimens with kindred spirits, had not made a marked advance, but we can never look upon the works of the greater writers of the mediæval period without the utmost respect. The common people of that day were eagerly searching after knowledge and the huge folios and encyclopædias that were freely published are a monument of the diligence and painstaking zeal, of the courage and enthusiasm of their teachers. That they made mistakes goes without saying, but to the full extent of their light they were honest seekers after truth.

While the statements of these early writers have been too frequently dismissed as fabulous and unreliable, it is only just to them to recall the fact that some of the details that have come into reproach have after all been found authentic. Sir Emerson Tennant in his work on Ceylon very justly observes that "we ought not to be too hasty in casting ridicule upon the narratives of ancient travellers. In a geographical point of view they possess great value, and if sometimes they contain statements which appear marvellous, the mystery is often explained away by a more minute and careful enquiry." The Troglodytes mentioned by Pliny, Aristotle and Herodotus yet exist in the Bosjesmen of to-day and still preserve many of the peculiarities and customs that those early writers described. Du Chaillu rediscovered the gorillas that Hanno, the ancient Carthaginian, endeavoured to capture, and Stanley encountered the pigmy tribes that are mentioned by travellers of a thousand years before. We accept in full faith the statements of such men as Captain Cook and Dr. Livingstone, and we may reasonably conclude that there have been many other and earlier travellers as scrupulously truthful. There have, undoubtedly, been travellers who have too credulously accepted mere hearsay in place of actual observation, and these, whether ancient, mediæval, or modern, are responsible for the stigma that has at times attached to "Travellers' tales": all that we are at present careful to assert is that the great bulk of travellers and authors in the Middle Ages—as in all other ages—were neither the fools nor the knaves that the malicious or the hypercritical would sometimes fain represent them.

We speedily find, on opening any of the books on natural history that were issued in the Middle Ages, that such ancient writers as Pliny, Aristotle, or Herodotus, and other venerable authorities are held in great reverence, and that the prefatory "as Pliny saith" gives at once dignity and authenticity to any statement advanced. Mediæval zoology is no more independent of the gatherings of previous centuries than the dogmas of nineteenth century Christianity are independent of the writings of Isaiah.

In comparing ancient or mediæval zoology with modern, we are conscious of a difference of aim and treatment. The study of the present day is largely devoted to the life-history of the creatures themselves, their structure, and so forth; while in former times the writer strove ordinarily after an entirely different aim, thinking much less of these external facts, but dwelling upon the value of the animal to mankind in one of two directions. While we occasionally in books of travels have the more modern and descriptive treatment, the main bulk of the writings on animals in mediæval days had ordinarily one of two objects: the healing of the body, or the saving of the soul. Hence the medical writers sought anxiously for "the vertues" that indicated their value to suffering humanity, and the theologians sought with equal zeal to implant a moral, and if the facts in this latter case did not lend themselves very happily to this treatment so much the worse for the facts.

As an illustration of this moral-pointing treatment we find in one of these old writers that "polypus is a fish with many feet, and a rounde head neare unto them: it is a great enemy to the lobster, and they can often change their colour, and by that project devoure other fishes. Their use and custom is to be lurking closely by the sides and roots of rocks, changing themselves into the colour of the same thing unto which they cleave: insomuch that they seem as a part of the rock; whither when the foolish fish swim they fall into danger, for whilst they dread nothing these polypodes suddenly prey upon them and devoure them. And indeede this is the constancie and unfeared treacherie which is often found in many men, who will be anything for their own ends. And nothing without them: sparing none for their own purposes, nor loving any but to effect them. Their heads, indeed, may well be neare their feet; for they prize the trash we trample on farre above the joyes of heaven; else they would never work their fond purposes by deceitfull meanes and damage others to help themselves." Another illustration of the same kind states that "although the mole be blinde all her lifetime, yet she beginneth to open her eyes in dying: whiche is a prettie embleme. This serveth to decypher the state of a worldly man, who neither seeth heaven nor thinketh of hell in his lifetime, untill he be dying: and then beginning to feel that which before he either not believed or not regarded, he looketh up and seeth. For even against his will he is then compelled to open his eyes and acknowledge his sinnes, although before he could not see them." We have taken these two passages from the "Speculum Mundi, or a Glasse representing the

Face of the World, whereunto is added a Discourse of the Creation, together with a Consideration of such things as are pertinent to each dayes Worke." It was written by one John Swan, and the copy before us as we write bears date 1635.* It is a good typical example of the theological treatment of natural history that was long so much in vogue. Many parables and fables in like manner deal with animals as so much raw material to be shaped to such moral end as the narrator or writer pleases.

The idea that it was permissible to sacrifice a lower truth to gain a higher one, and to make whatever modification was needed to turn a good moral into one still better was very frankly held, as the goodness of the intention was considered ample justification for any aberration from the actual facts. Thus Hippeau writes : " N'oublions pas que les pères de l'Eglise se préoccupèrent toujours beaucoup plus de la pureté des doctrines qu'ils avaient à développer, que de l'exactitude scientifique des notions sur lesquelles ils les

* The title pages of these old books should by no means be overlooked, as they are often full of interest and meaning. In the one before us we have at the top the Hebrew name for Jehovah within an equilateral triangle, and this again within a circle of rays. On one side is the sun shining in full splendour, on the other the moon and stars. From the triangle issues a narrow track that broadens as it goes, and finally returns to the triangle, its point of emergence being marked Alpha and the point of re-entry Omega. In the centre of this track is the world being rolled along by the foot of Time. On one side is a sitting figure, Theologia, book on knee, and having the tables of the law in one hand, and in the other a lantern, and on the other we find " Philosophia " with globe and compasses.

appuyaient. L'objet important pour nous, dit Saint Augustin, àpropos de l'aigle, qui disait on brise contre la pierre l'éxtrémité de son bec devenue trop long, est de considérer la signification d'un fait et non d'en discuter l'authenticité." This simple principle runs through the whole series of "Bestiaries" published under ecclesiastical influence, and, while it gives them a special interest of their own, deprives them of any scientific value.

The zoological lore of the mediæval writers was based, to some degree, upon actual observation, but was still more often largely borrowed from earlier writers, and was greatly influenced by various external influences, such as astrology. It was, moreover, a very credulous age, and men in all good faith wrote or read statements of wild improbability or of absolute impossibility; statements, too, that could so readily be brought to the test of experiment that one would have thought it impossible to gain a week's credence for them, and yet which are gravely transferred from one book to another for centuries. Numerous examples of such statements will necessarily crop up throughout our pages, but we may by way of immediate illustration quote a couple. These are both taken from a work entitled "Alberti Parvi Lucii Libellus de Mirabilibus Naturæ Arcanis," which was once very popular, was translated into French and English, and held in high repute. We merely quote these instances as we find them in the first book that comes to our hand; it would be easy from a score of other books to give a hundred of like character. The first of these would be invaluable to athletes if only it would bear the test of experience. "Gather some of the herb called motherwort, when the sun is entering the first degree of the sign of Capricorn : let it dry a little in the shade, and make some garters of the skin of a young hare ; that is to say, having cut the skin of the hare into strips two inches wide, double them, sew the before-mentioned herb between, and wear them on your legs. No horse can long keep up with a man on foot who is furnished with those garters." There is evidently here an idea that the speed of the hare can be somehow bestowed on the man who wears its skin, and this notion of transfer crops up repeatedly in these old recipes. Our next extract points to a time of some little peril, and gives welcome means of avoiding the evils that might befall the traveller. "Gather, on the morrow of All Saints, a strong branch of willow, of which you will make a staff, fashioned to your liking. Hollow it out, by removing the pith from within, after having furnished the lower end with an iron ferrule. Put into the bottom of the staff the two eyes of a young wolf, the tongue and heart of a dog, three green lizards, and the hearts of two young swallows. These must all be dried in the sun between two papers, having been first sprinkled with finely ground saltpetre. Besides all these, put into the staff seven leaves of vervain, gathered on the eve of St. John the Baptist, with a stone of divers colours, which you will find in the nest of the lapwing, and stop the end of the staff with a panel of box, or of any other material you please, and be assured that this staff will preserve you from the perils which befall the traveller, either from robbers, wild beasts, mad dogs, or venomous animals. It will also procure you the goodwill of those with whom you lodge." The dread of mad dogs, of scorpions and other venomous creatures seems to have been extreme in the Middle Ages, every medical book and herbal abounding in preservatives from, and antidotes for, such perils to the traveller. It will be noted in these and such like receipts that no little amount of trouble was necessarily entailed in providing the necessary ingredients, and in providing them at the special season that increased their efficacy. The necessary items in the foregoing receipt, a calendar to tell when the Saints' days come round, a willow stick, a wolf, two swallows, and a dog to be slain, lizards to be captured, paper, saltpetre, iron ferrule and plug of box to be procured, vervain leaves to be gathered, and lapwing's nest to be found and ransacked, are really few in number and easy of attainment compared to those required in many preparations. In the famous vermifuge and antidote to all animal poisons that was known as " Venice treacle," there were seventy-three ingredients. This was retained in the London Pharmacopeia up to little more than a century ago. The fourteenth-century equivalent of the well-known legend of the nineteenth-century chemist, " prescriptions carefully prepared," must have carried with it a tremendous responsibility in mediæval days.

Another potent influence with the older writers was the delight in what is abnormal and wonderful, and here again a ready credulity found ample material. The love of the marvellous is deeply engraved in human nature. We may see abundant proof of this in such classic myths as the Sirens, in the monstrous forms carved or depicted in the temples of Egypt or Mexico, in the popularity of such books as the Arabian Nights' Tales, or the adventures of Gulliver or Munchausen down to the fearful joy of the youngsters in the nursery in the sanguinary giant whose food was the blood of Englishmen.

> " Far away in the twilight time
> Of every people, in every clime,
> Dragons and griffins and monsters dire,
> Born of water, or air, or fire,
> Crawl and wriggle and foam with rage,
> Through dark tradition and ballad age."

The fell harpies, the monstrous roc, the death-dealing basilisk, the phœnix, the chimæra, the monstrous kraken, the deadly cockatrice, the fire-drake, dragon, half-man half-fish, the vulture-headed Nisroch, the treacherous Lorelei, sweet Queen Mab of Fairyland, fiery dragons, ghastly wehr-wolves, mermaids, centaurs, together with the great sea-serpent, the toad embedded for countless centuries in the rock, and other wonders that still turn up from time to time during the dull season in the newspapers, are but a few examples that at once occur to one's thoughts. Ovid and Pliny in their day went to very considerable lengths to satisfy this love of the marvellous; in the Middle Ages writers not a few discoursed of dog-headed men, of pigmies, of "the anthropophagi, and men whose heads do grow beneath their shoulders," while no country fair in this present year of grace would be considered by its patrons at all up to date unless it included a giant and a dwarf, together with a two-headed calf, or some such monstrosity.

The writings of Chaucer, Shakespeare, and other poets abound in allusions to the folk-lore of the time. Thus in the lines—

"When beggars die there are no comets seen,
The heavens themselves blaze forth the death of princes,"

we have an interesting reference to the old belief that all things, terrestrial or celestial, were created for the service of man and were profitable in some way or other to him. Much of the early medical treatment was a strange mixture of astrological, zoological and botanical lore. Thus Chaucer tells us of his Doctour of Phisik that—

"In al this world ne was ther non him lyk
To speke of phisik and of surgerye :
For he was grounded in astronomye."

Not only did he put his trust in "drugges and letuaries," but—

"He kepte his pacient wonderfully wel
In houres by his magik naturel.
Wel coude be fortunen the ascendent
Of his ymages for his pacient."

We have seen that it was a necessary condition

in the preparation of the receipt that we have given that the sun should be in a particular position in the heavens prior to gathering one of the ingredients, and the saturnine, jovial, martial, or mercurial qualities of various substances employed in the healing art owed their potency to a due regard to the starry influences.

In a quaint old book " Imprinted in London at Flete Streate, nyghe unto Saint Dunstones Churche," by one Thomas Marshe, and published by him in the year 1565, we have " goodlye Doctrine and Instruction necessarye to be marked and folowed of all true chirurgeons, gathered and diligently set forth by John Halle, Chyrurgeon," under the title of "An Historicall Expostulation against the Beastlye Abuses, both of Chyrurgerie and Physicke in oure tyme."* He sums up the requirements of the "chyrurgeon" properly equipped for his work in the following lines—

> " Not onlye in chirurgery
> Thou oughtest to be experte,
> But also in astronomye
> Bothe prevye and aperte.

* The titles of many of these old books are sufficiently quaint and striking. Sometimes a spade is called a spade with the most startling directness; while at others the title is a mystical conceit that needs interpretation. The following are some few that we have come across :—" The flaming sword of Justice unsheathed," " Matches lighted at the Divine Fire," " The shop of the Spiritual Apothecary," " The Scraper of Vanity, a Spiritual Pillow necessary to exterpate Vice and to plant Virtue." There would appear to be here some little confusion of metaphor: anyone desiring to plant anything would scarcely find a pillow a serviceable tool for the purpose.

> In naturall philosophye
> Thy studye shoulde be bente :
> To knowe eche herbe, shrubbe, root, and tree,
> Muste be thy good intente.
>
> Eche beaste and foule, wyth worme and fishe,
> And all that beareth lyfe :
> Their vertues and their natures bothe
> With thee oughte to be rife."

The acquisition of this varied fund of knowledge shall prove itself enjoyable, helpful, and profitable, for—

> " Whereby of knowledge and greate skill
> Thou shalt obteine the fruit :
> And men to thee in generall,
> For helpe shall make their sute."

One interesting result of searching in these old tomes is that amidst much that the world has now outlived one often finds interesting references that show how unchanging some customs are, and how some of the things that we have regarded as recent discoveries were, after all, well known centuries ago. It is somewhat startling, for instance, to see the great African lakes—the Victoria and Albert Nyanza, and others that have only comparatively lately been re-discovered—quite clearly marked in some ancient maps; and the whole course of the Nile, from source to sea, as definitely given as that of Thames or Tiber.

We speak of the " unchanging East," and adopt the phrase with more or less of thoughtful acquiescence, but it is distinctly interesting in the pages of Jordanus, for example, to find the Parsee funeral customs and the Tower of Silence thus referred to :—"There be pagan folk in this India who worship fire; they bury not their dead, neither do they burn them, but cast them into the midst of a certain roofless tower, and there expose them totally uncovered to the fowls of heaven." He was present also at Suttee, for he says:—" I have sometimes seen for one dead man who was burnt, five living women take their places on the fire with their dead, and for the love of their husbands and for eternal life burn along with them, with as much joy as if they were going to be wedded."

This Jordanus was a missionary bishop in India. He was appointed to the bishopric of Columbum by Pope John XXII., by a Bull bearing date April 5th, 1330. There are indications that there was at that time a considerable body of Christians at Columbum, but the locality is now entirely unknown. Many conflicting theories have been held, and each one demolished as hopeless by the holders of the others. His book, entitled "Mirabilia descripta," was written in Latin. "Like many other old writers," very justly observes Colonel Henry Yule, who published an English translation of his book from which we quote, " whilst endeavouring to speak only truth of what he had seen, Jordanus retails fables enough from hearsay. What he did see in his travels was so marvellous to him that he was quite ready to accept what was told him of regions more remote from Christendom, when it seemed but in reasonable proportion more marvellous." Of the truth of this we shall doubtless find illustration in subsequent references to his book.

Maundevile in like manner in his "Voiage and Travaile" gives us another insight into the unchangeable nature of the customs of the East. We recognize at once the sacrifice made to Juggernaut when we read that "at the thronynge of the Ydole all the Contree aboute meten there to gidere: and thei setten this Ydole upon a Chare with gret reverence, wel arranged with Clothes of gold, of riche Clothes of Tartarye and other precyous Clothes: and thei leden him aboute the Cytee with gret solempnytee. And before the Chare gon first in processioun alle the Maydennes of the Contree two and two to gidere, fulle ordynately. Aftre the Maydennes gon the Pilgrymes. And sume of hem falle down undre the Wheles of the Chare and let the Chare gon over hem, so that thei ben dede anon. And sume hav here Armes or here Lymes alle to broken and sume the sydes: and alle this done thei for love of hire God, in gret Dovocioun. And he thinkethe that the more peyne, and the more tribulacioun that thei suffren for love of here God the more ioye thei schulle have in an other World." We read also of the snake charmers, of the small misshapen feet of the Chinese ladies, the talon-like nails of their lords and masters. He tells us too of the incubation by artificial means, "withouten Henne, Goos or Doke or ony other Foul," of eggs "at Cayre," which our readers will readily recognize as Cairo. It will no doubt be remembered by many who may scan these pages, how large a use the French made of pigeons, when, during the siege of Paris in the Franco-German war, they desired to communicate with the outside world, and this is clearly no new thing under the sun, for Maundevile tells us that "in Judæa and other Contrees beyonde thei hav a Custom, whan thei schulle usen Werre, and whan men holden Sege abouten Cytee or Castelle, and thei with innen dur not senden out Messagers with Letters for to aske Sokour thei bynden here Lettres to the Nekke of a Colver* and leten the Colver flee, and the Colveren ben so taughte that thei fleen with the Lettres to the verry place that Men wolde sende hem to."

As we shall from time to time have occasion to refer to Maundevile's book, we may, on this first mention of it, very advantageously introduce some few details respecting it. The "Voiage and Travaile" of Sir John Maundevile was professedly a book for the guidance of pilgrims and travellers journeying to Jerusalem, but on the same principle that it has been asserted that all roads lead to Rome so all seemed to have centred in the capital of Judæa; hence his book is comprehensive enough to include the "Marvayles of Inde," and a very full description of China. The book was one of the most popular

---

* Culver is derived from the Anglo-Saxon culfre, a pigeon. The Culver cliffs in the Isle of Wight are so called from the great numbers of wild pigeons that nest there, while the Columbine, Lat. Columba, a pigeon, so named from the resemblance of its flowers to a ring of birds, is also known as the Culverwort.

works of the Middle Ages, and passed through many editions both in England and on the continent,* first in manuscript form and afterwards as a printed book. Of no book, with the exception of the Scriptures, can more MSS. be found of the end of the fourteenth and beginning of the fifteenth century. Nineteen manuscript copies of it, four being in Latin and nine in French, are in the library of the British Museum, and others at Oxford, Cambridge, and in various other libraries. In one of the copies in the British Museum, a small vellum folio of the fourteenth century, its *raison d'être* is thus defined—" Here bygynneth the book of John Maundevile, Knyght of Inglelond, that was y-bore in the toun of Seynt Albons, and travelide aboute in the worlde in manye diverse countreis to se mervailes and customes of countreis and diversiteis of folkys and diverse shap of men and of beistis, and all the mervaill that he say he wrot and tellitte in this book." The book is made up from his personal experiences, supplemented by gossip and hearsay, while at times he appropriated freely from the works of other authors. Much of what he tells of China and India is markedly similar, for instance, to the narrative of Friar Odoric, the narration of whose travels in those lands was given to the world in the year 1331. When Maundevile has an exceptionally improbable story

* Thus we find a Strasburg copy dated 1484; Bologna, 1488; Venice, 1491; Florence, 1492; Antwerp, 1494; Venice again. 1496; Milan, 1497; another Bologna edition, 1497; and so on.

to narrate he evades personal responsibility by prefacing it with the formula, "thei seyn." He set out on his travels on Michaelmas day in 1322, and was absent from England for thirty-four years, being "ravished with a mightie desire to see the greater part of the world," and in that lengthened period of absence going far towards the attainment of his ideal.

As regards the mention by various old authors of divers things that we have a way of considering quite recent discoveries we may give as an illustration the coca plant. This has been within the last few years brought to the front and highly commended as a stimulant, from its undoubted power of enabling one to sustain strength and endurance during any exceptional bodily exertion, but on taking down Burton's "Miracles of Art and Nature" from our bookshelf, we find that over two hundred years ago (our copy is dated 1678) all this was as thoroughly known as it is to-day. After mentioning in his description of Peru, divers curious animals, he goes on to say—"Some as deservedly account the coca for a wonder, the leaves whereof being dried and formed into Lozenges, or little pellets, are exceedingly useful in a Journey: for melting in the mouth, they satisfie both hunger and thirst, and preserve a man in his strength and his Spirits in vigour: and are generally esteemed of such Soveraign use that it is thought no less than 100,000 Baskets full of the leaves of this tree are sold yearly at the Mines of Potosi only, each of which at some other places would yield 12*d* or 18*d* apiece."

Burton's book, "Miracles of Art and Nature, or a Brief Description of the several varieties of Birds, Beasts, Fishes, Plants, and Fruits of other Countreys, Together with Severall Remarkable Things in the World," contains much curious and interesting matter, and we shall find occasion to quote from it from time to time in our subsequent pages. The scope and aim of the book may be very well gathered from the following extract from the preface—" Candid Reader, what thou findest herein are Collections out of feverall Antient Authors, which (with no fmall trouble) I have carefully and diligently Collected and Comprifed into this fmall Book at fome vacant hours, for the divertifement of fuch as thyfelf, who are difposed to read it: For the feveral Climates of the World, have not only influenced the Inhabitants, but the very Beafts, with Natures different from one another: So haft thou here, not only a Description of the feveral Shapes and Natures of Variety of Birds, Beafts, Fifhes, Plants, and Fruits: but alfo of the Difpofitions and Cuftoms (though fome of them Barbarous and Inhuman) of feverall People, who Inhabit many pleafing and other parts of the World. I think there is not a Chapter wherein thou wilt not find various and remarkable things worth thy obfervation: and fuch (take the Book throughout) that thou canft not have in any one Author, at leaft Modern, and of this Volume. 'Tis probable they are not fo Methodically difpof'd as fome hands might have done : Yet for Variety and Pleasure-ſake, they are (I hope) pleaſingly enough intermixed. And as I find this accepted ſo I ſhall proceed. Farewel." That the disposition is not altogether methodical is speedily evident, as opening the book at random we find chapters following each other on " Norwey, Assiria, Quivira in California, Germany, Nova Zelina."

The influence of Pliny is of immense weight with the writers of mediæval days, and even when the well-used formula " as Pliny saith," is not given, anyone who is familiar with his labours will have no difficulty in recognizing the utilization of his material by his successors. Thus Pliny tells us that many wonderful things which he specifies are to be found in Ethiopia, hence Ethiopia has been discovered by many subsequent writers to be a marvellous land, and the wondrous things they detail of it have strange similarity with those of the older writer. This need not in all cases imply plagiarism ; if a writer five hundred years ago, in describing the Bay of Naples, introduced a volcano into his description, we do not resent all subsequent writers on the subject also seeing it, but when an ancient writer introduces a rank impossibility, and subsequent writers see that too, we may reasonably assume that they have been borrowing. As an illustration we may mention that we read in the pages of Pliny of single-footed men who possess this solitary feature of so gigantic a size that its owner utilizes it as a sunshade. Hence these people appear from time to time in the pages of divers travellers. Maundevile, for instance, without acknowledgment of the source of his information, which he allows us to think is the result of his personal observation, tells us that "in Ethiope ben many dyverse folk," and goes on to specify that "in that Contree ben folk that have but on foot : and thei gon so fast that it is marvayle, and the foot is so large that it schademethe all the Body agen the Sonne whanne thei wole lye and reste hem."

That Pliny was at times imposed upon by his informants is sufficiently obvious from the illustration that we have given, but when all deductions have been made his work was a very wonderful and valuable one, and a monument of painstaking industry, intellectual power and enormous erudition. The great naturalist Cuvier, no mean authority, calls it "one of the most precious monuments that have come down to us from ancient times." Buffon, no mean authority either, writes : "It is, so to say, a compilation from all that had been written before his time : a record of all that was excellent or useful : but his record has in it features so grand, this compilation contains matter grouped in a manner so novel, that it is preferable to most of the original works that treat upon similar subjects."

Seeing that it is the *fons et origo* of so much subsequent work, we may well devote some little space to its consideration, for mediæval natural history is largely Pliny, either frankly acknowledged, boldly appropriated without acknowledgment, or at least the nucleus around which other observations of more or less value are gathered.

Pliny's book is of the most comprehensive character, and even his table of contents runs into many pages. This table would appear at the time of its issue to have been almost a literary curiosity, as he prefaces it by saying that "as you* should be spared as far as possible from all trouble, I have subjoined the contents of the following books, and have used my best endeavours to prevent your being obliged to read them all through. And this, which was done for your benefit, will also serve the same purpose for others, so that anyone may search for what he wishes, and may know where to find it. This has been done before amongst us by Valerius Soranus, in his book which he entitled 'On Mysteries.'"

The following shortened list gives a notion of the general character of the various sections of this *magnum opus*. After the first book, which is occupied entirely by the elaborate preface to the Emperor, the author plunges at once into his subject, and devotes the second book to a general treatise on the elements and on the world and the heavenly bodies. The third and fourth books describe the great bays of Europe, while the fifth and sixth deal with Africa and Asia respectively. The seventh book is entirely devoted to man, and the eighth and ninth are on

* The Emperor Titus Vespasian, to whom the book was dedicated.

land and aquatic animals. The tenth treats of birds, and the eleventh of insects. The attention of the author and reader is then turned to matters botanical, and the twelfth book dwells upon odoriferous plants. The thirteenth is occupied with the consideration of the various exotic trees then known, while the fourteenth is devoted entirely to the vine, and the fifteenth to fruit trees generally. In the next book, the sixteenth, the author passes to a consideration of the various kinds of forest trees, and in the following, the seventeenth, to the plants raised in nurseries and gardens. The eighteenth book deals with the cultivation of corn and the general pursuits of the husbandman. The treatise then turns to economic and medicinal considerations, section nineteen taking up flax and other commercial plants, and twenty dealing with the herbs cultivated for food or medicine. The twenty-first and twenty-second are somewhat æsthetic, and dwell upon the flowers and plants proper for garlands. The twenty-third and twenty-fourth and twenty-fifth are devoted to the medicines made from cultivated trees, forest trees, and wild plants respectively. The twenty-sixth deals with new diseases and their appropriate treatment by herbs, and the twenty-seventh is a continuation and amplification of the twentieth. The twenty-eighth and twenty-ninth are devoted to the medicines derived from animals, and the thirtieth chapter deals with magic and the proper medicines for various parts of the body. The thirty-first and thirty-second sections are given up to the economic uses of various aquatic animals, one being entirely devoted to their medicinal value, and the next to their general commercial adaptability. The remaining chapters deal with the mineral kingdom, the thirty-third chapter being given up wholly to gold and silver, and the thirty-fourth to lead and copper. The thirty-fifth division is given up to pictures and colours and the painters and users thereof. The thirty-sixth chapter is occupied with marbles and various kinds of stone, while the concluding section deals with gems.

It will thus be seen that the work is of the most comprehensive character, and however far the world may since have travelled, and in its revolutions disproved much that when this book was written was held to be undoubted, the book nevertheless remains a noble monument of the zeal, energy, and thirst after knowledge of its author.

Caius Plinius Secundus, ordinarily called the Elder to distinguish him from his nephew, who was also an eminent man of letters, was born at Verona or Como, A.D. 23. As the son of a Roman of noble family, he was early devoted to a military career, and spent a considerable portion of his life in the army, where he gained distinction in various campaigns; and on his retirement from actual service, was appointed by the Emperor Procurator of Spain. Though much occupied in public work he was an enthusiastic student, and devoted all his intervals of relaxation to literature. During dinner he was either being read to or was busily engaged in taking notes, and when travelling his secretary was in constant attendance upon him. Even while enjoying his bath, he was busy dictating or imbibing knowledge. He was a tremendous worker, and besides the "Natural History," wrote a voluminous treatise on the German Campaign and various other books. He fell a victim to his love of science, as while commanding the fleet he was witness of the great eruption of Vesuvius that destroyed Pompeii and Herculaneum, and while making observations ashore he was overwhelmed in thick sulphurous vapour.

Pliny had an intense love of nature, and to his own researches he added those of a great body of other observers, sifting with infinite patience from their labours whatever he deemed of value, and accumulating vast stores of observation. That he at times drew false conclusions is sufficiently evident, but it is clearly not just to apply a nineteenth-century standard to his labours. He gave credence to many stories that have since been proved erroneous, but he always honestly strove after truth. When he tells us, for example, that the appearance of an owl is a portent of misfortune, he adds, " but I myself know that it hath perched upon many houses of private men and yet hath no evil followed."

At the beginning of each book Pliny is careful to give the names of the authors that he has consulted for it.* As the subjects that he treats of are very varied the total list of authorities is very large. Some of the names, such as Virgil, Archimedes, and others, are those of men still held in reverence; while many are naturally now but little known, their works having perished. As an illustration of the thoroughness of Pliny in the matter we will give an illustrative list—that which precedes his eighth book, dealing with land animals. He divides his lists always into two sections, and commences with the authors of his own country. These in this particular instance are Mutianus, Procilius, Verrius Flaccus, L. Piso, Cornelius Valerianus, Cato the Censor, Fenestella, Trogus, Actius, Columella, Virgil, Varro, Metellus Scipio, Cornelius Celsus, Nigidius, Trebius Niger, Pomponius Mela, and Manlius Sura. His foreign authorities are considerably more numerous, and are, naturally, most of them Greek writers: Polybius, Onesicritus, Isidorus, Antipater, Aristotle, Demetrius, Democritus, Theophrastus, Euanthes, Hiero, Duris, Ctesias, Philistus, Architas, Philarchus, Amphilochus the Athenian, Anaxipolis the Thasian, Apollodorus of Lemnos, Aristophanes the Milesian, Antigonus the Cymæan, and twenty-three others, whom it is needless to add to the

* "I conceive it," he says, "to be courteous, and to indicate an ingenious modesty, to acknowledge the source whence we have derived assistance, and not act as most of those have done whom I have examined. For I must inform you that in consulting various authors I have discovered that some of the most grave and of the latest writers, have transcribed word for word from former works without making any acknowledgment."

list, as it is already quite long enough to illustrate the care with which Pliny fortified his own knowledge with the best aid that he could procure.

Though, doubtless, in some cases, the bearers of these names were travellers and others who contributed but one or two items to the store of knowledge, the greater portion of the names are those of men who, to the best of their ability, were endeavouring to penetrate the secrets of nature. It is a striking fact that at this early period there should be such a body of scientific opinion to draw upon. Pliny tells us that he has dealt with twenty thousand subjects and that this has necessitated the perusal of over two thousand books.

Though the quaintness of some of the ideas we encounter in Pliny raises a smile, yet the real wonder is that he was able to produce a book so excellent, and the more one reads of it the more this truth is impressed upon one's mind. In many of his ideas he appears to have been far in advance of his age. Thus he distinctly declares that the world is round, and gives lucid reasons for his statement, and in an age of abounding polytheism, when temples innumerable each enshrined the image of some deity, he had the courage to declare that " to seek after any shape of God and to assign a form or image to him is a proof of man's folly. For God, wheresoever he be and in what part soever resident, all sense he is, all sight, all hearing. He is the whole of the life and of the soul, and to believe that there be gods innumerable, and those according to man's virtues, as chastity, concord, understanding, hope, honour, clemency, faith, these conceits render men's negligence the greater."

The unchanging nature of the East that we have already seen illustrated by extracts from mediæval writers is even visible in the work of this author of nearly two thousand years ago, for Pliny mentions the people called Seres, beyond Scythia, who fly the company of other people and who are famous for the fine silk that their woods yield. There can be no reasonable doubt but that these exclusive folk were the Chinese. He tells us that they collect this silk from the leaves of the trees, and, having steeped it in water, card it: it being a very pardonable error to conclude that this silk was the product of the tree itself rather than of the silkworm that spun its cocoon amongst its foliage. The men have feet of natural size, while the women's are so small that Pliny's informant described them as ostrich-footed. Here we can scarcely doubt that the strange custom of the Chinese in binding up the feet of the women is referred to, and granting this it is an interesting proof of the great antiquity of this barbarous proceeding.

In India, too, it was reported to Pliny that there were certain philosophers who from sunrise to sunset persevere in gazing upon the sun without once removing their eyes, and from morn to eve stand upon one leg on the burning sand. It is remarkable to observe how exactly these

austerities and others of like severity and
uselessness are still practised by the Fakirs of
India. He tells us too of others who had
strange influence over venomous serpents,
doubtless the snake-charmers whose descendants
still exhibit their skill, and refers to the people
of India hunting and taming the elephants and
using them as beasts of burden, as valuable aids
to locomotion and for purposes of war.

Pliny's book has gone through many editions
and translations. Of these we need but mention
that of Dalecamp in 1599 ; De Laet in 1635,
Gronovius, 1669 ; Pinet, 1566 ; and Poinsinet de
Sivri, 1771. An English version of delightful
quaintness of language and expression is the
translation issued by Dr. Philemon Holland in
the year 1601. He is the only writer who has
given a complete rendering of Pliny's book in
English.* Bostock also, in 1828, began a
translation and issued the first and thirty-third
books as a specimen of a proposed rendering of
the whole work. His death prevented the
accomplishment of the task. The reader in
subsequent passages will readily detect for
himself from which source any quotation we
give is derived, as the diction of Holland is far

---

* He only used one pen throughout, a circumstance which
he deemed sufficiently remarkable to be celebrated in these
lines which are prefixed to his book :—

"With one sole pen I wrote this book,
   Made of a grey goose quill.
 A pen it was when I it took,
   A pen I leave it still."

more quaint and old-fashioned than that of the later translator.

Several other writers of antiquity influenced the mediæval authors, but it is scarcely necessary to detail their labours at any length, since if they lived before Pliny he borrowed from them, and if they lived afterwards they borrowed from him, so that we practically in Pliny get the pith and cream of all. Herodotus, the "Historiarum parens," as Cicero terms him, was, we read, scarcely a historian, but one finds divers passages from time to time in his descriptions of Egypt and other lands that throw an interesting sidelight on the natural history of the country under consideration, and these have a certain value. A writer of greater direct importance is Aristotle, one of the most illustrious naturalists of antiquity. It will be remembered that his works supplanted the love of gold, of sumptuous apparel, even the charms of music in the breast of Chaucer's philosopher, and formed an all-sufficient solace for a light cash box, a sparse wardrobe, and the missing "fidel." The passage is interesting as it indicates the repute in which the works of the ancient writer were held in the days of the poet :—

> "For him was lever han at his beddes hed
> A twenty bokes, clothed in black and red,
> Of Aristotle, and his philosophie,
> Than robes rich, or fidel, or sautrie,
> But all be that he was a philosopher
> Yet hadde he but litel gold in cofre."

Aristotle had very exceptional opportunities of acquiring knowledge, as his royal patron and friend, the potent Alexander the Great, was able and willing to afford him aid that was invaluable to him. Thousands of men, huntsmen, fishermen, soldiers in distant garrisons of his far-stretching realm, by royal command were instructed to keep a keen outlook, and to forward to Aristotle anything that was curious or rare, or to procure him, if possible, any specimen he desired to possess. His book "De animalibus," though naturally not free from a certain amount of error, and the intrusion of second-hand hearsay, is a mine of industry and research and not unworthy of the special opportunities that gave it birth.

In the study of our subject during the Middle Ages, several sources of information are open to us. Of books on natural history, pure and simple, there are none; their day was not yet. The love of nature for its own sake was a later birth, but the books of travels often detail the zoology and botany of the lands journeyed through. Then there are the medical books, containing the most extraordinary remedies, or perhaps it would be safer to say, prescriptions, for the ills of suffering humanity, and which more or less fully describe the source and origin of the various ingredients in their gruesome pharmacopœia, and with these we may class the books on social economics, dealing with gastronomy, gardening, the distillation of essences, and so forth, and which necessarily deal in some degree with the life-history of the materials that are introduced. In addition to these we have what are termed bestiaries, books that treat the animals and plants as so many lay figures to be clothed upon with any moral that, with often scant regard to facts, will serve to enforce a dogma. To these must be added the armories or books on heraldry, where the lions, elephants, bears, and other devices of blazonry, are often very quaintly and graphically described for the benefit of those, doubtless a considerable majority, to whom they were little more than a name; or to whom, if they had seen them at the Tower of London in the royal collection, further information on creatures so strange was of great interest. In addition to these sources of instruction of more or less value we may fitly refer to the writings of the poets, since in the pages of Chaucer, Shakespeare and the lesser lights of poesy are abundant allusions to the beliefs of the time, in this as in other directions, and many of these are of great interest and value.

> " Oh for a booke and a shady nooke
> Eyther in doore or out,
> With the greene leaves whispering overhead,
> Or the streete cryes all about;
> Where I maie reade all at my ease,
> Both of the newe and old,
> For a jollie goode booke whereon to looke
> Is better to me than golde."*

---

* " I would rather be a poor man in a garret with plenty of books than a king who did not love reading."—*Macaulay*. Sir John Herschell in like manner tells us—" Were I to pay for a taste that should stand me in stead under every variety of circumstances, and be a source of happiness and cheerfulness to me during life, and a shield against its ills, however things might go amiss and the world frown upon me, it would be a taste for reading. Give a man this taste and the means of

The praise of good books. 33

It must surely have been of some quaint book of travel that this old English song-writer was

FIG. 1.

thinking when he thus discoursed on the pleasant debt we owe to books, when in the stirring days gratifying it, and you can hardly fail of making him a happy man; unless, indeed, you put into his hands a most perverse selection of books. You place him in contact with the best society in every period of history—with the wisest, the wittiest, the tenderest, the bravest, and the purest characters who have adorned humanity. You make him a denizen of all nations, a contemporary of all ages. The world has been created for him." But we must bear in mind, while we subscribe to the dictum of Carlyle, " Of all things which men do or make here below, by far the most momentous, wonderful, and worthy are the things we call books," the wise line of Shakespeare: " Learning is but an adjunct to oneself," lest haply we be classed with " the bookful blockhead " of Pope—ignorantly read, " with loads of learned lumber in his head."

of Frobisher, Drake and Raleigh, men's minds were expanding to all sorts of possibilities, and they read with avidity of the Eldorado of the west, and of the headless men, or those whose heads do grow beneath their shoulders. Such as were in all good faith held to be fairly represented by our illustration (fig. 1) from one of these old books. The writers of the day described too the wondrous creatures that peopled the torrid plains of Africa or India, or the lands of Prester John, or far Cathay; where so many things were new and true and wonderful that it seemed as if all things were possible, and a mermaid no more an unreasonable probability than a milkmaid.

Of Maundevile we have already made mention. It would be manifestly undesirable to dwell at the length that the ample materials to hand would permit. We will mention but one or two other books as samples of the bulk.

Munster's "Cosmography" is a book that all bibliophiles whose tastes incline in this direction should see. Sebastian Munster, the learned author, died of the plague at Basel in the year 1552, at the comparatively early age of sixty-three, almost immediately after he had completed his book. The copy before us we see was published at Basel in the year of his death. Everyone consulting such a book should always begin at the very beginning, as the old titles, as we have already indicated, are often full of interest and beauty. In the instance before us the centre of the page is filled up with the title, given with that elaborate fulness that is so characteristic of early books. The upper part of the page is devoted to the secular and spiritual princes of the Roman Empire, the former crowned, the latter wearing their mitres, and each having a shield of arms. Amongst the secular princes we find those of Cyprus, Ungar, Sicilia, Bohem, Neapol and Polon. The sides of the page are taken up with panels containing the rulers of Turkey, Tartary and such-like outlandish places, and at the bottom is a very comprehensive picture indeed. In the foreground, resting against a tree, is a man in grievous extremity, naked and forlorn, and to him advances a warlike savage with bow and arrow and, worse still, a manifest inclination to use them to the detriment of the traveller. Behind the prostrate figure is an elephant, while in rear of the savage are three trees, marked respectively Piper, Muscata and Gariofili. In the background is a river, or arm of the sea, from which dolphins emerge, and on the further shore are two towns and a range of mountains.

The book is very freely illustrated with maps, portraits, pictures of towns, animals, plants, and so forth. Some of the figures are really very good; there is one of the Moufflon, for instance, that is full of character and truth, while others are hopelessly wrong. The same pictures come over and over again at intervals in the text, thus a man with a great sword going to chop off the head of a man kneeling before him, stands for martyrdom or the doom of the traitor, and re-appears impartially on all occasions where the

3 *

text suggests such ideas. The same battle-scene often crops up to illustrate the various conflicts described, and there is a standard figure of a bishop with mitre and pastoral crook that serves as a portrait of divers ecclesiastics. The same lantern tower that does duty for Lucerne re-appears for Alexandria. It argues a quaint simplicity all round when the author could gravely furnish and his readers as gravely accept these few stock illustrations for all the varying conditions.

It is very interesting to see that in the map of Africa* the Nile takes its rise from three large lakes far south of the equator, but the map of the world is an extraordinary production, and shows, sources of the Nile notwithstanding, a strange ignorance of elementary facts. The South Atlantic is almost entirely filled up from Brazil to Africa by a great sea monster. In the map of Africa a gigantic elephant is introduced, a proceeding that was rather popular with these

---

* There are separate maps for the leading countries, giving towns, rivers, forests, mountains, and other features. The towns are not only named, but have actual buildings represented. We notice that in the map of Germany "Holand" and "Flandria" are at the bottom right-hand corner, but this arises from the reversal of the whole thing, the north being at the bottom of the page instead of the top. It is as Germany would look if we imagine the point of view in Southern Denmark. Italy in the same way shows Venice at the bottom of the map and Sicily at the top. In the description of Spain the so-called pillars of Hercules are treated as two actual pillars and in the illustration look very like two pawns from a set of chessmen.

older writers, and which is satirized in the well-known lines of Swift—

> "So geographers, in Afric maps,
> With savage pictures fill their gaps,
> And o'er inhabitable downs
> Place elephants for want of towns."

Even in the days of Plutarch a kindred device was not unknown, as we find him in the "Theseus" writing, "as geographers crowd into the edges of their maps parts of the world which they do not know about, adding notes in the margin to the effect that beyond this lies nothing but sandy deserts full of wild beasts and unapproachable bogs." Elsewhere in this map of Africa we see trees with enormous parrots (miles long if we judge them by the general scale of the map) perched in their branches, and the reputed home of the monoculi, the one-eyed men, is indicated by the introduction of one of them. In South America in the same way the home of the Canibali is marked by a hut of tree trunks and branches from which hang suspended, as in a larder, a human leg and a man's head. Many old beliefs obtain curious illustration, thus in one of the quaint pictures we see a man using the divining rod to detect subterranean water. That Swift knew the book seems probable from his happy allusion to the elephants in lieu of towns, and this probability grows almost into a certainty, when we read, in his "Tale of a Tub," his assertion that seamen have a custom, when they meet a whale, of flinging him out an empty tub by way of amuse-

38   *Natural History Lore and Legend.*

ment, to divert him from doing damage to the ship. In the "Cosmography" there is the picture of a ship to which a whale is approaching

FIG. 2.

somewhat too closely for the **nerves** of the crew, and they are, therefore, represented as throwing a tub overboard for it to play with. Neither the substitution of elephants for towns nor the notion of the ship-preserving tub are, however, the exclusive copyright of the Munster limners. The former are seen in various other old maps and the tub incident is introduced into the "Ship of Fools" and other old books.

The great value of these monsters, terrestrial or marine, in filling up bare spaces, and in giving an additional interest and reality, may be very well seen in the accompanying illustration (fig. 2) —a view of the Azores, where the strange water-monster fills up very adequately indeed a space where Nature failed to deposit an island. It is impossible to decide its species; at first sight it suggests the notion of a sawfish or water-unicorn. The old draughtsman was unwilling that any of it should be lost to us, so instead of placing it in the water, it, with perhaps the exception of the missing lower jaw, is entirely on the surface. The mysterious something that crosses it suggests the idea that the creature is going bathing, and has thrown its towel, schoolboy-fashion, over its back; but on fuller reflection we take it that that is meant to indicate the wave and turmoil that the creature makes in the otherwise placid sea as it rushes through it, or rather over it.

The figure is a facsimile of a drawing of a portion of the Azores, St. George and Flores being omitted by us. It is extracted from Sir Thomas Herbert's book, "Some Yeares Travels into Africa and Asia the Great, especially the famous Empires of Persia and Industant." The edition we consult was printed in London in the year 1677. After the usual dedicatory letter we find the following appeal to the reader :—

> "Here thou at greater ease than he
> Mayst behold what he did see;
> Thou participat'st his gains,
> But he alone reserves the pains.
> He travell'd not with lucre sotted,
> He went for knowledge, and he got it.
> Then thank the Author: thanks is light,
> Who hath presented to thy sight
> Seas, Lands, Men, Beasts, Fishes, and Birds,
> The rarest that the world affords."

Personally we have much pleasure in paying the suggested tribute of courteous thanks, and we think that any of our readers who may encounter the book will in like manner confess their obligations to the old writer for his labours. We would fain hope that the trip had many brighter spots in it than he seems quite willing to allow.

It has been the custom with many writers to depreciate the labours of Marco Polo,* and to impute to him a lack of trustworthiness, but it appears to us, after a careful perusal of his book, that such censure is scarcely deserved. He made

---

* His accounts were at the time considered so incredible, that the Venetians gave him the *sobriquet* of "Millioni," from the frequent recurrence of millions in his statements; and amongst other traducers Herbert says that "Geographers have filled their maps and globes with the names of Tenduc, Tangutt, Tamfur, Cando, Camul, and other hobgobling words obtruded upon the World by those three arrant Monks, Haython, Marc Parc the Venetian, and Vartoman, who fearing no imputations make strange discoveries as well as descriptions of places." This from the sea-monsterist of the Azores!

mistakes, but he is poles asunder from such
writers as Maundevile or Pinto.* His travels
in the east are narrated with much fidelity,
and are almost entirely free from the gross
misstatements that are met with so freely in
many books of travel, not only at this early date
but for centuries afterwards. The original was
probably written in the Venetian dialect, but the
earliest manuscript now known, that of 1320, is
in Latin. A copy of this is in the magnificent
library of the British Museum, another is in the
Royal Berlin Library, another in the Paris
Library, and some few others are in private
collections. Other MSS. of it exist, and it was
also freely printed on the advent of the printing
press, as for instance, at Basle in 1522; in Venice
in 1496, 1508, 1597, and 1611; in Brescia in
1500; Paris, 1556; Nuremberg, 1477; Strasburg, 1534; Leipzig, 1611; Lisbon, 1502;
Seville, 1520; London, 1597, 1625; Amsterdam, 1664. As these various editions were in
the languages of the respective places of publication it indicates a widespread interest, and it
may be taken as a proof, too, that the book was
held to possess solid value: no book of the
Munchausen type can show such a record as

* Ferdinand Mendez Pinto was a celebrated Portuguese
navigator, who published a description of his travels of so
marvellous a nature that his name became a synonym for
extravagant fiction. We meet with him, for instance, in
Congreve's play of "Love for Love," where the passage occurs:
"Ferdinand Mendez Pinto was but a type of thee, thou liar of
the first magnitude."

this. An excellent English edition, very freely illustrated by notes, is that of William Marsden, published in 1818 : to this the editor prefixes a very complete biography of the old author.

Master Peter Heylyn, geographer, who flourished during the reigns of Charles I., Cromwell, and Charles II., tells us of many marvellous journeys in his volume, and introduces much that is curious in his notes of the natural history of the countries visited. India was in those days an inscrutable and little-known land, where the wildest imagination had full play and was in but little danger of being dispossessed by cold reality. Wonderful, however, as the tales were that came to Heylyn's ears he found some of them almost beyond credit, and after telling us of "men with dogges heads : of men with one legge onely, of such as live by sent ; of men that had but one eye, and that in their foreheads ; and of others whose eares did reach unto the ground," he is careful to add—" But of these relations and the rest of this straine I doubt not but the understanding reader knoweth how to judge and what to believe." He tells us, too, of an Indian people that by eating dragon's heart and liver attain to the understanding of the languages of beasts, who can make themselves, when they will, invisible, and who have "two tubbes, whereof the one opened yields winde, and the other raine," but here, too, he hesitates to take the responsibility of these tales and leaves their credence or rejection to the faith or scepticism of his readers. In the Moluccas, too, he hears of many wonders : a river, for instance, that is plentifully stored with fish, yet the water so hot that it immediately scalds the skin off any beast that is thrown into it; of men with "tayles"; of fruit that whosoever eateth shall for the space of twelve hours be out of his wits; of "a tree which all the day-time hath not a floure on it, but within half an hour after sunne-set is full of them." These, however, and several other wonders of the land, he concludes by embracing in one simple category—"All huge and monstrous lies." He tells of a people of Libya, the Psylli, so venomous in themselves that they could poison a snake ! One can fancy the immense disgust of some poisonous reptile of death-dealing powers when he found that he had at length met more than his match, and that his attempt on the life of one of these very objectionable Libyans was recoiling with fatal effect upon himself.

The America of those days was a very different place from the America of to-day. Primeval forest covered much of the land, the red man and the buffalo were in full possession, and the pilgrim fathers had but lately landed on its shores from the little "Mayflower." As the remote is always associated with the wonderful, and monstrosities and marvels flourish in such congenial soil, Heylyn finds in America no less than in Asia and Africa a rich crop of marvels. Into these we need not, however, go ; those who care to seek out this old author will find much of quaint interest, tradition blending with solid history and fable with fact in his pages.

Sir Walter Raleigh's book on Guiana—"The discoverie of the large, rich and bewtiful Empire of Gviana, with a relation of the great and golden City of Manoa, which the Spaniards call El Dorado, performed in the year 1595," gives much curious information, and should not be overlooked. We may read in it of the Amazons, the Cannibals, the headless people, and other strange creatures of this wondrous land. Hakluyt's black-letter folio, "The Principal Navigations, Voiages and Discoveries of the English Nation, made by Sea or over Land to the most remote and farthest distant Quarters of the earth at any time within the compass of these fifteen hundred yeeres," published in 1589, and "Purchas his Pilgrimage, or Relations of the World, Asia, Africa, and America, and the Ilands adiacent," published in London in the year 1614, are both quaint and interesting old books. Struys' "Perillous and most Unhappy Voiages through Moscovia, Tartary, Italy, Greece, Persia, and Japan," is another delightful old volume. It was published in the year 1638, and is illustrated by divers curious plates. To this list we need only add the "Natvrall and Morall Historie of the East and West Indies," by Joseph Acosta, published in 1604, and "Intreating of the Remarkable things of Heaven, of the Elements, Mettalls, Plants, and Beasts which are proper to that Country." Where we have given a date it is simply that of the copy that has come under our own cognisance ; many of those works were of sufficient popularity to run through several editions, sometimes several years apart ; still the dates we give will afford an approximate notion of the age of the books in question. This slight sketch of mediæval books of travel might very readily be extended ; we do but introduce them as illustrations and samples of the mass of material available.

The medical treatises of our forefathers were very numerous. Such books as Potter's "Booke of Phisicke and Chirurgery," or Cogan's "Haven of Health," may advantageously be consulted. The copy of the first of these that lies open before us as we write is dated "the yeare of our Lorde God, 1610," and like almost all these old books is more or less of a compilation, full of divers interesting matters "necessary to be knowne and collected out of sundry olde written bookes." Cogan is very frank on this point. He says, "Yet one thing I desire of all them that shall reade this booke ; if they finde whole sentences taken out of Master Eliot his Castle of Heath, or out of Schola Salerni, or any other author whatsoever, that they will not condemne me of vaine glorie, as if I meant to set forth for mine owne workes that which other men have devised ; for I confess that I have taken verbatim out of other wher it served for my purpose, but I have so interlaced it with mine owne, that (as I think) it may be the better perceived, and therefore seeing all my travaile tendeth to common commodity I trust every man will interpret all to the best." His statement that his ingenious interweaving of other men's work with his own makes the plagiarism and appropriation the more readily detected, is somewhat difficult to follow.

Cogan did, however, plagiarism notwithstanding, take up a somewhat special ground that supplied the *raison d'être* of his book, since he tells us that "it was chiefly gathered for the comfort of students, and consequently of all those that have a care for their health." There are repeated references to the Oxford scholars : thus, under the head of quinces he gives a receipt for marmalade, " because the making of marmalade is a pretty conceit, and may perhaps delight some painefull student that will be his own Apothecarie." Elsewhere we are told of " Cinamon-water " that " it hath innumerable vertues, wherefore I reckon it a great treasure for a student to have by him in his closet, to take now and then a spoonfull." One gets some interesting side-light thrown on the University life of that day—Cogan's book we may mention was published in 1636,—as for instance when we are told that " when foure houres bee past after breakefast a man may safely take his dinner, and the most convenient time for dinner is aboute eleven of the clocke before noone. At Oxford in my time they used commonly at dinner boyled beefe* with pottage, bread, and beere and no

---

* Beefe is a good meate for an Englysshe man, so be it the beest be yonge, and that it be not kowe-flesshe : for olde beefe and kowe-flesshe doth ingender melancholye and leperouse humoures. Yf it be moderatly powderyd, that the groose blode by salte may be exhaustyd it doth make an Englysshe man stronge."—*Andrew Boorde's "Dyetary."*

more. The quantitie of beefe was in value one halfepenny for one man, and sometimes if hunger constrained they would double their commons." Judging by the "battels" we have had the felicity of paying we may take it that this tariff has undergone considerable alteration since 1636.

The working and superintendence of the printing press has up to comparatively recent years been considered such essentially masculine labour that it is rather curious to find on the title-page of Cogan's book that it was " printed by Anna Griffin for Roger Ball, and are to be sold at his shop without Temple-Barre at the Golden Anchor."

As the ingredients used as remedies by our ancestors came largely from the animal and vegetable kingdoms, we get in these medical works a good deal, indirectly, of natural history lore. Thus Cogan strongly commends the eating of cabbage leaves as a "preservative of the stomache from surfetting and the head from drunkennesse." " Raw Cabage with Vinegar so much as he list." The philosophy of the thing is that "the Vine and the Coleworts be so contrarie by Nature that if you plant Coleworts neare to the rootes of the Vine of it selfe it will flee from them, therefore it is no maruaile if Coleworts be of such force against drunkennesse." Macer tells of the virtue of fennel as a restorative of youth, and bases his treatment on the assertion that " Serpentis whan thei are olde and willing to wexe stronge, myghty, and yongly agean thei gon and eten ofte fenel and thei become yongliche and myghty." Coles, in his "Adam in Eden," commends the Eyebright as a remedy for weak eyes, on the all-sufficient ground that goldfinches, linnets, and other birds eat of this plant to strengthen their sight.

Many of these prescriptions of our grand-fathers' great-grandfathers would have supplied ample justification for action on the part of the Society for the Prevention of Cruelty to Animals, had so invaluable a society been extant in those good old times of bull-baiting, cock-throwing brutality. Thus, in one remedy, the first step is to "take a red cock, pluck him alive, and bruise him in a mortar," in another we must take a cat, cut off her ears and tail and mix the blood thereof with a little new milk, while the victim to tight boots must find relief for his blistered heel by skinning a mouse alive and laying the skin, while still warm, upon the injured spot. Scores of such instances of selfish indifference to suffering could readily be adduced.

We need scarcely pause to dwell on books dealing with cookery, distillation, gardening, and such like household economics, though it will be readily seen how in these again the natural history knowledge—or want of it—of our ancestors finds room for its display, but pass on to the books that deal with animals and the works of nature generally, from the theological point of view.

The "Bestiare Divin" of Guillaume, a Norman priest, is a very good example of the attempts that were made by the ecclesiastics to show that all the works of Nature were symbols and teachers of great Divine truths. The MS. of Guillaume dates from the thirteenth century, and is at present preserved in the National Library in Paris. The work has been very well reproduced in a French dress by Hippeau, a compatriot of the author of it. The statements of the compiler of such a book as the one under consideration are essentially unreliable, since it was very difficult for him to ascertain the truth, and he had in addition no great desire to be literally exact, and was at any moment prepared to sacrifice the actual facts for what he would consider a higher stratum of truth. He could not be accurate if he would, and would not if he could. Hence Hippeau, in estimating the value of the book, very justly says: "N'oublions pas que les pères de l'Eglise se préoccupèrent toujours beaucoup plus de la pureté des doctrines qu'ils avaient à développer, que de l'exactitude scientifique des notions sur lesquelles ils les appuyaient;" and we have already seen that Augustine considered the significance that could be wrung out of a statement of very much more importance than any adherence to the facts of the case. " Dans la vaste étendue des Cieux, au sien des mers profondes, sur tous les points du globe terrestre, il n'est par un phénomène, pas une étoile, pas un quadrupède, pas un oiseau, pas une plante, pas une pierre, qui n'éveille quelque souvenir biblique, qui ne fournisse la matière d'un enseignement moral, qui ne donne lieu à quelqu'effusion du cœur, qui n'ait à révéler quelque secret de Dieu." It is evident that whatever of value or interest may be evolved on the strength of such sentiments, the result can hardly be called natural history—a decision that we have already arrived at in our consideration of the "Speculum Mundi."

The "Bestiary" of De Thaun is a book of like nature. Only one copy of the MS. is known, that in the Cottonian collection. Of another of his books, the "Livre des Creatures," seven copies are extant. The author had as his great patron Adelaide of Louvain, the second queen of Henry I. of England, and to her he dedicated his books. The language in which they are written is very archaic, but an excellent reproduction of the book for English readers has been made by Thomas Wright, F.S.A. We give six lines as an illustration of the original MS., and of its rendering into the rugged English that best gives its character :—

> "En un livre divin, que apelum Genesim,
> Iloc lisant truvum que Dés fist par raisun
> Le soleil e la lune, e estoile chescune.
> Pur cel me plaist à dire, d'ico est ma materie,
> Que demusterai e à clers e à lai,
> Chi grant busuin en unt, e pur mei perierunt."

> "In a divine book, which is called Genesis,
> There reading, we find that God made by reason
> The sun and the moon, and every star.
> On this account it pleases me to speak, of this is my matter,
> Which I will show both to clerks and to laics,
> Who have great need of it, and will perish without it."

As an example of moral-making we may

instance "the ylio, a little beast made like a lizard," and which we imagine must be the salamander. De Thaun says that "it is of such a nature that if it come by chance where there shall be burning fire it will immediately extinguish it. The beast is so cold and of such a quality that fire will not be able to burn where it shall enter, nor will trouble happen in the place where it shall be. A beast of such quality signifies such men as was Ananias, as was Azarias, as was Misael: these three issued from the fire praising God. He who has faith only will never have hurt from fire." Of the Aspis he tells us that "it is a serpent cunning, sly and aware of evil. When it perceives people who make enchantment, who want to take and snare it, it will stop very well the ears it has. It will press one against the earth: in the other it will stuff its tail firmly, so that it hears nothing. In this manner do the rich people of the world: one ear they have on earth to obtain riches, the other Sin stops up: yet they will see a day, the day of Judgment. This is the signification of the Aspis without doubt." In like manner a moral is tacked on to every creature, and all creation is shown to be a text-book wherein man may read to some little degree of the mercy, but much more fully of the penal judgments, of the God the writer thus blindly professes to honour.

The old Armories are a very happy hunting ground for the student who would learn somewhat of the beliefs of our ancestors on matters zoological and botanical, as the writers while

introducing the various creatures and pla[nts]
charges often take the opportunity to add
explanatory details for the benefit of tho[se]
whom they were unknown. Guillim's boo[k]
Display of Heraldrie, manifesting a more
accesse to the knowledge thereof than has
hitherto published by any," is a mine of v[alue]
on this score. The original edition appea[red]
the year 1611, but it was a very popular
for a long time, and other copies bear the
1632, 1638, 1660, 1679, and 1724. A[n]
interesting book of the same class wa[s]
"Accedence of Armorie" of Legh, a consid[erably]
earlier work, as it first appeared in 1562.
also was a very favourite book and was
frequently reprinted, as for instance in
1576, 1591, 1597, &c. It is nevertheless [a]
rare book. Bossewell's "Works of Arm[s]"
and many other quaint old volumes o[f]
character might readily be dwelt on, but o[ur]
is but to mention some few books in
section, and we care not to make our list
exhaustive or exhausting.

Having then dwelt at some little length
various books from which we shall have oc[casion]
later on to draw illustrations, we propose n[ow]
deal with some few of the creatures more c[ommonly]
familiar to these old writers, commencing
mankind and touching successively upon
birds, fishes, and, finally, reptiles. Guillim
book before mentioned greatly prides h[imself]
upon his "method." For this he claims
over and over again. "Whosoever," he sa[ys]

example, "shall address himself to write of Matters of Instruction, or of any other Argument of Importance, it behoveth him that he should resolutely determine with himself in what Order he will handle the same, so shall he best accomplish that he hath undertaken, and inform the Understanding and help the Memory of the Reader." In the spirit of this teaching we would humbly desire to walk, and having quite resolutely determined the order of our going we will endeavour so far as in us lies to make our labour a profit to those who honour us with their perusal.

CHAPTER II.

The pygmies—Ancient and modern writers thereon—Conflicts with the cranes—Counterfeits—Modern travel, confirming the statements of the ancient geographers—Pygmy races now existing—The "Monstrorum Historia" of Aldrovandus—Crane-headed men—Men with tails—The Gorilloi—The dog-headed people—The canine king—The many-eyed men—The giants of Dondum—The snake-eaters—The Ipotayne—Mermaids—Syren myth—Storm-raisers—The mermaids of artists and poets—Shakespeare thereupon—As heraldic device—The mermaids of voyagers—The seal and walrus theory—Mermaids in captivity—Mermaids as food—Counterfeit mermaids—Mermaid in Chancery—The "Pseudodoxia Epidemica" of Browne—Oannes or Dagon—Mermaids and Matrimony—Lycanthropy—The "Metamorphoses" of Ovid—The fate of Lykaon—Nine years of wolfdom—Wehr-wolves—Mewing nuns—Olaus Magnus—The doctrine of metempsychosis—Influence of enchantment - The dragon maiden—The power of a kiss—Witchcraft—Scot and Glanvil, for and against it—The good old times.

Shakespeare, whose writings form a mine of wisdom from which one can dig an appropriate wisdom-chip for every occasion, avers truly enough in the "Merchant of Venice," that "Nature hath fram'd strange fellows in her time," while the credulity of mankind has added to this goodly company many others too impossible even for the wildest freaks of nature to be held responsible for.

Of some of these abnormal forms we propose now to treat, and commence our chapter with some short reference to the pygmies. References to these are to be found in the works of many of the ancient writers, such as Homer, Pliny, Herodotus, Philostratus, Oppian, Juvenal and Aristotle. Strabo mentions them in his geography, but regards the belief in them as a mere fable, while some of the older authors suggest that very possibly exceptionally large monkeys* might have been mistaken for exceptionally small men. While most writers affirmed that such a race was to be met with in Africa—Aristotle, for instance, locating them at the head of the Nile —some authors placed them in the extreme north, where the rigour of the climate was held a sufficient explanation of their stunted growth. Philostratus assigned them a home on the banks of the Ganges, and Pliny gave them local habitation in Scythia. Shakespeare, not only the fount of countless stores of quotation, but also the storehouse of ancient and mediæval lore, mentions the pygmies, though he gives us no hint as to their home. "Will your Grace command me any service to the world's end? I will go on the slightest errand now to the Antipodes that you can devise to send me on: I will fetch you a toothpicker now from the furthest inch of Asia; bring you the length of Prester John's foot; fetch you a hair off the great Cham's beard; do you any embassage to the Pygmies!"

Homer, in the third book of the Iliad, refers

---

* There can be little question but that the ancient fictions of satyrs, cynocephali and other supposed monstrous forms of humanity arose in vague accounts of different species of apes.

to the conflicts between the pygmies and the cranes :—

> " When inclement winters vex the plain
> With piercing frosts, or thick-descending rain,
> To warmer seas the cranes embodied fly,
> With noise and order,* through the midway sky :
> To pygmy nations wounds and death they bring."

Our readers may possibly wonder, as we have done, why the cranes should bear the pygmies such ill-will, but Pliny in his seventh book supplies the justification for the feud, as it appears that in the springtime the pygmies sally forth in great troops, riding upon goats, searching for and devouring the eggs of the cranes, a state of things that no creature of proper parental instincts could be expected to submit quietly to.

Sir Thomas Browne, in his excellent book on vulgar errors, says that "Homer, using often similes as well to delight the ear as to illustrate his matter, compareth the Trojanes unto Cranes when they descend against the Pigmies ;† which was more largely set out by Oppian, Juvenall and many Poets since ; and being only a pleasant figment in the fountain, became a solemn story in the stream and current still among us." He declines to give credence to the pygmies and the tales that appertain to

---

* " Marking the tracts of air, the clamorous cranes
Wheel their due flight in varied ranks descried ;
And each with outstretched neck his rank maintains
In marshalled order through the ethereal void."

† The word is spelt sometimes as pigmy, and at others as pygmy ; the latter is the more correct, as the word is from the Greek name for them, the pygmaioi.

them and says that "Julius Scaliger, a diligent enquirer, accounts thereof but as a poeticall fiction. Ulysses Aldrovandus, a most careful zoographer, in an expresse discourse thereon, concludes the story fabulous. Albertus Magnus, a man ofttimes too credulous, was herein more than dubious," and though he quotes the statement of Pigafeta that pygmies were found in the Moluccas, and that of Olaus Magnus as to their being encountered in Greenland, he declares that "yet wanting confirmation in a matter so confirmable, their affirmation carrieth but slow perswation."

Maundevile, of course, is as fully prepared to believe in the existence of pygmies as of most other things, provided they be sufficiently outside ordinary experience. In his book he takes us "throghe the Lond of Pigmaus, wher that the folk ben of lytylle Stature, that ben but three span long; and thei ben right faire and gentylle. Thei marven hem whan thei ben half Yere of Age, and thei lyven not but six yeer or seven at the moste, and he that lyvethe eight yeer men holden him there righte passynge olde. Thei han often times Werre with the Briddes of the Contree that thei taken and eten. This litylle folk nouther labouren in Londes ne in Vynes, but thei han grete men amonges hem, of one Stature, that tylen the Lond and labouren amonges the Vynes for hem. And of the men of our Stature han thei as grete skorne and wondre as we wolde have among us of Geauntes if thei weren among us. And alle be it that the Pygmeyes ben lytylle yet thei ben full resonable aftre here Age: connen bothen **Wytt** and gode and malice." Another people of somewhat similar character that Maundevile professed to have met with in his travels were still more remarkable, for they "ne tyle not, ne labouren not the Erthe for thei eten no manere thing, and thei ben of gode colour and of faire schap aftre hire gretnesse, but the be smale as Dwerghes, but not so lytylle as ben the Pigmeyes. These men lyven be the smelle of wylde Apples, and whan thei gon ony far weye thei beren the Apples with hem. For if thei hadde lost the savour of the Apples thei scholde dyen anon." Unfortunately he can only say of these interesting people that "thei ne ben not full resonable, but thei ben symple and bestyalle."

Bishop Jordanus, in his "Mirabilia descripta," tells of pygmies in "an exceeding great island what is called Jaua," which our readers who are at all used to the substitution of the letter u for v, will at once recognize as Java, "where are many world's wonders. Among which, beside the finest aromatic spices, this is one, to wit, that there be found pygmy men of the size of a boy of three or four years old, all shaggy like a goat." He adds that they dwell in the woods, and we may not unreasonably conclude that these hirsute arboreals were a species of ape.

In the conflict of testimony, some affirming and some denying the existence of such a people, Marco Polo, writing it will be remembered in the thirteenth century, warns us that we must beware of counterfeits that are palmed off on

The Manufacture of Sham Pygmies. 59

the unwary as the real thing. "It should be known," says he, "that what is reported respecting the dried bodies of diminutive human creatures or pigmies, brought from India, is an

FIG. 3.

idle tale, such pretended men being manufactured in the following manner. The country produces a species of monkey of a tolerable size, and having a countenance resembling that of a man. Those persons who make it their business to catch them shave off the hair, leaving it only about the chin and those other parts where it naturally grows on the human body. They then dry and preserve them with camphor and other drugs, and having prepared them in such a mode that they have exactly the appearance of little men, they put them into wooden boxes and sell them to trading people, who carry them to all parts of the world. But this is an imposition, and neither in India nor in any other country, however wild or little known, have pigmies been found of a form so diminutive as these exhibited." It will be noted that the very fact of a counterfeit implies a something to be counterfeited, and Marco Polo is clearly quite prepared to give in his adhesion to the affirmative side.

The belief in a pygmy race, first declared centuries before the Christian era, was held most fully in mediæval days; and modern travel and research has amply proved that—various elements of the marvellous stripped away—the belief was a sound one. Du Chaillu in Western Equatorial Africa met with a diminutive race of which the average height of the individuals who would submit to measurement was four feet five inches; and readers of Stanley's books will recall his experiences with a similar people. On the authority of Dr. Parke, the Mikaba average four feet one inch, the Batwas four feet three inches, and the Akkas four feet six inches. Related to them in shortness of stature are the Bushmen of

Southern Africa, averaging about four feet seven inches in height ; and elsewhere, the Lapps, the Fuegians, the Ainos of Japan, and the Veddahs—all people of notoriously short stature.

Probably the Bushmen, or Bosjesmen, are the modern representatives of the Pygmaioi, for in their cave-dwelling, reptile-eating, and other peculiarities they agree entirely with the descriptions given by Herodotus, Pliny, and other ancient writers. The Bosjesmen are found, with all the peculiarities of their dwarfish race intact, as far north as Guinea. Winwood Reade, in his "Savage Africa," gives many interesting details concerning them, and holds the view that they were the aboriginal race in Africa. Dr. Stuhlmann, Emin Pacha's companion in many of his wanderings, succeeded for the first time in bringing pygmies alive to Europe, some members of the Akka tribe being brought to Berlin, where they were regarded with immense interest by the professors of anthropology.

The truthfulness of the ancient geographers being thus confirmed, it is quite possible that the tales of the conflicts of the pygmies with great birds may have a more solid foundation of fact than we are quite prepared to admit. The Maori traditions tell of the contests with the moa and other gigantic birds which formerly inhabited the islands of New Zealand ; while the Jesuit missionaries give accounts of enormous birds once found in Abyssinia and Madagascar. All these are now extinct, but it may well be that to a dwarf race, armed only with bows and arrows, such birds would be foes by no means to be despised. One finds the trustworthiness of the old writers often so curiously confirmed that one hesitates in the case of many of them to assume too readily either gross credulity or a wilful misstatement.

Amidst the millions of births in the animal creation there is scarcely any conceivable malformation, excess, or defect of parts, that has not at some time or other occurred ; anyone turning to the medical and surgical journals will find many strange illustrations of this, or our readers may find much interesting information on this subject, and given in a less technical form, in the " Histoire Générale des Anomalies" of Geoffroi de St. Hilaire. But such malformations occur singly and at comparatively remote intervals ; the anomalous departure from the type, the eccentricity of structure, is not hereditarily produced, does not become the starting-point of a new species. No natural malformation, allowance being made for the very restricted influence of hybridism, ever passes outside the species in which it is found or combines with it the character of any other creature, while even the limited possibilities of hybridism have a tendency to die out, owing to the sterility that is so marked a characteristic. Such monsters as Aldrovandus figures are utterly impossible, such as the body of a man conjoined to the head of an ass, and having one foot that of an eagle, and the other that of an elephant.

Abundant illustrations of the most un-natural

history may be found in the works of Aldrovandus; his voluminous works on animals are very curious and interesting, and are richly illustrated with engravings at least as quaint in character as the text. His "Monstrorum Historia," published in folio at Bologna in 1642, is a perfect treasure-house of rank impossibilities. Another book of very similar character is Boiastuau's "Histoires Prodigeuses," published in Paris in the year 1561, a strange assemblage of curious and monstrous figures.

The wondrous creatures of Aldrovandus, and it must be borne in mind that these are given in the most perfect good faith as contributions towards a better knowledge of natural history, are divisible into three classes:—creatures that are absolute impossibilities, such as fig. 3, a man having the head and neck of a crane; secondly, various species of malformation and abnormal growth, which do undoubtedly occur from time to time; and thirdly, other forms suggested by this second class, but carried to altogether impossible excess.

It is of course easy, having realized that a lizard with a forked tail is somewhat of a curiosity, to make a much greater wonder by representing, as he does, a ten-tailed lizard; and while a boy born without arms is a painful possibility, the wonder is undoubtedly greatly increased by also cutting off his legs, as Aldrovandus does, and replacing them with the tail of a fish.

The creature he calls hippopos, having the head,

arms, and body of a man, but terminating below in the legs and hoofs of a horse, was (though here only two-legged,) probably suggested by the centaur myth. Amongst the other impossibilities which we must nevertheless again remind our readers the old writer brings forward in the most perfect sincerity as valuable aids to a better

FIG. 4.

knowledge of the wonders of creation, is a man of normal growth, except that he has the head of a wolf, the lady, fig. 4, who is distinctly of harpy type, a ram-headed individual, and a boy with the head of an elephant.

This notion of the substitution of heads has a great charm for Aldrovandus. He gives us, elsewhere, a bird-headed boy, and horses, goats, pigs, and lions, all with human heads; while the "monstrum triceps capite vulpis, draconis et aquilæ" is, we venture to think, a creature that neither Aldrovandus, nor anyone else, ever did see or ever will see. According to the picture it had a human body and legs, differing however from those of ordinary humanity in being clothed with large scales. One arm was like that of a man, the other was the wing of an eagle, and a horse's tail in rear was another distinctly abnormal growth, while surmounting all were three heads, those of a wolf, a dragon, and an eagle. There are many other such atrocities; while they are curious as showing the depth of credulity our forefathers could reach, it will readily be seen that they are the dullest things possible. Anyone with a slight knowledge of zoology could create them by the score, placing, for instance, on the neck of a giraffe the head of an elephant, giving it the body of an alligator, and finishing off all neatly with the tail of a peacock.

The multiplication, or suppression, or distortion of various parts is a very strong point with Aldrovandus. He illustrates for our benefit four-legged ducks and pigeons, and two-headed pigs, sheep, cows, and fishes; calves, dogs, hares, each walking erect on their hind legs and having no front ones, and pigs, cats, dogs, chickens, double-bodied but single-headed. He also tells us of headless men, and gives us a drawing of one, neckless, having the ears rising from the shoulders, mouthless, the nose a proboscis a foot or so in length; this and the eyes are on the back of the figure. Fig. 5 we may fairly

FIG. 5.

include as an example of distortion, while fig. 6 is a monstrosity produced by suppression. In

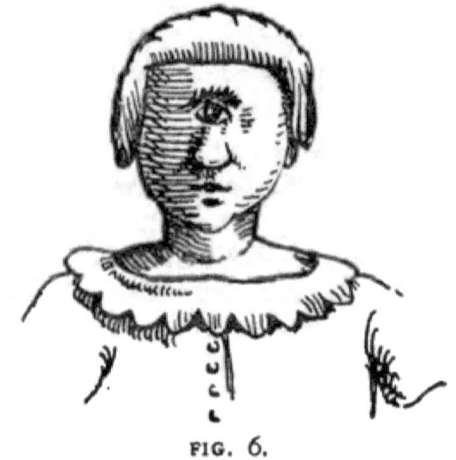

FIG. 6.

another place he gives a drawing of a man having two eyes in their natural position, and beyond each of these another, so that we have four in a row.

One quaint picture shows us two men wearing large ruffs and habited in quite the costume of "the upper ten" of the seventeenth century, but their faces are covered with thickly matted hair, their eyes peeping out like those of a skye-terrier. This idea was too grotesque not to utilize to the uttermost, so the next picture in the book is that of a young lady in the same plight.

The notion of hairy men, tailed men, and the like has no doubt arisen from the first introduction of the early writers and voyagers to various species of monkeys. Duris, one of the ancients, professed to know of the existence of an Indian tribe of shaggy, tailed men, while Ctesias, not to fall short in this pursuit of the marvellous, tells us of a certain Indian valley, or more probably a very uncertain one and exceedingly difficult to locate, where the inhabitants lived two hundred years, having in their youth white hair, which, with the ravages of time, gradually became quite black. In the "Periplus" of Hanno, about five hundred years before the Christian era, we have an unquestionable reference to the apes. "For three days," says the Carthaginian admiral, "we passed along a burning coast, and at length reached a bay called the Southern Horn. In the bottom of this bay we found an island which was inhabited by wild men. The greater number of those we saw were females; they were covered with hair, and our interpreters called them Gorilloi.* We were unable to secure any of the men, as they fled to the mountains, and defended themselves with stones. As to the women we caught three of them, but they so bit and scratched us that we found it impossible to bring them along: we therefore killed and flayed them, and carried their hides to Carthage." Rather a cool proceeding this, granting either that they were really human or that the Carthaginians regarded them as such. We should at all events so regard it nowadays if, for instance, the crew of a whaler flayed some Eskimo ladies and brought their hides to Dundee.

Burton and other early English writers thoroughly believe in the existence of tailed men, and it has long been an article of belief that divers men even in this realm of England were born with tails. The Devonshire men stoutly contended that their Cornish neighbours were thus distinguished. According to Polydore Vergil, some at least of the men of Kent shared this peculiarity, and he very definitely asserts that it was a Divine judgment upon them for insulting one of His servants, Thomas à Becket. He tells us that when that prelate fell into disgrace with his sovereign, many people treated him with but little respect, and in Rochester he met with such contempt that amongst other marks of contumely the tail of the horse on which he was riding was cut off. By this profane

* These great anthropoid apes are found in the forests that extend southward for a thousand miles or so from the gulf of Guinea. The gorilla is not found beyond this limit.

inhospitality they reaped deserved reproach, for all the offspring of the men who did or connived at this thing were born with tails like horses. This mark of infamy we are told only disappeared with the gradual extinction of those whose forefathers had incurred this notorious and shameful penalty. In the "Loyal Scot" of Andrew Marvel we find the line, "For Becket's sake, Kent always shall have tails." As a line or two before this he has written "Deliver us from a Bishop's wrath," it is sufficiently evident that the passage alludes to the legend referred to.

John Bale, the writer of the "Actes of English Votaries," is righteously indignant on the point. He writes as follows in his book, "John Capgrave and Alexander of Esseby sayth that for castynge of fyshe tayles at thys Augustyne, Dorsettshyre men had tayles ever after, but Polydorus applieth it unto Kentish men at Strood by Rochester, for cuttynge of Thomas Becket's horse's tail. Thus hath England in all other land a perpetual infamy of tayles by these wrytten legendes of lyes. An Englyshman cannot now travayle in another land by way of marchandyse or any other honest occupynge, but it is most contumeliously thrown in his teethe that all Englyshmen have tayles. That uncomely note and report hath the nation gotten, without recover, by these laisy and idle lubbers, the monkes and the priestes, which could find no matters to advance their gaines by, or their saintes, as they call them, but manifest lies and knaveries." John Bale was a post-Reformation

Bishop, holding the see of Ossory during the reign of Edward VI, and was especially notable for his zeal in spreading the principles of the Reformed Church.

John Struys, a Dutchman, who visited Formosa in the year 1677, gives a description of a tailed man that is strongly suggestive of the monkey theory, except that he endows him with intelligible speech. He tells us that before he visited this island he had often heard of men therein who had long tails, but that he had never been able to credit it. Seeing, however, is proverbially believing. "I should now have difficulty in accepting it," he writes, "if my own senses had not removed from me every pretence for doubting the fact, by the following strange adventure. The inhabitants of Formosa, being used to see us, were in the habit of receiving us on terms which left nothing to apprehend on either side; so that, although mere foreigners, we always believed ourselves to be in safety, and had grown familiar enough to ramble at large without an escort, when grave experience taught us that in so doing we were hazarding too much. As some of our party were one day taking a stroll, one of them had occasion to withdraw about a stone's-throw from the rest, who being at the moment engaged in an eager conversation, proceeded without heeding the disappearance of their companion. After awhile, however, his absence was observed, and the party paused, thinking he would rejoin them. They waited some time, but at last, tired of the delay, they returned in the direction of the spot where they remembered to have seen him last. Arriving there, they were horrified to find his mangled body lying on the ground. While some remained to watch the dead body, others went off in search of the murderer, and these had not gone far when they came upon a man of peculiar appearance, who, finding himself enclosed by the exploring party, so as to make escape from them impossible, began to foam with rage, and by cries and wild gesticulations to intimate that he would make anyone repent the attempt who should venture to meddle with him, The fierceness of his desperation, for a time, kept our people at bay ; but as his fury gradually subsided they gathered more closely around him, and at length seized him. As the crime was so atrocious, and if allowed to pass with impunity might entail even more serious consequences, it was determined to burn the man. He was tied up to a stake, where he was kept for some hours before the time of execution arrived. It was then that I beheld what I had never thought to see. He had a tail more than a foot long, covered with red hair, and very much like that of a cow. When he saw the surprise that this discovery created amongst the European spectators, he informed us that his tail was the effect of climate, for that all the inhabitants of the southern side of the island, where they then were, were provided with like appendages." The measure of burning the man to avoid any future unpleasantness, seems a somewhat strong one, and attended with a very considerable element of risk to themselves, besides the grave personal inconvenience to the victim. The account is a very circumstantial one; how is it to be explained? One cannot accept the tail—or the tale; and yet it is painful to feel that the alternative is to brand John Struys as deliberately errant from the truth; and brave men who take their lives in their hands are above the meanness of vapouring or lying. In such a case one agrees entirely with Dr. Johnson: "Of a standing fact, sir, there ought to be no controversy. If there are men with tails, catch a homo caudatus."

Africa and India, the two great wonder-lands of our forefathers, were the home of many strange specimens of humanity. Far away towards the sources of the Nile were the Nigriæ, ruled by a king who had but one eye, and that in the midst of his forehead. There, too, were found the Agriophagi, a people who lived on the flesh of lions and panthers: the Anthropophagi that fed on the flesh of men, and the Pomphagi that, like the modern schoolboy, eat all things. In that mysterious land too dwelt the Cynamolgi, whose heads were those of dogs. One old writer tells us that there was a tribe of one hundred and twenty thousand of these dog-headed men: they wore the skins of wild animals as their clothing, and carried on conversation in true canine style by yelps and barks. Sir John Maundevile, of course, knew all about these folk, since he found a great and fair island somewhere, called Nacumera, that was more than a thousand miles in circuit, and which had no other population. He tells us that they were a very reasonable people and of good understanding, the only fault that he finds with them being that they worship an ox as their god. Jordanus, Burton and others locate these peculiar people in India. Jordanus says that there are many different islands in which the men have the heads of dogs, but the women are purely human, and, moreover, very beautiful, whereat he very justly observes, "I cease not to marvel." Ibn Bakuta, describing the people of Barah-nakar, says "their men are of the same form as ourselves, except that their mouths are like those of dogs, but the women have mouths like other folks." Aldrovandus naturally does not miss such a chance as the dog-headed people afford him. Vicentius places them in Tartary, and Marco Polo heard of them in the island of Angaman. In Ethiopia we hear of a tribe of men that elected a dog as their king, and judged as best they might by his actions and barking the royal commands.

Ethiopia was a land of marvels, the focus and centre of all the wonders of Africa. It was held that the strange and monstrous forms there produced arose from "the agility of the fiery heat to frame bodies and to carve them into strange shapes." It was reported by some that far within the interior of the country were to be found whole nations of noseless men, and that others were without the upper lip, while others again were without speech, and only made communication by signs. It is easy to see how the notion of a noseless people originated, since the negro physiognomy often has the nose a very flattened feature, while the people who could only make signs to the strangers that came amongst them evidently did so from a full realization of the hopelessness of speech. The negro lip is ordinarily a very conspicuous feature, so that the lipless people were a legitimate object of wonder. In one district all the four-footed beasts were without ears, even the elephants, the old author is careful to add, being in the same plight. Our readers will doubtless remember that the ears of the African elephant, outside this district, are of enormous size, and form one marked difference between him and his Asiatic brother. Elsewhere in this wondrous land we hear of men having three and four eyes, but the old traveller carefully explains that this tale merely arose—" not because they are thus furnished, but because they are excellent archers." The "because" is not very evident, as the keenness and excellence of sight that would be of such value to an archer is scarcely to be obtained by the multiplication of eyes : it is quality rather than quantity that is needed here, and the old writer is careful to add, "thus much must I advertise my readers, that I will not pawn my credit for many things that I shall deliver." What he saw for himself he could vouch for, and these things were themselves so strange that he could scarcely refuse to credit some of the wonders that were by hearsay, but he very justly declines responsibility.

Another old writer, Burton, in the same way

cautiously evades fathering all the wonderful tales he tells of the men who live by scent alone,* of those who by eating the heart and liver of a dragon attain to the understanding of the language of beasts, of those who have the power of making themselves "invisible, and so forth," "but of these I doubt not but that the understanding reader knoweth how to judge and what to believe."

On the isle called Dondum, an island that Maundevile seems to have discovered, or developed from his inner consciousness, are "folk of gret stature, as Geauntes: and thei ben hidouse for to loke upon: and thei han but on eye, and that is in the myddylle of the Front, and thei eten no thing but raw Flessche and raw Fyssche. And in another yle towards the Southe duellen folk of foule Stature and of cursed kynde that han no Hedes: and here Eyen ben in here Scholdres." These are both mentioned by Pliny, but this passage of Maundevile must not be considered as confirmatory of Pliny's wonders, as it is considerably

---

* Burton probably got this notion from Megasthenes, an old writer who, not to be outdone in the introduction of the marvellous, tells us of a nation in the extreme East of India that are wholly mouthless, and that live only by the smells that they draw in at their nostrils, partaking of no food whatever, but flourishing on the pleasant odours given off by various roots, blossoms, and fruits that they are careful to carry about with them when travelling. Unfortunately, if the scent be too strong it deprives them of life and they die as effectually of a surfeit of good things as the famous British sovereign who overdid his devotion to lamprey stew.

less probable that the mediæval writer had seen these monsters than that he had seen the olden book, and transferred its wonders to his own pages. He, in fact, distinctly tells us that his nerves would not stand an interview with these giants, "sume of forty-five Fote or fifty Fote long. I saghe none of tho, for I had no lust to go"! He tells us, however, of the "Geauntes Scheep als gret as Oxen here, and thei beren gret Wolle and roughe. Of these Scheep I have seyn many tymes." These we may reasonably conclude to have been Yak. As he tells us that men have often seen "the Geauntes taken men in the Sea out of hire Schippes and broughte hem to lond, two in one hond and two in another, etynge hem goynge alle rawe and alle quyk," we can readily understand his reluctance to visit them. Elsewhere he professes to have found "wylde men hidouse to loken on for thei ben horned, and thei speken nought, but thei gronten as Pygges." In yet "another Yle ben folk,"—so at least Maundevile tells us, though it may be but a traveller's tale,—that are "of such fasceon and Schapp, that han the Lippe above the Mouthe so gret that whan thei slepen in the Sonne thei kovoren alle the face with that Lippe." This story again is probably less a personal experience than a proof of scholarship, as Strabo describes such a people in his writings.

These great-lipped people have as neighbours "lytylle folk that han no Mouthe, but in stede therof thei han a lytylle round hole: and whan thei schalle eten or drynken thei taken throughe a Pipe or a Penne or suche a thing and sowken it in. Thei han no Tonge and therefor thei speke not but thei maken a manner of hyssynge, as a Neddre dothe."

Pliny, Isidore, Strabo and other ancient authorities on the subject, tell of a tribe that have ears so long and pendulous that they reach to their knees, and therefore Maundevile knew of them too, and as Pliny knew of the Hippopodes so the mediæval writer tells us of "folk that han Hors Feet." These, thanks we may assume to this peculiarity, are a nation of very swift runners, easily beating the record of any of our modern athletes, hence they are able to capture "wylde Bestes with rennyng" and add them to their bill of fare.

Amongst other strange specimens of humanity that we encounter in the pages of Maundevile, if not in the flesh, are the peculiarly strange "folk that gon upon hire Hondes and hire Feet as Bestes,* and thei ben all skynned and fedred, and thei lepen als lightly in to Trees and fro Tree to Tree as it were Squyrelles." In one district the people subsist chiefly on adders, partly because there is "gret plentee" of them, but more especially from appreciation. "Thei eten them at gret sollempnytees, and he that makethe there a Feste, be it nevere so costifous, and he han no Neddres, he hathe no thanke for his travaylle." It would in

---

* These doubtless would be some of the larger apes, that, sufficiently human in general form to suggest the notion of a man, drop upon their fore-paws and travel across the open spaces of the forest as quadrupeds.

fact be a parallel atrocity to a gathering of the City Fathers at the Mansion House and no turtle soup provided.

The long-headed people that formed part of the strange African fraternity we may reasonably conclude to have owed their peculiarity to the habit of employing pressure to mould the head into the compressed and elongated form, in just the same way that in recent times the heads of some of the tribes of North American Indians were manipulated. We may not unreasonably conclude, too, that some at least of the various curious people referred to by the ancient and mediæval writers were but accidental monstrosities, malformations of rare or casual occurrence. Such an one appearing amongst strangers would be regarded with great curiosity, and it would be but a short step farther to the lover of the marvellous to assume that somewhere or other in the region from whence he sprang, was a whole tribe or nation of such. The accidental resemblances, too, that we sometimes see in the human physiognomy to animals would be suggestive material to those in search of the wonderful. Porta's book, "De Humana Physiognomonica," gives many illustrations of heads, animal and human, showing resemblance of the men's heads to those of the owl, lion, ox, and other creatures. Some of these are very clever, while others are absurdly forced and exaggerated.

Munster, under the section De mirabilibus et monstrosis creaturis quæ in interioribus Africæ inueniuntur, gives a picture in his book, where our old friend the man with the single immense foot, the one-eyed man, a two-headed fellow, the headless man with his eyes and other features in his chest,* whose acquaintance we have made in fig. 1, and a wolf-headed man, are all grouped together as a matter of course, leaving the observer to conclude that anyone strolling through Central Africa would any day expect to come across such a gathering.

The classic myth of the centuar crops up again in the mediæval Ipotayne. These " dwellen somtymes in the Watre and somtyme on the Lond, and thei ben half Man and half Hors, and thei eten men† whan thei may take hem." Pliny writes of the Ægipanæ, half beasts, "shaped as you see them commonly painted," a terse description that may have been amply sufficient for his original readers, but which leaves later generations considerably in the dark.

The belief in the mermaid was to our ancestors as real as the belief in the mackerel; and though

---

* " Who would believe that there were mountaineers,
  Dewlapped like bulls, whose throats had hanging at them
  Wallets of flesh ? Or that there were such men
  Whose heads stood in their breasts ?"
                    GONZALE *in the " Tempest."*

† Robertson, in his "History of America," Vol. II., p. 525, says of the Spaniards, "that they and their horses were objects of the greatest astonishment to all the people of New Spain. At first they imagined the horse and his rider, like the centaurs of the ancients, to be some monstrous animal of a terrible form. Even after they had discovered the mistake they believed the horses devoured men in battle, and when they neighed, thought that they were demanding their prey."

we have in these later days surrounded all with an air of romance, the mermaid was to them no myth or poetic fancy, but as genuine an article of credence as any other creature of earth, or air, or sea. Phisiologus simply calls it "a beast of the sea," which is a very unpoetic definition indeed; while Boswell in like manner calls it "a sea beast wonderfully shapen." Nowadays one's notion of a mermaid is of a fair creature, half woman half fish, basking amongst the rocks or rocking on the waves, and engaged in nothing more arduous than alternately combing her flowing golden tresses in the sunlight, and gazing in her constant travelling companion, her mirror, to study the effect of her work. The mediæval mermaid was of sterner temper; one old writer says that "they please shipmen greatly with their song that they draw them to peril and shipwreck;" while another affirms that "this beast is glad and merry in tempest, and heavy and sad in faire weather." Bœwulf, the Saxon poet, styles the mermaid—

> "The sea-wolf of the abyss,
> The mighty sea-woman."

The syren myth of the ancients is clearly the origin of this belief in the malevolence of the mermaid. These syrens, to quote Spencer's "Fairie Queen,"

> "Were faire ladies, till they fondly strived
> With th' Heliconian Maides for mastery:
> Of whom they overcomen were depriv'd
> Of their proud beautie, and th' one moyity

Transform'd to fish, for their bold surquedry :
But th' upper half their hew retayned still,
And their sweet skill in wonted melody
Which ever after they abused to ill,*
T" allure weake travellers whom gotten they did kill."

The writer of the "Speculum Mundi" believed in mermaids as firmly as his contemporaries did, but he departs somewhat from the traditional lines of belief, and instead of making his mermaids brewers of the storms, sees in them merely rather exceptionally weather-wise and gifted prophets of the coming tempest. He says of them : " The mermaids and men-fish seem to me the most strange fish in the waters. Some have supposed them to be devils or spirits, in regard of their whooping noise that they make. For (as if they had power to raise extraordinary storms and tempests) the windes blow, seas rage, and clouds drop presently after they seem to call." This was the popular belief, but he explains matters as follows :—"Questionlesse that Nature's instinct makes in them a quicker insight and more sudden feeling and foresight of those things than is in man, which we see even in other creatures upon earth, as fowles, who feeling the alteration of the aire in their feathers and quills, do plainly prognosticate a change of weather before it appeareth to us." So that really the bellowing of these maidens is brought down to the level of

* In the " Eastern Travels of John of Hesse," amongst perils of voyage, we read :—"We came to a stony mountain, where we heard syrens singing, meermaids who draw ships into danger by their songs. We saw there many horrible monsters and were in great fear."

cock-crowing, the braying of the ass,* or the scream of the peacock, as indications of weather-changes.

The classic writers limited the number of their syrens to three ordinarily, though they were not quite unanimous as to the exact number, while the mediæval mermaids were simply as unnumbered and as un-named denizens of the deep as the cod-fish. In mediæval times the mermaidens were not ordinarily credited with any particular musical gifts, though we remember seeing a Gothic carving of one playing on a violin. It will be remembered that with their antique prototypes the musical part of the entertainment was a very conspicuous feature :—

"Withe pleasaunte tunes the syrenes did allure,
Vlisses wise, to listen to theire songe :
But nothinge could his manlie harte procure,
He sailde awaie, and scaped their charming stronge,
The face he likde; the nether parte did loathe,
For woman's shape, and fishes, had they bothe.
Which showes to us, when Bewtie seeks to snare
The carelesse man, who dothe no daunger dreede,
That he should flie, and should in time beware,
And not on lookes his fickle fancie feede:
Such Mairemaides liue, that promise onelie ioyes,
But he that yeldes at lengthe him selffe distroies." †

We will consider first the mermaid of the artist and the poet, and then see how the poetic

---

* As the old adage hath it :—
"When that the ass begins to bray,
Be sure we shall have rain that day."

† "A maiden strangely fair, but strangely formed,
Rises from out the pool, and by her songs
And heavenly beauty lures to shameful death
The luckless wight who hears her melodies."—*Kirke*.

and artistic type tallies with, or differs from, the mermaid as the ancient voyager vouches for her from ocular demonstration. Naturally the poets were unwilling to surrender the sweet song of the mermaid, and the bellowing and whooping of the matter-of-fact naturalists becomes with the poets a "dulcet and harmonious breath." All our readers must be familiar with the beautiful passage in the "Midsummer Night's Dream":—

> "I sat upon a promontory,
> And heard a mermaid on a dolphin's back
> Uttering such dulcet and harmonious breath,
> That the rude sea grew civil at her song;
> And certain stars shot madly from their spheres
> To hear the sea-maid's music."*

Several other allusions to the mermaid will be found in the writings of Shakespeare and many others of our poets, though it would be somewhat foreign to our purpose to quote them at any length, fascinating as the subject would be. Our present prosaic intent is but to introduce the poets as witnesses to the widespread belief in such a creature as the mermaid and to show their sympathy with it.

In mediæval heraldry the mermaid frequently appears as a charge upon the shield, as a supporter of the arms, and as the surmounting crest. Any book upon heraldry will supply illustrations

---

* Allusive to Mary Queen of Scots and to the Duke of Norfolk, and the Earls of Westmoreland and Northumberland, who fell from their allegiance to Elizabeth by the witchery of Mary. She was celebrated for the melody of her singing. The reference to the dolphin alludes to her marriage with the Dauphin of France.

of this. We need only now refer to the allusive use of the charge in the arms of the ancient family of De La Mere, and to its occurrence as one of the badges adopted by the Black Prince. By his will in 1376 the Prince left to his son some hangings "de worstede embroidery avec mermyns de mier." The mermaid is found, too, sometimes on paving tiles, bells, and in Gothic stone and wood-carving. It may be seen, for example, in a boss at Exeter Cathedral. In Winchester Cathedral the mermaid holds the accustomed comb, while her companion merman grasps a captured fish. In Lyons Cathedral a mermaid, or we may perhaps more justly say a mer-matron, nurses a mer-baby. A mermaid will be found carved on one of the misereres of Henry VII.'s chapel. Another may be seen at Exeter Cathedral, and a very good one again on a bench end at Sherringham church.* It is also well known as a tavern sign, and the first literary club ever founded in England, including amongst its members Shakespeare, Ben Jonson, Beaumont, Fletcher, Selden and Carew, was established in 1603 at the Mermaid in Bread Street, Cheapside.

Scoresby in his account of the arctic regions says that the head of the young walrus is very human in appearance ; the creature has a way too of rearing itself well out of water to gaze at ships and other objects in a way that proves very suggestive of the mermaid idea. " I have myself,"

* See some good figures, too, in the "Book of Emblems" of Alciatus, 1551.

he remarks, "seen one in such a position and under such circumstances, that it required very little stretch of imagination to mistake it for a human being. So like, indeed, was it, that the surgeon of the ship actually reported to me his having seen a man with his head just appearing above the water." It is probable that the various species of seals, too, are responsible for many of the mermaid and triton stories, as at a little distance, and amidst the spray dashing over the rocks, they are very human-looking—at all events, perhaps sufficiently so to satisfy the credulity of those whose superstition made them susceptible to such ideas. On the other hand, a whaler or other old salt who has seen thousands of seals should scarcely be imposed upon in this way under any possible circumstances. Let us turn, however, to some of the experiences of those who profess to have seen the real thing in the way of mermaids, and see what they can tell us.

Hudson, the great navigator, whose narrative is strikingly free from any touch of imagination, and may in fact almost without fear of libel be called dry and tedious, tells us, in the following words, of a curious incident that happened to them while forcing a passage through the ice near Nova Zembla: "This morning one of our company, looking overboard, saw a mermaid, and calling up some of the company to see her, one more came up, and by that time she was come close to the ship's side, looking earnestly on the men. A little while after a sea came and overturned her. From the navel upward her back and breast were like a woman's, as they say that saw her; her body as big as one of ours; her skin very white, and long hair hanging down behind, of colour black. In her going down they saw her tail, which was like the tail of a porpoise, and speckled like a mackerel. Their names that saw her were Thomas Hilles and Robert Rayney." "Whatever explanation," says Gosse, in commenting on this story of the old voyager in his "Romance of Natural History," "may be attempted of this apparition, the ordinary resource of seal and walrus will not avail here. Seals and walruses must have been as familiar to these polar mariners as cows to a milkmaid. Unless the whole story was a concocted lie between the two men, reasonless and objectless, and the worthy old navigator doubtless knew the character of his men, they must have seen some form of being as yet unrecognized."

In the "Speculum Regale," an Icelandic work of the twelfth century, we read of a creature that was to be found off the shores of Greenland —"like a woman as far down as her waist, long hands, and soft hair, the neck and head in all respects like those of a human being. The hands seem to be long, and the fingers not to be pointed, but united into a web like that on the feet of water birds. From the waist downwards this monster resembles a fish, with scales, tail, and fins. This shows itself, especially before heavy storms. The habit of this creature is to dive frequently and rise again to the surface with fishes in its hands. When sailors see it playing with the fish, or throwing them towards the ship, they fear that they are doomed to lose several of the crew ; but when it casts the fish from the vessel, then the sailors take it as a good omen that they will not suffer loss in the impending storm. This monster has a very horrible face, with broad brow and piercing eyes, a wide mouth and double chin." This is clearly a creature to be dreaded : we may, in fact, lay down the broad principle that the attractive and fascinating mermaid is the creation of the landsman and poet, while the sterner type is that of the mariner.

Pontoppidan, in his " Natural History of Norway," has his mermaid story, but it is too long to quote, and it is, moreover, needless to do so, as all these narratives follow much the same general lines. Captain John Smith, too, in his account of his expedition to America in 1614, has a similar experience to relate, and many narratives of like tenour might be found in various old writers, but we will now turn to one or two that not merely describe a mermaid and merman seen, but the creature actually captured.

The following news item, from the *Scots Magazine* for the year 1739, refers to a creature less piscine than the typical form, but coming sufficiently near it for inclusion. "They write from Vigo, in Spain, that some fishermen lately took on that coast a sort of monster, or merman, five feet and a half long from its foot to its head, which is like that of a goat. It has a long beard and moustachios, and black skin somewhat hairy, a very long neck, short arms, and hands longer than they ought to be in proportion to the rest of the body : long fingers like those of a man, with nails like claws ; very long toes, joined like the feet of a duck, and the heels furnished with fins resembling the winged feet with which painters represent Mercury." We get considerably nearer the ideal in the seven mermaids that were said to be entrapped by some fishermen in their nets off Ceylon in the year 1560. Of these, several Jesuits, and the physician to the Viceroy of Goa, professed to be eye-witnesses, and the latter having dissected them with great care asserts that both the internal and external structure resembled that of human beings. Of the piscine moiety he appears to make no mention.

In the "Speculum Mundi" we have a very circumstantial account indeed of a mermaid who drifted inland through a broken dyke on the Dutch coast during a heavy storm, "and floating up and down and not finding a passage out againe (by reason that the breach was stopped after the flood), was espied by certain women and their servants as they went to milke their kine in the neighbouring pastures, who at the first were afraide of her, but seeing her often, they resolved to take her, which they did, and bringing her home, she suffered herself to be clothed and fed with bread and milk and other meats, and would often strive to steal again into the sea, but being carefully watched, she could not : moreover, she learned to spinne and perform other pettie offices of women, but at the first they cleansed her of her sea-mosse, which did sticke about her. She never spake, but lived dumbe, and continued alive fifteene yeares; then she died. They tooke her in the yeare of our Lord, 1403." One can scarcely wonder at the poor sea-maid endeavouring to escape; the scraping down to get off the seaweed and barnacles prior to the introduction to the rough dress of a Dutch peasant and the homely lessons in spinning, bread-making, and other domestic cares, were a sad contrast to the life of wild freedom of yore amidst the rolling billows of the wild North Sea. We read, too, that she was taught to kneel before a crucifix—a task in itself, we should imagine, of considerable difficulty to a mermaid. When we read in another old author that "in the island Mauritius they eat of the mermaid, its taste is not unlike veal," the last vestige of the poetry of the belief vanishes, while the added detail that "when they are first taken they cry and grieve with great sensibility" seems to bring the indulgence in such diet almost to cannibalism.

From veal to the "maiden clothed alone in loveliness," of whom the poet sings, is a contrast indeed, and even the scraped mermaid turned Dutch vrouw is a very different creature to her whose—

> " Golden hair fell o'er her shoulders white
> And curled in amorous ringlets round her breasts;
> Her eyes were melting into love, her lips
> Had made the very roses envious;
> Withal a voice so full and yet so clear,
> So tender, made for loving dialoges.

> And then she sang—sang of undying love
> That waited them within her coral groves
> Beneath the deep blue sea, and all the bliss
> That mortals made immortal could enjoy,
> Who lived with her in sweet community."

In an advertisement in the London *Daily Post*, of January 23rd, 1738, we read that there is "To be Seen, next door to the Crown Tavern in Threadneedle Street, behind the Royal Exchange, at One Shilling each, the Surprising Fish or Maremaid, taken by eight Fishermen on Friday the 9th of September last, at Topsham Bar, near Exeter, and has been shewn to several Gentlemen, and those of the Faculty, in the Cities of Exeter, Bath, and Bristol, who declare never to have seen the like, so remarkable is this Curiosity amongst the Wonders of Creation. This uncommon Species of Nature represents from the Collarbone down the Body what the Antients called a Maremaid, has a Wing to each Shoulder like those of a Cherubim mentioned in History, with regular Ribs, Breasts, Thighs, and Feet, the Joints thereto having their proper Motions, and to each Thigh a Fin; the Tail resembles a Dolphin's, which turns up to the Shoulders, the forepart of the Body very smooth, but the skin of the Back rough; the back part of the Head like a Lyon, has a large Mouth, sharp Teeth, two Eyes, Spout holes, Nostrils, and a thick Neck." This we may not uncharitably assume was less a mermaid than a swindle. While the advertisement tells us that the creature in question has been seen by several of the faculty, it does not tell us what the faculty said when they saw it! This is a very serious omission. This "Maremaid" does not altogether conform to the accepted type, feet, spout-holes, and cherubic wings being all abnormal developments.

There are, of course, at all times plenty of skilful knaves and unprincipled adventurers ready in divers ways to take advantage of the credulity of the public, and a belief in many absurdities has been maintained by the apparent evidence which the conniving of such persons has from time to time furnished. To say nothing of the impostures constantly practised at fairs and by travelling show-people, it was announced in the earlier days of the century that a party had arrived from abroad with a mermaid, and that it was to be exhibited in one of the leading streets in the West End of London. A good round fee was demanded for admission, and the dupes were shown a strange-looking object in a glass case, which was unblushingly declared to be a mermaid. But the imposture was too gross to last long; it was ascertained to be the dried skin of the head and shoulders of a monkey attached to the skin of a fish of the salmon kind, with the head cut off, the whole being stuffed and highly varnished. This grotesque object was taken by a Dutch vessel from on board a native Malacca boat, and from the reverence shown it by the sailors it was probably an idol or fetish, the incarnation of some river-god of their mythology. Repulsive as the creature was, we have an illustration of it before us in a newspaper of the year 1836. It achieved a great popularity, and the profits that accrued from the exhibition were, for some time, considerable, but the owners presently quarrelled amongst themselves, and the unpoetic ending of this monkey mermaiden was that she became the subject of a suit in Chancery. When one remembers the success that Barnum achieved amongst the credulous in very much more recent times with a stuffed mermaid, we can only feel that Carlyle was right in his liberal percentage of fools, and though in this case it was the cute Yankee and not the unsuspecting Britisher that succumbed, the truth of Southey's assertion that " man is a dupeable animal " holds equally good, and is of far-reaching application.

The " Pseudodoxia Epidemica, or Enquiries into very many received Tenents and commonly Presumed Truths, by Thomas Browne, Doctor of Physick," is a book far in advance of its time, and very interesting in showing what extraordinary beliefs were held at the time it was written. The copy open before us is the second edition, and is dated 1650. Some of the ideas combatted are " that Crystall is nothing else but Ice strongly congealed ; the legend of the Wandering Jew ; that a diamond is made soft by the blood of a goat ; that an elephant hath no joynts ; that a salamander lives in the fire ; that storks will only live in republics." To these fancies many others might be added, and some few of them that deal with the animal kingdom we shall have occasion to touch upon in the course of our book.

We naturally turn to Browne's remarks upon

mermaids, but we scarcely gather from them any definite idea as to his belief in the matter. Before quoting his remarks we must premise that his style of composition is somewhat stilted and pedantic. "Few eyes," saith he, "have escaped the Picture of Mermaids; that is, according to Horace, his monster, with woman's head above and fishing extremity below; and this is conceived to answer the shape of the ancient Syrens that attempted upon Ulysses. Which notwithstanding were of another description, containing no fishy composure, but made up of Man and Bird; the human mediety being variously placed not only above but also below. These pieces so common among us doe rather derive their originall, and are indeed the very description of Dagon; which was made with humane figure above and fishy shape below, of the shape of Atergates or Derceto with the Phœnicians, in whose fishy and feminine mixture as some conceive, were implied the Moon and the Sun, or the Deity of the waters, from whence were probably occasioned the pictures of Nereides and Tritons among the Grecians."[*]

[*] A writer in the *Gentleman's Magazine*, in the year 1771, says of Browne's book on "Vulgar Errors," "Of all the books recommended to our youth after their academical studies, I do not know a better than this of Sir Thomas's to excite their curiosity, to put them upon thinking and inquiring, and to guard them against taking anything upon trust from opinion and authority. His language has, indeed, a little air of affectation which is apt to disgust young persons, and it would be doing a very great service to that class if some gentlemen of learning would take the pains to smooth and adapt it a little

Browne had the wisdom at a period when immense faith was attached to tradition to investigate matters for himself whenever it was possible, and the courage to declare the result whether it fell in with the statements of previous authorities or not. Thus he tells us that "the Antipathy between a Toad and a Spider—and that they poisonously destroy each other—is very famous, and Solemne Stories have been written of their combats, wherin most commonly the Victory is given unto the Spider." This definite statement of antipathy would appear to be an assertion very capable of proof or disproof, but it never seems to have occurred to the philosophers to bring the matter to test, it being so much simpler to copy throughout the centuries from each other.* "But what we have observed herein," quoth Browne, "we cannot in reason conceale ; who having in a glasse included a Toad with severall Spiders, we beheld the Spiders without resistance to sit upon his head and passe over all his body, which at last upon advantage he swallowed down, and that in a few

more to modern ears,"—a comment which we do not at all endorse, as the individual style of the old writer has a quaint charm of its own.

* "There is scarce any tradition or popular error but stands also delivered by some good authors, who though excellent and usefull, yet being merely transcriptive, or following common relations, their accounts are not to be swallowed at large, or entertained without a prudent circumspection. In whome the *ipse dixit*, though it be no powerfull argument in any, is yet lesse authentick than in many others, because they deliver not their own experiences, but others' affirmations."—*Browne.*

houres unto the number of seven." Thus in ten minutes of practical observation collapsed a legend that had held its ground for over a thousand years.

Such results gave him full right to speak out, and he analyses the works of the ancients very freely, yet withal very justly and temperately. Thus he terms Dioscorides "an Author of good Antiquity, preferred by Galen before all that attempted the like before him : yet all he delivered therin is not to be conceived oraculous." Concerning Ælianus he tells us that he was "an elegant Author, he hath left two books which are in the hands of every one— his 'History of Animals' and his 'Varia Historia,' wherein are contained many things suspicious, not a few false, some impossible." Of Pliny himself, the great holdfast and sheet-anchor of all previous writers on natural history, he writes : "A man of great elegance and industry indefatigable, as may appear by his writings, which are never like to perish, not even with learning itself. Now what is very strange, there is scarce a popular error passant in our daies which is not either directly expressed or diductively contained in his 'Natural History,' which being in the hands of most men, hath proved a powerful occasion of their propagation." The labours of Browne should ever be held in great esteem, as he had the true scientific spirit, and, regardless of all minor considerations, sought eagerly for the truth.

In fig. 7 we have a representation of the

Oannes of the Chaldeans, the Philistine Dagon,* the fish On, as shown on one of the slabs from the Palace of Khorsabad. While one may readily admit that the mediæval mermaid is a

FIG. 7.

direct descendant from the tritons and sea-nymphs of classic mythology and fancy, and that these in turn may have descended from the yet older civilizations and creeds of Egypt and Assyria, we can hardly ascribe any close associa-

* " Dagon his name, sea-monster, upward man, and downward, fish."—*Milton.*

tion between the Chaldean Oannes and the popular notion as to mermaids. The former is divine, and is necessarily but one, while the latter claim no divinity and no individuality, but are both numerous and nameless. The work of Oannes was moreover wholly beneficent; he taught men the arts of life—to construct cities, to found temples, to compile laws. He was a solar deity equivalent to Osiris and Apollo, bringing light and life to all. He was fabled to visit earth each morning, and at evening to plunge into the sea; a poetic description of the rising and setting of the sun. Hence his semi-piscine form was an expression of the belief that half his time was spent on earth and half below the waves. Hence, too, the moon-goddess, Derceto, that Browne refers to as at times manifesting herself to the eyes of men, at times plunged beneath the waves, was represented as half-woman, half-fish, and may be thus still seen on the coins of Ascalon. The kindly influence of solar and lunar deities—in other words, the beneficent influence of Nature and of the times and seasons—on the works of men is an altogether nobler idea than belief in classic syren or mediæval Lorelei, who charm but to destroy.

Fig. 8 is a curious variant from the accepted notion of a mermaid. We have extracted it from one of the maps in Munster's Cosmography. It is placed where in more modern charts Australia would be found, south of the islands of "Iaua" and "Porne," names which the discrimination of our readers, who are at all accustomed to the transposition and substitution of letters in these old records, will no doubt readily resolve into Java and Borneo. One can easily imagine that the double tail, like the twin screws of an ironclad or ocean liner, might be of great assistance in steering, though some few millions of the lowlier inhabitants of the deep

FIG. 8.

have nevertheless for ages got along very fairly without this special development.*

We are told in mediæval story that a young man wandering along the rocky beach suddenly encountered a mermaid and seized her before she was able to reach the water. Her personal charms so worked upon his ardent temperament that he then and there proposed matrimony, and his suit was successful. Would that we could

* A very similar figure may be seen amongst the designs of the mosaic pavements at the Roman villa discovered at Brading.

conclude in true story-book style, and declare that they lived happy ever after! After years of wedded bliss, a great longing came over her to see her own people once more, and, on the distinct understanding that the parting was to be a very short one, she embraced her husband and children and plunged into the sea and never reappeared, it being charitably assumed by those responsible for the story that the waters, like those of Lethe, washed away all remembrance of the past, and buried in oblivion the years she had spent so happily on earth.

The power that this story and the next one we propose to tell presupposes—the power of being able to change one's nature—is responsible for some of the most terrible beliefs, notably those where men and women were changed into animals, such as dragons or the wehr-wolf. In the following story, though the outcome was lamentable, the weird horror of so many of these tales is absent. Like the previous story, it deals with the tender passion, and the ardent lover and the charming damsel reappear on our page. The lady, before acceding to the wishes of her suitor, stipulated that she should have, without question, the whole of every Saturday to herself, and the request was acceded to and honourably observed for some years. At last one day, stung by the remarks of some mischief-makers, he intruded upon his wife's privacy, and found her in mermaid form disporting herself in her bath. She gave one piercing shriek, and then vanished for ever. In fig. 9

100 *Natural History Lore and Legend.*

we see in the foreground the astonished husband, and to the left of the picture the meddlesome neighbour riding off, while, with the quaint *naïveté*

FIG. 9.

of Gothic art, all that intervenes between us and the chamber of mystery is removed, and there is unmistakable evidence that the fatal and final Saturday, after years of wedded bliss, has dawned. The tempting peep-hole that facilitated the tragedy will be seen by the side of the man's head, and it speaks well for the honourable feeling of the promise-giver that so easy a means of clearing up the weekly mystery was for years unused. It is difficult now to realize that such a story could ever be seriously believed, and that the possibility of some such incident might befall oneself, or occur, quite as a matter of course, in the circle of one's friends.

The terrible belief in lycanthropy, the transmutation of men into wolves, was one of the most widely spread of the weird fancies of the Middle Ages. The idea of the changing of men into various animals is a very ancient one. Herodotus tells us that the Scythians affirm that the whole nation of the Neuri change themselves once a year into wolves, and our readers will readily recall the transformation of the companions of Ulysses into swine, of Actæon into a stag, and divers other gruesome stories of like nature. Ovid, for example, in the "Metamorphoses" tells how Zeus visited Lykaon, the King of Arcadia, and how the king placed a dish of roasted human flesh before his guest to test his omniscience. The daring experiment was promptly detected, and the monarch as a punishment was changed into a wolf by the offended deity in order that henceforth he should himself feed on the flesh he had so impiously offered.

> "In vain he attempted to speak; from that very instant
> His jaws were bespluttered with foam, and only he thirsted
> For blood, as he ranged amongst flocks and panted for slaughter.
> His vesture was changed into hair, his limbs became crooked,
> A wolf—he retains yet large trace of his ancient expression,
> Hoary he is as afore, his countenance rabid,
> His eyes glitter savagely still, the picture of fury." *

Euanthes, an early Greek writer, tells a very circumstantial story indeed of a certain tribe where one of its members must each year be chosen by lot to become a wolf. Why this should be at all necessary he does not stop to explain. The conditions are very precise. The day and the man having been selected he is taken to the border of a large lake, and his clothes removed, and hung upon an oak tree. He then swims across the lake and disappears into the gloomy woods that come down on the further side to the water's edge, and then and there changes into a wolf. Should he forbear for nine years to eat the flesh of man he may return to the lake and recross it, changing back, as he lands, into his manhood again, and only differing from his former self in the fact that he will look nine years older. Should he, on the

---

* Agriopas tells a gruesome story of a man who, at the sacrifice of a human being to the gods, surreptitiously tasted a piece of the flesh and was turned into a wolf. Whether as a punishment for his cannibalism, or because by abstracting a portion of the victim he was sacrilegiously robbing the altar, we are not informed.

general principle of doing at Rome as the Romans do, share with his vulpine companions in any feast of human flesh, a wolf he must remain to the end of his days. As very probably, however, he would find amongst his comrades some few who, like himself, were human beings undergoing this temporary metamorphosis, he would be encouraged to persevere in this restriction of his diet by their example and encouragement, and also escape the painful singularity that his genuinely wolf associates would very possibly resent.

One Fabius, having an inquiring mind and fired with curiosity as to why the man should carefully suspend his clothes in an oak tree, is able to add as the result of his inquiries, that those are the clothes that the man resumes when he emerges from the lake. Whether they had been miraculously preserved or whether they had undergone such deterioration as would otherwise arise from their suspension in a tree exposed to all weathers for nine years he does not inform us. The point is a distinctly interesting one, and especially to the man reclaiming his wardrobe.

One great feature of terror in the belief in lycanthropy and such like metamorphosis is that the man still retains his human reason, memory, and knowledge of himself and his surroundings, and is, in addition, imbued with the fierce animal instincts of the ravenous brute into which he has been transformed.

The wolf is the prominent animal in the

history of this belief in Europe, since in this part of the world it was the creature that caused the greatest devastation, but in India the transformation is to the tiger or the serpent, in South America to the jaguar, in Africa to the lion, the leopard, or the hyæna. In some cases this change would appear to be a terrible punishment for wrong done, in others a transformation at pleasure by wicked men seeking in the new guise to inflict terror, loss, and death. Amongst some peoples it was believed that brave and noble men became lions and eagles, while mean and treacherous ones changed to snakes, jackals, or hyænas. The belief in one form or another reappears in endless fables in circulation amongst the natives of almost every country the wide world over.

Insanity, monomania, bodily disease, hydrophobia, are doubtless responsible for much in this matter. In many cases, we can scarcely doubt, the people charged with being wehr-wolves were entirely innocent of offence, the charge, like that of witchcraft, being brought against them by those who either in blind terror and superstition or some motive of craft or greed were desirous to get them removed out of the way. In some cases fierce lunatics, not as now confined in asylums, but roaming the country at large, in homicidal mania destroyed human life and became invested in the eyes of men with strange and terrible powers. Often, too, the reputed wehr-wolves under pressure of torture would in their agony confess to anything their tormentors suggested, simply as a means of obtaining some temporary respite for their sufferings, or in the ravings of delirium utter things that superstition could readily distort into admission and confession. We must remember, too, that many of the most horrible stories are narrated by writers whose veracity is by no means on a par with their credulity, and while their statements, outrageous as they are, were no doubt in most cases honestly intended, the reader must by no means suspend the right of private judgment.

It is historic fact that in the year 1600 multitudes of men were seized with the hallucination that they were changed into wolves, and retreating into caves and dark recesses of the forests, issued thence howling and foaming in mad lust of blood.* Many helpless men, women, and children were destroyed by them during this frightful epidemic, and many hundreds of those possessed were executed on their own confession or on the testimony of the panic-stricken.

> " In those that are possess'd with't there o'erflows
> Such melancholy humour they imagine
> Themselves to be transform'd into woolves ;
> Steale forth to churchyards in the dead of night,

---

* Such hallucinations are often very contagious. A nun in a large convent got the idea into her head that she was a cat, and began to mew. Shortly afterwards other nuns also mewed, until at last the great majority of them were mewing for hours at a time. The matter got to the ears of the town authorities, and on the removal of the monomaniac and the promise of a good whipping to anyone who mewed again, the concert at once died out.

> And dig dead bodies up ; as, two nights since
> One met the Duke 'bout midnight, in a lane
> Behind St. Markes Church, with the leg of a man
> Upon his shoulder ; and he howl'd fearfully;
> Said he was a woolfe ; only the difference
> Was, a woolfes skinne is hairy on the outside,
> His on the inside, bade them take their swords,
> Rip up his flesh and try. Straight I was sent for ;
> And, having ministered unto him, found his Grace
> Very well recover'd."

Some commentators have held that Nebuchadnezzar, when driven from the presence of man, was suffering from a like form of madness, and fancying himself to be a beast.

It was a common belief in ancient times that the wehr-wolf simply effected the change from man to beast by turning his skin inside out, hence he was sometimes called Versipellis, a term equivalent to skin-turner. In mediæval days it was thought that the wolf's skin was beneath the human, and any unfortunate individual who was suspected of lycanthropy was very likely to find himself being hacked at by seekers after truth in search of this inner hairy covering.

Olaus Magnus,* in the early part of the sixteenth century, tells us a story of a nobleman and his retinue who lost their way in journeying

---

* "There is a book, De Mirabilibus narrationibus, written by Antigonus, another also of the same title by Trallianus, which make good the promise of their titles, and may be read with caution, which if any man shall likewise observe in the Lecture of Philostratus, or not only in ancient Writers but shall carry a wary eye on Paulus Venetus, Olaus Magnus, and many another, I think his circumspection laudable, and he may hereby decline occasion of Error."—*Browne.*

through a wild forest and presently found themselves hopelessly foodless and shelterless. In the urgency of their need, one of his servants disclosed to him in confidence that he had the power of turning himself at will into a wolf, and doubted not but that, if his master would kindly excuse him awhile, he would be able to find the party some provision. Permission being given, the man disappeared into the forest under semblance of a wolf, and very quickly returned with a lamb in his mouth, and then, having fulfilled his mission, resumed his human shape. The forest would provide unlimited fuel, while their knives would supply the cutlery. Some member of the party, it is to be hoped, had a tinder-box, or the repast after all would have to consist of cold raw lamb. As hunger is proverbially said to be the best sauce, the absence of mint would be of little moment at this vulpine banquet.

The belief in man's power thus to change his form and nature is obviously derived from the widely-spread doctrine of metempsychosis, the passing of the soul after the human life is ended into an animal, or a series of animals. This change is ordinarily in harmony with the character of the deceased, the timid nervous folk reappearing on earth as hares and such-like creatures, the gluttonous as swine or vultures and other foul-feeders. Thus the soul, the eternal principle, in the words of the poet :

"Fills with fresh energy another form,
And towers an elephant or glides a worm

> Swims as an eagle in the eye of noon
> Or wails a screech-owl to the deaf cold moon,
> Or haunts the brakes where serpents hiss and glare,
> Or hums, a glittering insect, in the air."

John of Nuremberg relates, in his book "De Miraculis," how a man, lost at night in a strange country, directed his steps towards a fire that he saw before him. On reaching it he found a wolf sitting enjoying its warmth, and was informed by him that he was really as human as himself, but that he was compelled for a certain number of years, like all his countrymen, to assume the shape of a wolf. A strange country, indeed, where wolves when the evenings grow chilly light a fire, and in the comfort of its ruddy glow are found quite ready to entertain the passing traveller with their conversation.

In the year 1573 one Garnier, a native of Lyons, who had led a very secluded life, excited the suspicions of his neighbours, and was dragged before the tribunals on the charge of being a *loup-garou*, the French equivalent term for wehr-wolf. It was affirmed that he prowled about at night and in vulpine form devoured infants. He was arrested, and put to the torture, confessed everything that was charged against him, and was burnt at the stake. It was no joke in mediæval days to be a little retiring in disposition: the worst construction was put upon it, and one's neighbours, at short notice, were able to report having seen a black cat about the place, or some equally convincing proof of evil possession, and from thence it was a short passage to the river or the fire.

The Belief in Enchantment.   109

Within a few years afterwards a man named Roulet was tried at Angers on the charge of having slain and partially devoured a boy. Evidence was given that he was seen in wolf form tearing the body, and on being pursued, he took refuge in a thicket. Here he was surrounded and captured, but when caught he had resumed the human form. He was condemned to death, but the sentence was afterwards changed to life-long confinement.

In Auvergne in 1588, a nobleman, in returning from the chase, was stopped by a stranger, who told him that he had been furiously attacked by a savage wolf, but had been fortunate enough to save himself by slashing off one of its fore-paws. This he produced as a trophy, when, to the astonishment of both, it was found to have become the delicate hand of a lady. The noble felt so sure that he recognized a ring upon it, that he hurried to the castle, and there found his wife sitting with her arm tied up, and on removing the wrappers the hand was missing. She had to stand her trial as a *loup-garou*, and being convicted, perished at the stake. Stories of the type of those given might readily be multiplied indefinitely.

A belief in enchantment introduced a new complication. Things we are taught are not always what they seem, and certainly in the writings of the Middle Ages we find many illustrations of the truth of this adage, since the pages of those authors abound with examples of the transformation of men and women into various uncanny creatures by mystic spells. The story of Beauty and the Beast is a survival of these. Sir John Maundevile, to give but one illustration, tells us, in his very wonderful travels, of a dragon that was to be seen in the island of Cos, a creature which the people of the island called the Lady of the Land, being in fact "the Doughtre of Ypocras in forme and lykenesse of a gret Dragoun, that is an hundred Fadme of lengthe. Sche lyethe in an old Castelle, in a Cave, and schewethe twyse or thryes in the yeer. Sche was thus chaunged and transformed from a fayre Damysele in to lykenesse of a Dragoun be a Goddesse that was clept Deane." This Deane our readers may perhaps scarcely recognize as Diana. How it was that Damysele and Deane had between them brought about such a state of things the history does not tell us. Centuries after Deane was an exploded myth we find this evidence of a bygone feud still in existence, testifying to the virulence of the goddess's temper and the power of enchantment. "Men seyn that sche schalle so endure in that forme of a Dragoun unto the tyme that a Knyghte come that is so hardy that dare come to hir and kisse hir on the mouthe, and then schalle sche turne agen to hire owne Kynde and ben a Woman agen. It is not long sith then that a Knyghte of Rodes that was hardy and doughtie in Armes seyde that he wolde kyssen hire, and whan he entred into the Cave the Dragoun lifte up hire Had agenst him, and whan the Knyghte saw hire in that Forme so hidous and so horrible he fleyghe awey." The dragon-maiden naturally resented this slight upon her charms, and pursued and killed him. Presently, a young man who knew nothing of all this, for "he wente out of a Schippe" and was a stranger in those parts, came to the cave, and there found a charming "Damysele that Kembed hire Hede and lokede in a Myrour." She asked him if he were a knight, and when he answered her that he was but a poor mariner, she told him to go and get knighted, and come again on the morrow, "and kysse hir on the Mouthe and have no Drede, for I schalle do the no maner harm, alle beit that thou see me in Lykenesse of a Dragoun." She went on to assure him that she was the victim of enchantment, and that if he would free her from this he should be her lord, and have in addition much treasure. How his "Felowes in the Schippe" were able to dub him knight does not appear; but he, at all events, presented himself on the morrow "for to kysse this Damysele." But his nerve failed him at the critical moment, for "whan he saughe hir comen out of the Cave so hidouse and so horrible, he hadde so gret dred that he flyhte agen to the Schippe." For anything we learn to the contrary, the charm was never broken, for all that Maundevile can tell us more is that "whan a Knyghte comethe that is so hardy as to kysse hir he schalle not dye, but he schalle turne the Damysele in to hir righte Forme and Kyndely Schapp, and he schal be Lord of alle the

Contreye and Isles." In our illustration, fig. 10, we see the newly-made knight making his way back again to his vessel with all convenient speed, his courage having entirely failed him at the critical moment.

A belief in witches, fairies, and divers other uncanny folk was a strong article of faith with

FIG. 10.

our ancestors, but to go at any just length into these points would lead us further afield than our title would perhaps justify. As we have already referred to the suspicion that attached itself to anyone who led a life somewhat outside the ordinary groove, we append an excellent illustrative passage from Spenser's "Faerie Queene," as it admirably conveys the popular idea. There in a gloomy hollow glen she found :—

> "A little cottage built of sticks and reedes
> In homely wise, and walled with sod around,
> In which a Witch did dwell, in loathly weedes
> And wilful want, all careless of her needes ;
> So choosing solitarie to abide
> Far from all neighbours, that her devilish deedes
> And hellish arts from people she might hide,
> And hurt far off unknowne whom ever she envide."

Those who care to look the subject up may turn to Reginald Scot's "Discoverie of Witchcraft," "wherein the lewde dealing of Witches and Witchmongers is notablie detected, the knauerie of coniurors, the Curiositie of figure-casters, and many other things are opened which have long lien hidden ;"* or perhaps, better still, to the book entitled "Saducismus Triumphatus, or full and plain Evidence concerning Witches and Apparitions, proving partly by Holy Scripture, partly by a choice Collection of modern Relations, the Real Existence of Apparitions, Spirits and Witches, by Jos. Glanvil, late Chaplain to His Majesty, and Fellow of the Royal Society." The copy before us is dated 1658, and is full of tales of familiar spirits in the forms of toads, rabbits, hares, dogs, &c., diver incantations to provoke evil or to shield from it, and the like, all gravely narrated. The author, in fact, holds it rank atheism to doubt such tales, since

* The first edition of Scot's book was published in the year 1584.

witches are moved by evil spirits, and if people do not believe in one they do not in the other, and therefore not in spirits at all, and therefore not in God!

In the days of our forefathers the ideas held were of a very primitive and unscientific character, and what knowledge there was was largely mixed up with mysticism, gross superstition, rank credulity, sheer guesswork. The common people saw in everything outside their common experience some grave portent, some prophecy of coming evil, and filled the forest glades, the wild moorland, the dark recesses of the mine, the air, the waters, with strange forms of life, sometimes in sympathy with mankind, but more frequently hostile. We may, on the whole, be very thankful that our lot was not cast in the "good old times."

CHAPTER III.

THE lion, king of beasts—Unbelievers in him—Aldrovandus on the lion—The lion of the heralds—The "Blazon of Gentrie"—Guillim as an authority—The lion's medicine—The lion's antipathies—Why some lions are maneless—De Thaun's symbolic lion—Lion's cubs born dead—The theory of Creation held during the Middle Ages—Degenerate lions of Barbary—The Leontophonos—Hostility between lion and unicorn—Literary references to the unicorn—Martin's "Philosophical Grammar"—How to capture the unicorn—The value of the horn—The elephant—The capture thereof—Feud between elephant and dragon—Use of elephant in war—Performing elephants—Moon-worshippers—Knowledge of the value of their tusks—The first elephant seen in England—Sagacity of the elephant—Kindliness to lost travellers—Ethiopian huntresses—Difference between the creations of Fancy and of Nature—Elephants cold-blooded—Hippopotamus prescribing himself blood-letting—The river-horse of Munster—The panther—Powers of fascination—Beauty of coat—Fragrance—Red panthers of Cathay—Aromatic spices as diet—Antipathies between various animals—Antipathetic medicines—Porta's "Natural Magick"—The hyæna—Counterfeiting human speech—The wolf—Producing speechlessness—The dragon's parentage—Enmity between wolf and sheep—Value of wolf-skin garments—The stag-wolf—The bear—Licking cubs into shape—Bees and honey—The hare—Cruelty of many mediæval remedies—The hedgehog—The deer—Stories with morals—The boar—Swine-stone—The ermine—The goat—The malevolent shrew-mouse—The horse—Why oxen should drink before horses—The donkey—The sparrow's aversion—The dog—The cat—Rats and mice.

Having in the preceding chapters dealt with some few of the abnormal forms of humanity, we propose now to give some little consideration to the ideas that have clustered round various animals, dealing first with the beasts, the royal lion, the elephant, and various others; then passing through the various stages of birds, fishes, and reptiles, to the conclusion of our labours.

The lion claims our first regard, since he has, by the naturalists, poets, moralists, fable-writers, been unanimously crowned the King of Beasts, and has been duly accredited with every royal virtue, such as magnanimity, courage, generosity; while in art he has always taken the same exalted position, crowning the gates of Mycenæ, flanking the entrances of the palaces of Nineveh, enhancing the dignity of the Pharaohs, guarding the steps of the throne of Solomon, typifying in the lion of Lucerne undaunted bravery, and around the column of Nelson in Trafalgar Square, or on the Royal Standard of England, symbolising all that Britons associate with the grandeur and might of their country.

The lion alone of all wild beasts, we are told, is gentle to those that humble themselves to him, and even when his wrath is awakened, and the pangs of hunger call for relief, his chivalrous nature is such that he will not attack a woman without the greatest provocation or necessity. Another interesting fact that the ancient writers ascertained is that the blood of the lion is black. That he is not in any derogatory sense black-hearted, is one of the most heartily accepted articles of belief since the magnanimity of the lion is the trait in his character that is most fully dwelt upon.

There have, nevertheless, arisen unbelievers in these latter days who have endeavoured to belittle the royal beast, and to make out that he is, after all, not much better than a sneaking coward, that his courage springs from a knowledge of his superior power, and that his forbearance and generosity are but indications that the creature at the time he displayed these estimable qualities had lately dined. Even in the following passage from an early writer we get some little hint of this feeling: "He despiseth the darts and defendeth himself by his terror only, and, as if bearing witness that he is forced to his own defence, he riseth up in fury, not as at last compelled by the peril, but is made angry by their folly. But this more noble display of courage is shown in that, however great may be the strength of hounds and hunters, while in the open plains, and where he may be seen, he retireth only by degrees, and with scorn; but when he hath got amongst the thickets and woods, then he hurrieth away, as if the place concealed his shame." Perhaps, however, we should assign this strategic movement to the rear to the discretion that we are proverbially told is such an excellent supplement to mere valour, or a wise acquiescence in the dictum: "He that fights and runs away will live to fight another day."* The ideal lion, however, is a very noble beast indeed, and very few of the early writers do aught but sing his praises.

* "The Lion is not so fierce as painted."—*Thos. Fuller.*
"The Lion is not so fierce as they paint him."—*Herbert.*

Aldrovandus in his book on animals—not the "Monstrorum Historia," but the volume that treats of matter-of-fact creatures—deals very fully with his subject. The Lion stands first, and our readers will gather some notion of the fulness of the treatment when we state that the royal beast takes up sixty-three folio pages. The book is written wholly in Latin, and the various details are arranged in sections. Amongst these we find "Descriptio, Anatomica, Differentiæ, Locvs, Natvra, Mores, Magnanimitas, Vox, Sympathia et Antipathia, Historica, Mystica et allegorica, Hieroglyphica, Moralia, Nvmismata, Insignia Gentilitia et Militaria, Simvlacra statvæ, Fabvlosa, Proverbia, Vsvs in Medicina, Vsvs in Lvdis et Trivmphis, Vsvs in Venatione et in Bello." Even this does not exhaust the exceedingly comprehensive treatment, though amply sufficient to illustrate it. The leopard, lynx, dog, and other beasts are in proportion as fully treated of, though the subjects of the sections of course vary; thus in the dog we find much information under the heading Fidelitas and Amor, sections that would be entirely out of place in the description of the wolf.

The Aldrovandus picture of the lion is rather a poor one, while the tiger is very fairly good, and the wolf is capital. It is rather curious too that the hippopotamus, the first living specimen of which, as far as we know, came to Europe over two hundred years after the publication of the book in question, is represented by very fair figures, by which it can readily be identified.

There are three of these altogether, and one of them has seized a crocodile by the tail. Several of the beasts are also given in skeleton form, thus we have the osteology of the wolf, squirrel, mole, and many others carefully rendered. The effect is sometimes rather quaint, thus, for instance, the skeleton of the hare is given, and the creature in this osseous condition is represented as gnawing a plant. The mole is figured with very conspicuous eyes. Any plant that can be at all associated with an animal is always introduced, thus we have a very good drawing of the rabbit nibbling clover, and the legend appended "cuniculus cinereus cum trifolio pratensi, quo maxime delectatus," a statement that many a luckless farmer would **very** heartily endorse; then we have the weasel standing **by** a plant of rue, and the legend "qua omnes mustelæ adversus serpentes se defendunt," in allusion to the old belief that a weasel well fortified with rue was able to wage successful war against venomous serpents. Many kinds of dogs are shown, the greyhound, the water spaniel, the poodle with his collar, **and so** forth; one, to show his fidelity to his master, carries two keys in his mouth, while another is termed "canis bellicosus," and certainly looks the **character.**

"The Lyon," says Ferne, in his "Blazon of Gentrie, 1586," "is the most worthiest of all beastes; yea, **he** standeth as the king, and is feared above all the beastes of the fielde. So that by the Lyon is signified principallitie, dominion, and rule. Fortitude and magnanimity is denoted in the Lyon." Coats, another heraldic authority of somewhat later date, affirms that "the lion is the most magnanimous, the most generous, the most bold and fierce of all the four-footed race, and therefore he has been chosen to represent the greatest heroes. This noble creature represents also Command and Monarchical Dominion, as likewise the Magnanimity of Majesty, at once exercising Awe and Clemency, subduing those that resist, and sparing those that humble themselves." In the "Indice Armorial" of Geliot, published in Paris in the year 1635, we read: "Si ca est auec raison que les anciens ont donné a l'aigle la qualité de Roy des oyseaux et au dauphin celuy des poissons, il y a plus de sujet de qualifier du nom de Roy le lyon, non seulement pour **estre** plus fort et le plus genereux des animaux terrestres, mais principalement à cause des qualitez royales qui sont en luy. Le **lyon ne dort** iamais, ou bien s'il dort c'est auec si peu de repos qu'il ne laisse pas d'auoir les yeux ouverts. C'est ce que l'on remarque de genereux au lyon que iamais il n'offence ceux qui s'humilient deuant luy, qu'il **ne** touche **point** aux petits enfants et porta qu'entre les hommes et les femmes il s'addresse plutost aux hommes, et entre **ceux qui les** prouoquent il choisira tousiours celuy qui l'aura blessé, comme mespriant les autres." **Guillim**, in his "Display of Heraldry," a most popular book, running through many editions, scarcely gives so exalted an idea of the king of beasts, since he tells us that "the lion, when he mindeth to assail his enemy, stirreth up himself by often beating of his back and sides with his tail, and thereby stirreth up his courage to the end to do nothing faintly or cowardly. The lion, when he is hunted, carefully provideth for his safety, labouring to frustrate the pursuit of the hunters by sweeping out his footsteps with his tail as he goeth, that no appearance of his track may be discovered. When he hunteth after his prey he roareth vehemently, whereat the beasts, being astonished, do make a stand, while he with his tail makes a circuit around them in the sand, which circle they dare not transgress, which done, out of them he maketh choice of prey at his leisure." Thus the lion's tail is at once a stimulus to valour, an aid to concealment when the valour has oozed away, and a ring-fence for the enclosure of his prey.

Gerard Legh, author of the "Accedens of Armorie," a book originally published in 1562, and so popular that within half a century five editions were called for, tells us that when lions are born "they sleepe continually three long Egyptian daies. Whereat the Lyonesse, making such terrible roring as the erth trembleth therewith, raiseth them by force thereof out of that deadlie sleepe, ministering foode, which of sleepe before they could not take. Aristotle writeth that in his marching he setteth foorth his right pawe first, and beareth in himselfe a princelie port. When he pursueth aunie beast he rampeth on them, for then he is in most force. In nothing so much appeareth the princelie minde of the haughtie Lyon as in this, that where other beastes do herd and rowte together the Lyon will not do so, neither will hee haue any soueraigne, such is the haughtie courage of his high stomache that he accomteth himselfe without peere; when he is sicke he healeth himselfe with the bloud of an Ape.* In age when his strength faileth him he becommeth enemie to man, and not before, but neuer to children. There is little marrow in his bones, for when they are smitten together fier flieth out of them as from a flint stone. Therefore in the olde time they made shields for horsemen of Lyon's bones." Another old writer tells us that "the lion is never sick but of loathing." This we may presume is a kind of biliousness or sick headache, and a general disinclination for food. Whatever it may be, the Faculty are equal to the occasion, as the simple "way to cure him is to tie to him the apes, which with their wanton mocking drive him to madness, and then when he hath tasted their blood it acts as a remedy." Legh's remedy and this one do not quite agree, but this latter is clearly intended for the lion in a state of captivity, when his unnatural surroundings necessitate severer treatment.

When a lion is wounded we are told that he

* "A lion being sick of a quartane Ague eats and devours Apes, and so is healed; hence we know that Apes' blood is good against an ague."—*Porta*.

has a remarkable quickness of observation in detecting which amongst the hunters is to be held responsible for the injury, and, no matter what the size of the hunting party, he singles out this particular individual for his attack, but if a man has merely thrown a dart at him without wounding him it is sufficient punishment for his audacity to be struck down and well shaken. Lions, Pliny tells us, are destitute of craft and suspicion; "they never look aslant, and they love not to be looked at in that manner." The lion was believed by the ancients to be afraid at the turning of a wheel, and more especially at the crowing of a cock. These ancient naturalists had excellent opportunities of studying the lion. For one thing he was found in Greece, Palestine, and many other districts where he is now never seen, and then, too, the sports and combats of the amphitheatre and the desire of the rulers to gain popularity by pleasing the multitude with various shows led to their free introduction. Thus we read that Pompey the Great caused six hundred lions to be exhibited together to the Roman people, while Cæsar the Dictator exhibited four hundred, and many others in authority had smaller collections gathered together for the gratification of the populace.

That there were maneless lions was a fact known to the ancient writers, as they are mentioned by Pliny, Aristotle, and others, but the reason they give for this peculiarity, that they had panthers as their sires, is erroneous.* The lions found in Persia and Arabia are almost maneless, and the lions of Gujerat have simply on the middle line of the back of the neck some hairs that stand erect like the mane of a quagga. It would probably be one or both of these varieties that had come under the notice of the ancient authors. Amongst other mixed breeds that these writers believed in was the camelopardilis, the reputed offspring of the camel and the leopard or panther, and the hartebeest, springing from the union of the antelope and the buffalo.

In the "Livre des Creatures," the quaint old MS. of Philip de Thaun, the lion is treated symbolically, and as this tone of thought greatly influenced the art and literature of the period we may very legitimately quote the passage. "The lion," writes our old author, "in many ways rules over many beasts, therefore is the lion king. He has a frightful face, the neck great and hairy; he has the breast before square, hardy and pugnacious; his shape behind is slender, his tail of large fashion, and he has flat legs, and haired down to the feet; he has the feet large and cloven, the claws long and curved. When he is hungry or ill-disposed he devours

* A much later writer, Porta, includes some strange animals in his treatise: thus the leopard is the offspring, according to him, of the panther and lioness: the crocuta of the hyæna and lioness; the thoes of the panther and the wolf; the jumar of the bull and ass; the musinus of the goat and ram; the cinirus of the he-goat and ewe. The figures of these are sufficiently curious.

animals without discrimination, as he does the ass which resists and brays. Now hear, without doubt, the significance of this. The lion signifies the Son of Mary. He is King of all people without any gainsay. He is powerful by nature over every creature, and fierce in appearance, and with fierce look He will appear to the Jews, when He shall judge them. The square breast shows strength of the Deity. The shape which he has behind, of very slender make, shows humanity, which He had with the Deity. By the foot, which is cloven, is demonstrance of God, who will clasp the world and hold it in His fist." It is needless to follow De Thaun any further in his laboured mysticism; the passage quoted suffices to show the method adopted. The idea that the lion's cubs were brought to life three days after their birth was a belief that very readily became transformed into a symbolism of the Resurrection of Christ from the sleep of death,* while the notion that the lion always

* "However erroneous it may now be considered, the theory of creation held during the Middle Ages, was both beautiful and noble, and in a fairly accurate manner may be summarized as follows: On the fall of the tenth legion of the citizens of heaven, God resolved to create man to take the place of the fallen angels. He evolved this world for the home of the new creation, and all things that He then made. The celestial bodies, the vegetable and animal kingdoms were formed solely and entirely for man alone, as the centre round which the whole of creation revolved. There was no idea then that the world in which man was placed formed only one of many such inhabited homes, and that our sphere was simply an insignificant fragment of a vast universe. The celestial bodies, it was held, were created not only to give light and heat to generate metals and

126 *Natural History Lore and Legend.*

FIG. 11.

precious stones, but to govern the affairs of men, and enable them to foretell events. The vegetable kingdom was to furnish food and medicine not only for man's body but likewise for his mind. Lastly, the animal creation provided him with servants, with food for his bodily wants, and with moral lessons and examples for those of his soul. This I venture to advance as a tolerably accurate summary of the theory of creation held during the Middle Ages and until nearly the close of the seventeenth century, and, if correct, it will appear from it that each part of creation was viewed not only in an outward and material manner, but also in an interior and spiritual one."—*André.*

slept with its eyes open made it a symbol of watchfulness, and led to its introduction in the sculptures of early Christian churches, and especially those under Lombard influence, where it is not infrequently found as a sentinel at the doors, as the base to pillars, or at the foot of the pulpits.

According to Burton, in his "Miracles of Art and Nature," in Barbary "'tis said they have Lyons so tame that they will gather up Bones in the Street like Dogs, without hurting any Body; and other Lyons that are of so cowardly a Nature that they will run away at the Voice of the least child." Munster's notion of the African lion, fig. 11, is impressive, though it is perhaps less nearly allied to the lion of real life than to the lion of the herald, of which fig. 12, from the effigy of Prince John of Eltham, brother of Edward III, in Westminster Abbey, may be taken as a characteristic example. Munster's lion* would satisfy even the country heraldic painter, who was so irate when shown a lion in a travelling menagerie. "What!" cried he, "tell me that's a lion! Why I've painted lions rampant, lions passant, and all sorts of lions these five-and-twenty years, and for sure I ought to know what a lion is like better than that!" This lion of Munster is a very different beast to the degenerate lions of Barbary that find a precarious sustenance in collecting discarded

* "De leonibus, quaram copia est in Africa." The illustration is a facsimile of the one given in this section of Munster's book.

bones from the gutter, and slink away at the chiding of some Arab brat who is inclined to break in upon their sordid repast.

Nature, when not interfered with by man, ever keeps the balance true: hence "the Leontophonos is only bred where lions are found," and if the old writers may be trusted (and there

FIG. 12.

is much virtue in an "if"), we have in this an excellent antidote to the bane that a plague of lions would undoubtedly be. The king of beasts, we are told, regards the leontophonos with deadly hatred and crushes the life out of it with its paw, as the smallest portion of its flesh is immediate death to him. To checkmate this decisive action of the lion, we learn from our ancient author that in districts that have a plague of lions the people of the place burn the leontophonos and sprinkle the ashes on other pieces of flesh, and these they lay about as a bait with fatal effect. By this happy arrangement they are free at once of Leo and Leontophonos.

One of the greatest enemies of the lion would appear to be the unicorn; for though the two appear to get on amicably enough as supporters of the royal arms, appearances, it is well known, are often deceptive, and they are really deadly foes. Gesner, in his "History of Animals," gives the whole story in a nutshell, for he tells us that "the Unicorn and the Lion being enemies by nature, as soon as the lion sees the unicorn he betakes himself to a tree." This strikes one as being a rather feeble performance on the part of the king of beasts—in fact, decidedly *infra dig.*; but the end is considered to justify the means, for "the unicorn in his fury, and with all the swiftness of his course, running at him, sticks his horn fast in the tree, and then the lion falls upon him and kills him." The indiscreet valour of the unicorn seems distinctly a nobler thing than the calculating craft of the lion. Spenser, in the "Faerie Queene," introduces the story as evidently a well-known fact in natural history :—

> " Like as a Lyon whose imperial powre
> A proud rebellious unicorn defyes,
> T'avoid the rash assault and wrathful stowre
> Of his fiers foe, him to a tree applyes,

> And when him rouning in full course he spyes
> He slips aside : the whiles that furious beast
> His precious horne, sought of his enemyes*
> Strikes in the stocke, ne thence can be releast,
> But to the mighty victor yields a bounteous feast " †

In "Timon of Athens" Shakespeare writes: "Wert thou the Unicorn pride and wrath would confound thee, and make thine own self the conquest of thy fury;" and in "Julius Cæsar" we find the line: "Unicorns may be betray'd with trees," both passages evidently referring to this legend.

Most furious of all beasts was the Monoceros; or, as Ælian calls it, the Cartazonos, a creature still having literary and heraldic existence as the unicorn; though in some few points the beast, as described by Pliny and others, does not altogether resemble in form the creature of the heralds that is so well known to us as joint supporter with the lion of our national arms. The ancient monoceros had the body of a horse, the head of a stag, the feet of an elephant, and the tail of a boar, and from the middle of his forehead projected a single horn.

The Monoceros, Unicornu, or Einhorn is described in Jonston's "Historia Naturalis," published in 1657, and Munster, in his description of

---

* Bussy D'Amboise, 1607, writes—
"An angry unicorne in his full career
Charged with too swift a foot a jeweller
That watch'd him for the treasure of his brow,
And ere he could get shelter of a tree
Nail'd him with his rich antler to the earth."

† Ctesias says that its flesh is so bitter that it cannot be eaten.

Asia,* gives a picture of the unicorn, a beast in all respects like a horse, save that it has one tremendous horn. Barrow, in his "Travels in Southern Africa," gives the figure of a head of a unicorn which he saw drawn on the side of a cavern, and appears to entertain no doubt that such an animal exists, while Burton tells us that in Æthiopia "some Kine there are which have Horns like Stags, others but one Horn only, and that in the Forehead, about a foot and a half long, but bending backwards," a departure this from the recognized type.

Figures of the unicorn are found on the archaic cylinder seals of Assyria and Babylonia, and throughout the whole course of ancient and mediæval history we find belief in the creature as much a matter of course as belief in horse or elephant, and it would not be difficult to bring forward a score or more of authors who have written even in comparatively recent times on the existence of the unicorn.†

In a curious old book on our shelf, the

---

* "Topsell nameth two kingdomes in India (the one called Niem, the other Lamber), which he likewise stored with them."
—*Speculum Mundi*.

† As for example : Bacci's book "Discorso dell' Alicorno," published at Florence in 1573, and the "De Unicornu Observationes novæ" of Thomas Bartholinus, bearing date 1645. Caspar Bartholinus had already, in 1628, written " De Unicornu ejusque affinibus." Then we have Bereus' "De Monoceroti," 1667 ; Catelan's "Histoire de la Licorne," 1624 ; Frenzel, "De Unicornu," 1675 ; Stolbergk's "Exercitatio de Unicornu," 1652 ; Sachs' "Monocerologia," 1676 ; and the "Notice en réfutation de la non-existence de la Licorne" of Laterrade, bearing the very recent date of 1826.

"Philosophical Grammar" of Benjamin Martin, published in 1753, the author raises the question as to whether such creatures as the phœnix, syrens, dragons, mermaids, fairies, and many others that he mentions really exist, and in the matter of the unicorn he evidently suspends judgment. "Most naturalists," he says, "have affirmed that there have been such creatures and give descriptions of them; but the sight of the creatures or credible relations of them having been so rare, has occasioned many to believe there never were any such animals in nature; at least it has made the history of them very doubtful. In all such ambiguous pieces of history 'tis better not to be positive, and sometimes to suspend our belief rather than credulously embrace every current report." In another book, however, published in 1786, and therefore not much more than a century ago, the unicorn is described in all sober seriousness as having equine body, a voice like the lowing of an ox, and his horn "as hard as iron and as rough as any file" to the touch.

Guillim declares that the unicorn cannot be taken alive, "the greatness of his mind is such that he chuseth rather to die," while De Thaun gives full directions for its capture. It would appear that the animal is of a particularly impressionable nature, and is always prepared to pay homage to maiden beauty and innocence, hence fierce as it is the wily hunter by taking advantage of this amiable trait in its character effects its capture, for "when a man intends to hunt and ensnare it he goes to the forest where is its repair, and there places a virgin. Then it comes to the virgin, falls asleep on her lap, and so comes to its death. The man arrives immediately and kills it in its sleep, or takes it alive, and does as he will with it." As this must be rather a trying experience for the young lady, "the Indian and Ethiopians," says a later writer, "catch of these unicornes which be in their country after the following manner. They take a goodly-strong and beautifull young man, whom they clothe in the apparell of a woman, besetting him with divers flowers and odoriferous spices, setting him where the Unicornes use to come, and when they see this young man they come very lovingly and lay their heads down in his lap (for above all creatures they do great reverence to young maids), and then the hunters having notice given them, suddenly come, and finding him asleep, they will deal so with him, as that before he goeth he must leave his horn behind him" and fall a victim to his guileful foes. Spenser speaks of "the maiden Unicorne," and Dallaway, too, refers to "their inviolable attachment to virginity," and many other writers speak in the same sense, or shall we rather say lack of it!

The horn was in great demand as it was made into drinking vessels that were held to possess the invaluable gift of detecting poison. Thus in the "Speculum Mundi" we read of it that "it hath many soveraigne virtues, insomuch that, being put upon a table furnished with many junkets and banqueting dishes, it will quickly descrie whether there be any poyson or venime among them, for if there be, the horne is presently covered with a kinde of sweat or dew." This belief in the efficacy of the horn of the unicorn as a test for poisons is seen by the frequent appearance of it in mediæval inventories. We gather from these no clue, no alternative name, for instance, to guide us, as to what the material so valued really was. In a book of travels by one Hentzner, a foreigner who visited England in the year 1598, mention is made of a horn of the unicorn that he was shown at Windsor Castle, and which he says was valued at over £1000, as indeed it very well might be, if Decker's line, "the unicorn whose horn is worth a city," written in 1609, gives anything like a fair estimate of its worth. In the "Comptes Royaux" of France for 1391 we find the entry: "Une manche d'or d'un essay de lincourne pour attoucher aux viandes de Monseigneur le Dauphin," and in the year 1536 in the inventory of the treasures of Charles V., we have: "Une touche de licorne, garnie d'or, pour faire essay." Many other examples of a similar nature might readily be brought forward. It seems strange that a belief in the efficacy of the horn of the unicorn to detect the presence of poisons should have endured for hundreds of years, when practical experiment would in half an hour have convicted the thing, whatever it was, of being a mockery, a delusion, and a snare.

Many curious beliefs have clustered around the elephant, his sagacity, great strength, and association with the wonderful countries of Africa and India giving occasion for much that is marvellous. One old writer tells that "the elephant is a beast of great strength, but greater wit, and greatest ambition; insomuch that some have written of them that if you praise them they will kill themselves with labour, and if you command another before them they will break their hearts with emulation. The beast is so proud of his strength that he never bows himself to any, and when he is once down (as it usually is with proud great ones) he cannot rise up again." The female elephant was supposed to rear her young one in deep water, for fear lest the dragon should find and devour it. Physiologus says that when the bone of an elephant shall be burnt, or his hair singed, the smell of it shall drive away serpents and all poison. Isidore informs us that the elephant is beyond measure great, and that it has the form of a goat, a statement that leads us to imagine that he writes rather from hearsay than from personal knowledge. He further tells us that the creature cannot lie down, a statement that is entirely opposed to fact, as they may be seen rolling to and fro with the greatest ease when bathing, and after their ablutions recovering their feet with great readiness. This supposed inability to lie down necessitated the elephant's leaning against a wall or tree while sleeping, and the people of the land, when they desired to capture one, had only to fell the tree or undermine the wall, while the elephant was in happy unconsciousness of the rude awakening that they were preparing for him.

> "The elephant so huge and strong to see
> No perill fear'd but thought a sleepe to gaine;
> But foes before had underminde the tree,
> And down he falls, and so by them was slaine.
> First trye, then truste; like goulde the copper showes;
> And Nero oft in Numa's clothinge goes."
> WHITNEY'S Emblems.

They are provoked to madness at the sight of blood or of the juice of the mulberry tree. They eat both leaves and stones, but if by inadvertence they swallow a chameleon the result is fatal, unless they can immediately afterwards eat some olives. As no elephant, being a vegetarian, would eat a chameleon knowingly, we are reduced to the alternative that he must eat him unconsciously, and would therefore feel nothing of the need of a prompt administration of antidote until the olives came too late.

In the family feud which was held to exist between the elephant and the dragon the reptile endeavoured to twist himself round the ponderous beast's feet and so bring him to the ground, but the sagacity of the elephant here stood him in good stead, and when he saw that his fall was inevitable, he also saw the great advantage of flattening the life out of his foe by falling with all his huge bulk upon him. The blood produced by these sanguinary combats soaked into the earth and thus yielded the cinnabar of commerce. Possibly some early observer may have seen a deadly struggle in the jungle between an elephant and some huge python or boa, and being content to view from some little distance, may have filled in the details from imagination and thus set the story afloat. When a tale of this nature once gained credence, one old writer after another inserted it in his work without further question. The elephant was said to be afraid of a mouse, though the ancient authors unfortunately fail to satisfy our very legitimate curiosity as to why this should be so; in an old romance, dealing with the wars of the great Alexander, the elephants of the enemy are put to rout by the squeaking of a herd of swine brought for the nonce on to the tented field.

The elephant was first used in war by Pyrrhus, who, B.C. 280, employed these animals in the war with Tarentum against the Romans. We learn also that the Carthaginians, in the time of Hannibal, B.C. 210, employed them in their wars; and we have modern illustrations of the like service amongst the various princes of India. When the Romans in Leucania first saw the elephants in the battle array of Pyrrhus, they called them Leucanian oxen. "Next the Poeni taught the horrible Leucanian oxen, with lowered body and snake-like head, to endure the wounds of war, and to throw into confusion the mighty ranks of Mars." Later on the Romans introduced them into their own service, and in one of the triumphal entries of Cæsar into Rome his chariot was drawn by forty elephants.

A little later on we read of their appearance in the arena, dancing and wrestling with each other, walking on stretched ropes, four of them carrying a fifth on their shoulders reposing on a litter or couch, and generally going through those performances that from the earliest times to the travelling show of to-day have been received by the vulgar with such favour. Both Pliny and Plutarch tell us that if any one elephant in such a gathering for any reason fails to do what is required of him he will study by night, in what a workman would call "his own time," to achieve success, and go through the performance of his own accord when the rest of the world is sleeping, until he has mastered it.

Sir John Maundevile, in his "Voiage and Travaile," gives an interesting mediæval reference to an Eastern potentate having "14,000 Olifauntz or mo. In cas that he had ony Werre agenst ony other Kynge aboute him than he makethe certyn men of Armes for to gon up in to the Castelles of Tree, made for the Werre, that craftily ben set uppe on the Olifauntes Bakkes, for to fryghten agen hire Enemyes." How very craftily these are set up may be seen in our illustration, fig. 13, from an early edition of the book. As we may reasonably assume from the look of the Castelle of tree that it is built in two storeys, we may judge the bulk of the elephant from imagining the size that the men must be who are quartered in the upper storey. It will be noticed that there is no suggestion of any method of fastening the Castelle to the Olifaunte. Were we amongst the men of arms who were expected to take up a position in this fortress, we should regard this as a peculiarly weak point in the arrangements. In marked contrast with this massive beast Munster has a funny picture of a man ploughing with an elephant, the elephant being, in proportion to the man, of about the size of a Shetland pony.

The ancient writers believed, or taught, that the elephant indulged in moon-worship. Ælian, amongst others, states that at the increase of the moon these creatures gathered long branches of trees in the forest, and held them up in adoration, with uplifted trunks, to the queen of night. Pliny, too, writes that "they have withall religious reverence, with a kind of devotion ; not only the starres and planets but the sunne and moone they also worship, and in very truth, writers there be who report thus much of them—that when the new moone beginneth to appeare fresh and bright,* they come doune by whole herds to a certaine river named Amelus in the deserts and forests of Mauritania, where, after that they are washed and solemnlie purified by sprinkling and dashing themselves all over with the water, and have saluted and adored

* Mutianus tells us that when the moon is on the wane the monkeys are sad, but that they adore the new moon with liveliest manifestations of delight.

after their manner their planet, they returne againe unto the woods and chases, carrying before them their young calves that be wearied and tired"—a grand and pious pilgrimage of pachyderms.

Another strange idea of the ancients was that the elephant when pursued by the hunters beats its tusks against the trees until they drop off, as he has a shrewd suspicion that it is his ivory rather than himself that they want. The elephant, sagacious beast, would appear to have as good a notion of the value of his tusks to the hunter as his pursuer himself has. We are told that "when they chance to be environed and compassed round with hunters they set foremoste in the ranke to bee seene those of the heard that have the least teeth, to the end that their price might not be thought worth the hazard and venture in chace for them. But afterwards, when they see the hunters eager and themselves over-matched and wearie, they breake them with running against the hard trees, and, leaving them behind, escape by this ransome as it were, out of their hands." Another curious fact is that "their skin is covered neither with haire nor bristle, no, not so much as in their taile, which might serve them in goode steade to driue away the busie and troublesome flie (for as vast and huge a beast as he is, the flie haunteth and stingeth him), but full their skinne is of crosse wrinckles lattiswise: and besides that, the smell thereof is able to draw and allure such vermine to it, and therefore when they are laid stretched along, and perceive the flies by whole swarmes settled on their skin, sodainly they draw those cranies and crevices together close, and so crush them all to death. This serues them instead of taile, maine and long haire,"—one striking instance the more of the wonderful compensatory powers of Nature !

It is by no means an incurious subject to trace the sources of information possessed by our

FIG. 13.

ancestors of subjects of natural history that have now become so familiar as to create a surprise that fables respecting them should so long have been currently received. In regard to the elephant, the earliest notions the people of the Middle Ages had of it must have been from the narratives of pilgrims and other travellers from the East.

The first instance, after classic times, of an elephant being brought to the West occurred in the year 807, when one was sent as a present from the famous Caliph Haroum al Raschid to the Emperor Charlemagne, and must have occasioned no small degree of astonishment. Matthew Prior mentions that the Soldan of Babylon, Malek el Kamel, sent an elephant as a choice present to the Emperor Frederic II. in the year 1229, but it was not till 1255 that the first specimen was seen in England: this was a present from the King of France to our Henry III. The chronicler, John of Oxenedes, gives full details of the arrival of this animal in London, and tells us of the enormous crowds that flocked together to behold it. The writ is still existing that was sent to the Sheriff of Kent, dated February 3rd, 1255, directing him to go in person to Dover, together with John Gouch, the king's servant, to arrange in what manner the king's present might most conveniently be brought over, and to find for the said John a ship and all things necessary; and if, by the advice of mariners and others, it could be brought by water, directing it to be so conveyed. It was, however, eventually landed at Sandwich, and walked thence to London. Another writ, dated the 26th of the same month, ordered the Sheriffs of London to cause to be built at the Tower a house for it, forty feet in length and twenty in breadth. The elephant itself was ten feet in height and ten years old. It only lived two years. Of this elephant Matthew Prior made a very good representation and his original drawing may still be seen amongst the Cottonian MSS. in the British Museum; this he expressly tells us was taken from the life *ipso elephante exemplariter assistente*. An equally good, but smaller, drawing occurs at the close of the chronicle of John de Walingeford, a monk in the Abbey of St. Albans. This also may be seen amongst the Cottonian collection. The historians of the time regarded the new arrival as a perfect prodigy, as they very well might do, when we remember how the British public, comparatively satiated with wild beasts, flocked in hundreds of thousands some few years ago to see the first hippopotamus. They gave long and detailed accounts of the habits of the elephant in a wild state, details which were eagerly read by the great multitude seeking for some information on this strange monster in their midst; these more or less trustworthy facts, though mingled with many obvious absurdities, would seem to show that a fair amount of knowledge of the creature had penetrated thus far. Some of the information was at least curious, as, for instance, that elephants will not enter a ship to cross the sea until an oath is taken before them by their conductor that they shall return, and that if they meet a man in the desert who has lost his bearings they will very courteously conduct him to the right path. Either of these indicate a high degree of sagacity, and a good knowledge of human speech. The latter proceeding was probably a delicate way of conveying to the wandering botanist or prospecting engineer that he was a trespasser on their domain, and a gentle hint to him that he would be on the right path when he took his leave and left them in undisturbed possession.*

There is no record in modern times of an African tribe endeavouring to domesticate the wild elephant, or to utilize it in warfare, but Marco Polo mentions that in the South-East of Africa the people are very warlike, and fight—having no horses—upon elephants and camels. Upon the backs of the former he tells us that they place castles capable of containing from fifteen to twenty armed men, and that, previous to the conflict, they give the elephants draughts of wine to make them more spirited and furious in the assault.† "There is no creature," saith the writer of the "Speculum Mundi," "amongst all the beasts of the world which hath so great

---

* "When trauaylers are out of their way the Oliphaunt will do all that hee can by familiar tokens to bring them in again. He is of much vertue and verie seruiceable with loue towardes man."—*Legh*. "Even the wilde ones living in deserts will direct and defend strangers and travellers. For if an Elephant shall finde a man wandering in his way, first of all that he may not be affrighted, the Elephant goeth a little wide out of the path and standeth still, then by little and little going before him, he shews him the way; and if a Dragon chance to meet this man thus travelling, the Elephant then opposeth himself to the Dragon and powerfully defendeth the helplesse man who is not able to defend himself."—*Speculum Mundi*.

† "And to the end they might provoke the elephants to

and ample demonstration of the power and wisdom of Almighty God as the Elephant, both from proportion of body and disposition of spirit; and it is admirable to behold the industrie of our ancient forefathers, and noble desire to benefit us their posteritie, by searching into the qualities of every beast, to discover what benefits and harms may come by them to mankinde; having never been afraid of the wildest, but they tamed them; and the greatest, but they also set upon them: witness this beast of which we now speak, being like a living mountaine in quantitie and outward appearance, yet by them so handled as no little dog could be made more serviceable, tame, and tractable."

According to the belief of one mediæval writer, at least, the capture of the elephant is not a matter of much difficulty, though, having caught him, he seems to find no better use for him than to kill him as so much raw material for the dyer's vat, instead of utilizing his gigantic strength and magnificent willingness for work[*] in the service of man. Nowadays, the men do

fight they shewed them the blood of grapes and mulberries."— 1 *Maccabees* vi. 34.

"And upon the beasts there were strong towers of wood, which covered every one of them, and were girt fast unto them with devices; there were also upon every one two and thirty strong men that fought upon them, besides the Indian that ruled him."—1 *Macc.* vi. 37.

[*] Miss Cobbe, in discussing the moral difference between the creatures of Fancy and those of Nature, remarks very truly that "the instincts which man has lent to the offspring of his imagination are infinitely worse and lower than those which are to be found in real eagles and tigers, which slay and eat their

most of the elephant-catching, but "among the Ethiopians," says one ancient authority on the subject, Bartholomew Anglicus, "in some countries elephants be hunted in this wise. There go in the desert two maidens, and one of them beareth a vessel and the other a sword. And these maidens begin to sing alone; and the beast hath liking when he heareth their song, and cometh to them, and falleth asleep anon for liking of the song," an explanation of the drowsiness that would scarcely nowaday be held satisfactory at any concert or social function of the kind; "then the one maid sticketh him in the throat or in the side with a sword, and the other taketh his blood in a vessel. And with that blood the people of the country dye cloth, and done colour it therewith." The writer prefaces his story by the assertion that it is "full wonderful;" and so it is, when regarded from our modern standpoint, but to anyone who could believe that unicorns could be captured in a very similar way, we should have thought that the narrative would have seemed most matter-of-fact and prosaic. The ladies of Ethiopia must have been of considerably stouter heart than some

natural prey to satisfy their hunger, and there make an end. But the perfidious and cruel Sphinxes, and Harpies, and Gorgons, and Gnomes, and Dragons, do mischief for mischief's sake, and are altogether merciless. The brutes of Fancy are merely brutal, with a spice of human malignity superadded. Man has created filthy Harpies, and relentless Hydras, and subtle and vindictive Sphinxes, but he has never, even in thought, created such an animal as the sagacious and friendly elephant, the kindly-natured horse, or the affectionate dog."

fair maidens of the present day, who dare not enter where the presence of mouse or cockroach is suspected.

Great good-natured beast as the elephant is, he has more than one most merciless and vindictive foe. "There ben Bestes," or Maundevile is in error, "men clepen hem Loerancz, and thei han a blak Hed and thre longe Hornes trenchant in the Front, scharpe as a Sword, and the body is sclender. And he is a fulle felonous Best, and he chacethe and sleethe the Olifaunt." What can have ever prompted and suggested the idea of such a very unpleasant tricorn it is impossible to say. In real life the elephant and the rhinoceros are sometimes at feud, but clearly the massive rhinoceros cannot be this very slender and objectionable three-horned beast. We have seen, too, that the dragon cannot let the elephant alone; he is to the full as "felonous" as the Loerancz. Pliny held that this constant unpleasantness on the part of the reptile was a "sport of nature." In other words, that Nature,—personified, as the Romans personified the winds, the mountain streams, and so forth,—felt a real delight in seeing a downright fight between two such doughty antagonists. As the dragon was always the aggressor, while the elephant only wished to be let alone, and merely used his strength in self-defence when so wantonly attacked, one's sympathies must necessarily be with the latter.

As this view degraded Nature to the level of an emperor feasting his eyes on the sanguinary horrors of a gladiatorial show, or to that of a bull-baiter or other member of "the fancy," it was not altogether acceptable to thinking men, as it must have been difficult to worship at the shrine of the Creator and Sustainer of all, and yet feel that one was in the grasp of a power so capricious, relentless, and unfair. Nor was the narration even fair to the dragon, as there was

FIG. 14.

no suggestion in it that the attack was made for the legitimate purpose of obtaining food; the story as it stood pointed to a depth of sheer vindictiveness that even a dragon with any self-respect would resent the imputation of. The theory therefore was started that while during the great heats of the dry season the dragon's blood was almost at boiling point the blood of the elephant was singularly and exceptionally cold, and thus made the creature a most welcome prey. The dragon, with parched throat and molten veins, therefore went as naturally for an elephant as the members of a picnic-party in July go for the iced lemonade or claret-cup.

Our ancestors had immense faith in bloodletting, but there is nothing new under the sun, and Pliny tells us that a hippopotamus, when good living has told upon him and he is suffering from plethora, goes ashore to where he has seen that the river reeds have been newly cut, and presses one of the sharp edges of a stem into his leg, and thus vigorously bleeds himself. When the process has given him the desired relief, and there is no immediate fear of gout or apoplexy, he smears the wound over with the Nile mud and quickly heals it. Munster's idea of the hippopotamus, as shown in his book, from which we have made the facsimile fig. 14, is a much more genuine notion of a river-horse than the beast as we see him in the Zoological Gardens. The way he is dashing up the stream around him as he gallops through the water is a caution.

The panther was believed to have an especial power of fascination, a gift ascribed by some to the beauty of his coat and by others to his odour. The savour of the larger species of felidæ, as we find it in zoological collections, is malodorous rather than fascinating, though the creatures could doubtless plead in their own defence that they were placed under artificial circumstances. In one of Spenser's sonnets we find the first theory upheld in the lines:—

"The panther knowing that his spotted hide
　　Doth please all beasts, but that his looks them fray,
Within a bush his dreadful head doth hide
　　To let them gaze, while he on them may prey."

In the eighth book of Pliny's "Natural History," the second theory is maintained. "It is said that all four-footed beasts are wonderfully delighted and enticed by the smell of panthers; but their hideous looke and crabbed countenance, which they bewray so soone as they show their heads, skareth them as much againe; and therefore their manner is to hide their heads, and when they have trained other beasts within their reach by their sweet savour, they flee upon them and worrie them."* In a MS. presented by Sir William Segar to King James I. and now No. 6085 in the Harleian collection, we come across a combination of the theories, the result being a fascination of the most killing description:—
"The panther is admired of all beasts for the beauty of his skyn, being spotted with variable colours, and beloued and followed of them for the sweetnesse of his breath, that streameth

---

* The panther was one of the beasts that was brought in great numbers to Rome. Pompey, for instance, exhibited to the citizens over four hundred of them on one occasion. The beast is figured in mosaic pavements, in the fresco paintings of Pompeii, &c., and was evidently so well under observation that it is remarkable how such erroneous ideas concerning it could have become current or stood their ground as articles of belief even for a day.

forth of his nostrils and ears like smoke, which our paynters mistaking corruptlie, doe make fire." This detail is given in the manuscript in explanation of one of the badges of King Henry VI.—a panther passant guardant argent, spotted of all colours, with **vapour** issuant from his mouth and ears.*

Sir John Maundevile professed to see in the capital of far Cathay a palace with its halls "covered with red skins of animals called panthers, fair beasts and well-smelling ; so that for the sweet odour of the skins no evil air may enter into the palace. The skins are as red as blood and shine so bright against the sun that a man may scarce look at them. And many people worship the beasts when they meet them first in a morning, for their great virtue and for the good smell that they have ; and the skins they value more than if they were plates of fine gold." This is very clearly not a statement springing from personal observation. Some old writers of imaginative turn of mind regarded the panther as the emblem of providence and foresight, the number of eye-like spots on his coat suggesting the idea that he was well able to look before, behind, and around him ; while others declared that he bore on his shoulder one particular spot of the shape of the moon, and that this passed through

---

* At a state banquet given by **Gaston** the Fifth we read that "there was brought in (for an enter-course) the shape of a beast called a Tiger, which by cunning art disgorged fire from his mouth and nostrils."

the various phases of form from crescent to full circle simultaneously with the moon itself.

The tastes of the panther would appear to be considerably more refined than those of the other great carnivoræ—an idea that we base on the statement of the author of the "Speculum Mundi." "Now, the reason why these beasts have such a sweet breath is in regard that they are so much delighted with the kinde of spices and daintie aromaticall trees; insomuch that (as some affirm) they will go many hundred miles in time of the yeare when these things are in season, and all for the love they bear to them. But above all, their chief delight is in the gumme of camphire, watching that tree very carefully, to the end they may preserve it for their owne use." The notion of the panther prowling round and keeping his eye on the camphor the while is distinctly quaint.

Porta tells us that the hyæna and the panther are in continual enmity, and that even the skin of a dead hyæna makes the panther run away, though we should ourselves have thought that the live hyæna, skin and all, would have been no match for the panther. Nay, this feeling is so intense, that one old author tells us that even if one hangs up the two skins together the antipathy outlives death itself, and the panther's skin will lose all the hair.

This notion of antipathy between various animals is a very strong point with old writers. "A lion's skin wasteth and eating out the skins of other beasts; and so doth the wolves skin eat up the lambs skin. Likewise the feathers of other fowles, being put among eagles feathers do rot and consume of themselves. The beast Florus and the bird Ægithus are at such mortal enmity that when they are dead their blood cannot be mingled together." Porta is very learned on this matter, and tells us that an elephant is afraid of a ram. This must clearly be from some invincible feeling of antipathy, for there is little doubt but that in fair fight the ram would be nowhere; yet we learn that, unmanageable as an elephant may be, "as soon as ever he seeth a ram he waxeth meek, and his fury ceaseth." One can only wonder, over and over again, how it comes that such ideas should gain credence for centuries, when the whole matter could so readily be brought to the touchstone of experience.

The doctrine of sympathy and antipathy, and more especially the latter half of it, was of immense value in mediæval medicine. As an example of sympathy we may instance the affection that was held to exist between the goat and the partridge; hence for whatever one of them was a remedy the other became equally available. The prescriptions were interchangeable, and one used one or the other in full faith that either was equally valuable, as indeed might very possibly be the case. As examples of the antipathetic treatment, one may instance the following :—
" The Ape of all things cannot abide a Snail ; now the Ape is a drunken beast, for they are wont to take an Ape by making him drunk

and a Snail well wash'd is a remedy against drunkenesse. The Wolf is afraid of the Urchin; thence if we wash our mouth and throat with Urchin's blood it will make our voice shrill, though before it were hoarse and dull like a Wolves voice. The Hart and the Serpent are at continuall enemity; the Serpent as soon as he seeth the Hart gets him into his hole, but the Hart draws him out again with the breath of his nostrils and devours him; hence it is that the fat and the blood of Harts, and the stones that grow in their eyes, are ministered as fit remedies against the biting and stinging of Serpents. Likewise the breath of Elephants draws Serpents out of their dens, and therefore the members of Elephants burned, drive away Serpents. So also the crowing of a Cock affrights the Basilisk, and he fights with Serpents to defend his hens, hence the broth of a Cock is good remedy against the poison of Serpents. The Stellion, which is a beast like a Lyzard, is an enemy to the Scorpions, and therefore the Oyle of him being purified is good to anoint the place which is stricken by the Scorpion. A Swine eats up a Salamander without danger, and is good against the poison thereof." All these and many other hints of like value may be found in the pages of Porta.

The edition of "Natural Magick," by John Baptist Porta, from which we have made these extracts, is a somewhat late one,* as the preface begins:—" Courteous Reader,—If this work

* It is dated 1658. The author was a Neapolitan.

made by me in my youth, when I was hardly fifteen years old, was so generally received, and with so great applause, that it was forthwith translated into many Languages, as Italian, French, Spanish, Arabick; and passed through the hands of incomparable men; I hope that now coming forth from me that am fifty years old, it shall be more dearly entertained. For when I saw the first fruits of my Labours received with so great Alacrity of mind, I was moved by these good Omens, and therefore have adventured to send it once more forth, but with an Equipage more Rich and Noble. From the first time it appeared it is now thirty-five years, and (without any derogation of my Modesty be it spoken) if ever any man laboured earnestly to disclose the secrets of Nature it was I."* After nearly forty years, therefore, of reflection, observation, and criticism he feels that his medical hints on this subject of anti-

* The "Natural Magick" is divided into what is called twenty Books, equivalent really to chapters, and they receive various headings according to their contents, but the twentieth Porta calls "Chaos," and he explains it by saying: "I determined from the beginning of my Book to unite Experiments that are contained in all Natural Sciences, but by my business that called me off, my mind was hindered, so that I could not accomplish what I attended. Since, therefore, I could not do what I would, I must be willing to do what I can. Therefore, I shut up in this Book those Experiments that could be included in no Classes, which were so diverse and various that they could not make up a Science or a Book; and, therefore, I have here them altogether confusedly as what I had overpassed, and, if God please, I will another time give you a more perfect Book. Now you must rest content with these."

pathy have borne the test of time, and may well take their place amongst the other secrets of Nature divulged for the benefit of humanity.

The hyæna was held to possess the power of counterfeiting man's speech, and of turning the gift to profitable account by going up at night to a shepherd's or woodman's hut and calling out the man's name.* Upon the man's going forth to see who wanted him, he was promptly torn to pieces. The Manticora also, according to Juba, possessed this uncanny power of imitating human speech, and turned its conversational powers to the same treacherous use. It was also held that if a hyæna made a circuit three times round any animal its victim lost all power of escape, and could not stir a foot. According to some ancient writers the animal had a stone called hyænia in its eye, and this being placed under a man's tongue imparted to him the gift of prophecy. Aristotle taught that the eyes of this creature could change colour a thousand times a day, and this is but a sample of many other curious and absurd stories concerning the beast. Sir Gardner Wilkinson mentions a strange fancy believed in by the Abyssinians that a race of people who inhabited their country had the power of changing their form at pleasure, being sometimes men and at others hyænas.

* We see this notion so lately as in a book entitled "An English Expositour," issued in 1680 by John Hayes, Printer to the University of Cambridge.

Wolf Causing Dumbness.

In the Middle Ages the wolf seems to have been in decidedly bad odour; he was probably too well-known to be respected, and in the long dreary nights of winter proved himself a terribly bad neighbour, and a very undesirable travelling companion for those who had to cross amidst the snows the almost trackless wastes. Amongst the Scandinavians the wolf held a conspicuous place in tradition and mythology. Eclipses of the sun and moon were held to be caused by two great wolves that were always pursuing them through the heavens.* The wolf, too, was the companion of Odin, the god of war, and at his feet these creatures crouched while he fed them with the flesh of his enemies.

It was an accepted belief that if a man encountered a wolf, and the creature caught sight of him before he saw it, he became dumb. Scott refers to this old notion in his "Quentin Durward," where, in the eighteenth chapter, Lady Hameline exclaims, "Our young companion has seen a wolf, and has lost his tongue in consequence." "The ground or occasionall originall thereof," Browne in his "Exposure of Vulgar Errors" would endeavour to persuade us, "was probably the amazement and sudden

---

* The northern peoples believed also in an enormous wolf, called Fernris, who was the offspring of Loki, the evil principle. This creature until the end of the world would be the cause of unnumbered ills to humanity, but at the crack of doom would, after a fearful struggle, be vanquished by the Gods, and a reign of universal peace would succeed his overthrow.

silence the unexpected appearance of wolves doe often put upon travellers, not by a supposed vapour or venomous emanation, but a vehement fear which naturally produceth obmutescence, and sometimes irrecoverable silence"; but it would appear to be a still simpler procedure, and one with a good deal to recommend it, to deny that there is an atom of truth in the story. In another old natural history before us, we read that "the wolf when he falls upon a hog or a goat, or such small beast, does not immediately kill them, but leads them by the ear, with all the speed he can, to a crew of ravenous wolves, who instantly tear them to pieces." We should have thought that the reverse had been more probable, and that the wolves that had nothing would have come with all the speed they could upon their more successful comrade; but if the old writer's story be true, it opens out a fine trait of hitherto unsuspected unselfishness in the character of the wolf.

John Leo, in his "History of Africa," declares that the dragon is the progeny of the eagle and wolf. Perhaps this may be so, but probably the conception that most of our readers have of the dragon is that he was a considerably more formidable beast than such a parentage, fierce as it is, quite suggests.

An old heraldic author tells us "how that the wolfe procureth all other beasts to fight and contention. He seeketh to deuour the sheepe, that beaste which is of all others the most hurtlesse, simple, and void of guile, thirsting continually after their blood. Yea, Nature hath planted so inveterate an hatred atweene the wolfe and the sheepe, that being dead, yet in the secrete operation of nature appeareth there a sufficient trial of their discording natures, so that the enimity betweene them seemeth not to dye with their bodies ; for if there be put vpon a harp or any such like instrument strings made of the intrailles of a sheepe, and amongst them but onely one made of the intraills of a wolfe, be the musician never so cuning in his skil, yet can he not reconcile them to an vnity and concorde of sounds, so discording alwayes is that string of the wolfe." The inveterate enmity between the two creatures is scarcely in accordance with the facts, for the wolf, from its appreciation of mutton as an article of diet, is really partial to the sheep, and is always glad to make its acquaintance.

Another old herald tells us that "the wolfe loveth to plaie with a child, and will not hurt it till it be extreme hungrie, what time he will not spare to devour it." He dwells also upon some of the animal's prejudices, as that "he watcheth much, and feareth fier and stones to be wherled at him," a feeling that one finds no difficulty in sympathizing with, and adds that "there is nothing that he hateth so much as the knocking togither of two flint stones, the which he feareth more than the hunters." He also mentions the curious physiological fact that "the wolf may not bend his neck backward in no moneth of the yere but in May," but gives us no inkling as to the reason for this.

The wearing of wolfskin was held to be a valuable preservative against epilepsy, but those who were unable to procure this, found an equally serviceable remedy in wearing a small portion of an ass's hoof in a ring. The wolfskin coat also was in request as a preservative against hydrophobia, and there was nothing better in the good old times than a wolf's head under the pillow to secure a good night's rest. Albertus Magnus, in his work " De Virtutibus Herbarum," tells us that if we wrap the tooth of a wolf in a bay leaf and carry it about with us no one will have the power to vex or annoy us.

According to Porta—and he, we have seen, professes to have gone into the secrets of nature as deeply as most men who pose as authorities*—the rook is killed by eating " the reliques of flesh the wolf hath fed on." This would appear to be a discovery of Porta's own : we do not find any suggestion of it, so far as we are aware, in any other author.

A creature called the stag-wolf, if we may credit these ancient authors (and there is much saving virtue in this if), had the curious peculiarity that if, while he was devouring his prey, he

---

* " Wherefore, studious Readers, accept my long Labours, that cost me much Study, Travel, Expense, and much Inconvenience, with the same Mind that I publish them; and remove all Blindness and Malice, which are wont to dazle the sight of the Minde, and hinder the Truth; weigh these Things with a right Judgement when you try what I have Written, for finding both Truth and Profit, you will (it may be) think better of my Pains."—*End of the Preface to Porta's " Natural Magick."*

chanced to look backward, he straightway forgot that he was already provided with a dinner, and would at once start off for one with all the zeal that his supposititious famishing condition called for.

The bear has not escaped the observation of the lover of the marvellous, though we should have thought that our forefathers, with their bear-baiting proclivities, would have had a sufficient knowledge of the creature to protect them from falling into gross error. One of the most firmly accepted beliefs in ancient and mediæval days was that the cubs were born a merely shapeless mass, and owed what after-beauty of form they possessed to the assiduous care of their mother. Hence, an ancient scribe hath it, "At the firste they seeme to be a lumpe of white flesh without any forme, little bigger than rattons, without eyes, and wanting hair. This rude lumpe, with licking, they fashion by little and little into some shape." Shakespeare it will be remembered compares Gloucester, in King Henry VI., to "an unlick'd bear-whelp," while Dryden writes :—

"The cubs of bears a living lump appear
When whelp'd, and no determined figure wear.
The mother licks them into shape, and gives
As much of form as she herself receives."

The device of the great Venetian painter, Titian, was a she-bear licking her cubs into shape.*

* In Dryden's poem, "The Hind and Panther," we find the reference :—
"The bloody bear, an independent beast,
Unlick'd to form, in groans her hate expressed."

Our readers will probably recall the lines in "Hudibras":—

> "A bear's a savage beast, of all
> Most ugly and unnatural;
> Whelp'd without form, until the dam
> Has lick'd it into shape and frame."

"Which opinion notwithstanding," quoth Browne in his assault on the vulgar errors of his day, "is not only repugnant unto the sense of everyone that shall enquire into it, but of exact and deliberate experiment. It is, moreover, injurious unto reason, and much impugneth the course and providence of nature to conceive a birth should be ordained before there is a formation. Besides, what few take notice of, men do hereby in a high measure vilifie the works of God, imputing that unto the tongue of a Beast." Browne's ideas were, we have already seen, far in advance of his time, and he took the trouble to do what many who wrote on the subject before him failed to do, went to look at some young bears. Though the belief in the idea has died away, the remembrance of the superstition still survives in the notion of licking youngsters into shape at school by such appeals to body or mind as may seem most efficacious and persuasive.

It was held that the bear found no little nutriment in sucking his own paws, and in old books on natural history he may often be found thus figured. Beaumont and Fletcher embody the old belief in their "Bonduca," where we read of those—

> "Just like a brace of bear-whelps, close and crafty,
> Sucking their fingers for their food."

Why Bears attack Beehives.

It has long been an accepted belief in rural England, that a child who has had a ride upon a bear will escape whooping cough, a belief that has had great pecuniary value to the Savoyards and others, who take a dancing bear through the villages, as the rustics gladly fee them for the privilege of a ride for their children, and the attendant immunity from one of the most infectious and distressing of the minor ailments of childhood.

We have long been familiar with the idea that bears attacked bee-hives, but we have accepted the notion that the bears did so from an appreciation of the honey that they found therein. It appears, however, that the bear does it really as a kind of stimulant, the stinging of the angry bees giving him just a welcome titillation, and arousing him from a certain torpidity that at times oppresses him, and which he rightly feels should be fought against. Others tell us that the outraged bees, justly angry at the overturning of their home and the pillage of their store, supply, by the energy of their attack and the keenness of their stings, just that pleasant piquant set-off to the epicurean bear that the over-richness and cloying sweetness of the honey seems to call for. Yet a third theory is that "they are many times subject to dimnesse of sight, for which cause especially they seeke after honeycombes, that the bees might settle upon them, and with their stings make them bleed about the head, and by that meanes discharge them of that heavinesse which troubleth their eyes." Possibly three more equally reasonable theories might be forthcoming on searching for them in the various old tomes in which the wisdom of our forefathers is enshrined.

A considerable amount of folk-lore has gathered round the hare. It was held to be a favourable omen to meet certain beasts early in the morning, but it was especially unfortunate to meet a hare. "Sume Bestes han gode meetynge, that is to seye for to meete with him first at Morne; and sume Bestes wykked meetynge : and that thei han proved ofte tyne tat the Hare hathe fulle evylle meetynge, and Swyn, and many othere Bestes. The Sparhauke and other Foules of Raveyne whan thei fleen aftre here preye and take it before men of Armes, it is a gode Signe ; and if he fayle of takynge his preye it is an evylle sygne, and also to such folke it is an eville meetynge of Ravennes." Carew, in his "Survey of Cornwall," mentions that "to talk of hares or such uncouth things" was regarded as omnious of coming ill by the fishermen ; and at some places on the coast until quite recently—or possibly even till to-day, for such notions die out very slowly—if a fisherman going down to his boat were to see a hare cross his path, he would not that day go to sea.

> "How superstitiously we mind our evils!
> The throwing down of salt, or crossing of a hare,
> Bleeding at nose, the stumbling of a horse,
> Or singing of a cricket, are of power
> To daunt whole man in us."

This superstition arose from the belief that

witches sometimes transformed themselves into hares. In Ellison's "Trip to Benwell," we find the following congratulatory lines:—

> " Nor did we meet, with nimble feet,
> One little fearful lepus;*
> That certain sign, as some divine,
> Of fortune bad to keep us."

In Aubrey's "Remaines of Gentilisme and Judaisme," written in the year 1586, it is stated, as " found by Experience, that when one keepes a Hare alive and feedeth him till he have occasion to eat him, if he telles before he killes him that he will doe so the hare will thereupon be found dead, having killed himself." One really scarcely sees what the creature gains by this proceeding.

Old writers tell us that when the hare is fainting with the heat, a state of things that one may hope does not often occur, it recruits its strength by munching up sowthistle. Topsell says that there is no leporine ailment that this plant will not cure, and that directly the hare feels a little unwell he seeks sowthistle and goes in for a course of diet. Askham goes so far as to say that "yf a hare eate of this herbe in somer when he is mad he shal be hole," but as hares are proverbially held to be specially *non compos mentis* in March, the treatment seems to come a little late. All boys who have kept rabbits will recall how appreciatively they nibble up the succulent sowthistle leaves and stems, and

---

* The scientific name of the hare is *Lepus timidus*. Dryden, in the " Hind and Panther," places " amongst the timerous kind the quaking hare."

probably it is just as welcome to the hares, not as a medicinal herb or a help to sanity, but as a toothsome item in the daily fare.

It will be remembered that in 1 Henry IV. i. 2, Shakespeare uses the expression "Melancholy as a hare," and as it was believed in mediæval days that those who partook of the flesh of any animal thereby partook also of its nature, the flesh of the hare was supposed to generate melancholia, and was therefore avoided. Why the hare should be considered of a desponding temperament no one seemed to know.

It seems curious in face of such an expression as "Mad as a March Hare" and such an epithet as "hare-brained" applied to anything especially wild and foolhardy, to find the great Bacon in his "Natural History" recommending the brains of hares as invaluable for strengthening the memory* and brightening up the faculties. Those who have "frekels,"† and would like to get rid of them, should "take the bloude of an hare, anoynte them with it, and it will doe them

---

* Magliabechi, the learned librarian, pinned his faith upon treacle to make his memory retentive. Grataroli, a famous physician of the sixteenth century, wrote a Latin treatise, "The Castle of Memory," wherein, amongst an enormous number of recipes, we find the internal application of bear's grease, a hazelnutful of mole's fat, and calcined human hair, strongly recommended by the learned author.

† It was held by our ancestors that freckles came in the early part of the year when the birds were laying their eggs, and that the same mysterious influence of Nature that spotted the eggs of the chaffinch, wren, robin, thrush, and other birds, freckled the human skin.

awaye." Another eccentric prescription is for the benefit of sufferers from rheumatism, and if it were only efficacious, its simplicity would be a great point in its favour, as it merely consists in the carrying in the pocket of the right fore-foot of a hare, the only caution to be exercised being that in the case of a man it must be the foot of a female hare, while a male hare must supply the remedy if the patient be a woman. Cogan, in his "Haven of Health," declares "thus much will I say as to the commendation of the hare, and of the defense of hunters' toyle, that no beast, be it never so great, is profitable to so many and so diverse uses in Physicke as the hare," and he then proceeds to give numerous prescriptions in which it is the principal feature. " The knee-bone of an Hare taken out alive and worne abute the necke is excellent against Convulsion fitts,"* we are told, and perhaps it may be so, but the point that more especially strikes us, and it impresses one over and over again in these mediæval recipes, is the cold-blooded cruelty and indifference to animal suffering that is shown in so many of them. Fried mice were considered a specific in small-pox, but it was necessary that they should be fried alive; while for cataract a fox should be captured, his tongue cut out, and the animal released; the member thus barbarously procured was placed in a bag of red cloth and hung round the man's neck. For erysipelas

* In another popular remedy for "fitts" one has to "take the furr of a living Bear's belly, boil it in Aqua Vitæ, take it out, squeeze it, and wrap it upon ye soales of ye Feete."

a favourite old remedy was to cut off one-half of the ear of a cat and let the blood drop on the part affected, while for fits one popular recipe was to take a mole alive, cut the tip of his nose off, and let nine drops of the blood fall on to a lump of sugar : the swallowing of this was held to be a certain cure. It would be easy to multiply these illustrations of atrocious cruelty by the score, since one comes across such barbarities in abundance.

Edward Topsell, in his "Historie of Fourefooted Beastes," published in the year 1607, discusses thus quaintly and pleasantly of the Hedgehog : "It is about the bignesse of a Cony, but more like to a Hogge, being beset and compassed all ouer with sharpe thorney haires, as well on the face as on the feete. When she is angred or gathereth her foode, she striketh them vp by an admirable instinct of nature, as sharp as pinnes or needles : these are haire at the beginning, but afterwards grow to be prickles, which is the lesse to be maruelled at, because there be Mise in Egypt which haue haire iike Hedgehogs. His meate is Apples, Wormes, and Grapes. When he findeth Apples or Grapes on the earth he rowleth himselfe vppon them, vntill he haue filled all his prickles, and then carrieth them home to his den. And if it fortun that one of them fall off by the way, he likewise shaketh off all the residue and waloweth vpon them afresh vntill they all be settled vpon his backe againe, so foorthe he goeth, makyng a noyse like a cart wheele. And if there be any young ones in his nest they pull off his load wherewithall he is loaded, eating thereof what they please, and laying uppe the residue for the time to come."

In the "Workes of Armorie" of Bossewell, published some thirty years or so before Topsell's book, we find an account so similar that we may conclude that some one or other wrote a sketch of the hedgehog that was considered so satisfactory that it became the nucleus for anybody else who wanted to deal with the subject. "The little Hiricion, with his sharpe pykes, is almost the least of all other Beastes. And of vs Englishmen he is termed an Irchin or Urcheon, a beast so-called for the roughness and sharpnesse of his pykes, which nature hath giuen him in steade of haire. And such hys pykes couereth his skinne, as the haire doth the other beastes, and be his weapon or armour wherewith he pricketh and greeveth them that take or touch him. He is a beaste of witte and good puruciance, for he clymeth vpon a Vine or an Apple tree, and biteth of their branches and twiggs, and when they be fallen doune he waloweth on them, and so they sticke to his prickles, and he beareth them into a hollow tree, or some other hole, and keepeth them for meate for himselfe and his young ones. If after he is so charged there happe any to fal from his pricks, then for indignation he throweth from his backe all the other and eftsoones returneth to the tree to charge him againe of newe."

These two old authors both refer, too, to the belief that the hedgehog had distinct gifts as a wind and weather prophet. Bossewell asserts that "the Urcheon is witty and wise in his knowledge of comming of Winds, North and South, for he changeth his Denne or hole, when he is ware that such windes come;" while Topsell has it that "when they hide themselves in their den they haue a naturall vnderstanding of the turning of the wind. They have two holes in their caue, the one North, the other South, obseruing to stop the mouth against the winde, as the skilful mariner to stiere and turn the rudder and sailes, for which some haue held opinion that they do naturally foreknow the change of weather."

> "The hedgehogge hath a sharp quicke thorned garment,
> That on his backe doth serue him for defence;
> He can presage the winds incontinent,
> And hath good knowledge in the difference
> Between the southerne and the northerne wind.
> These virtues are allotted him by kind,
> Whereon in Constantinople, that great city,
> A merchant in his garden gaue one nourishment;
> By which he knew that winds true certainty,
> Because the hedgehog gaue him just presagement."

So at all events declares Chester in his "Love's Martyr"; and Bodenham in the "Belvedere, or Garden of the Muses," A.D. 1600, testifies to the same belief in the lines :—

> "As hedgehogs doe foresee ensuinge stormes,
> So wise men are for fortune still prepared."

The author of "Poor Robin's Almanack," at the much more recent date of 1733, takes what one may consider quite a professional interest in the hedgehog as a weather prophet, and exclaims:—

> "If by some secret art the hedgehog know,
> So long before, which way the winds will blow,
> She has an art which many a person lacks,
> That thinks himself fit to make almanacks."

A remark that is certainly most true, though for the honour of the craft we should hardly have expected a calendar-maker to admit as much.

The medicinal virtues of the hedgehog were held to be very considerable in the days of faith, and some of the preparations were abominably nasty. "The flesh being stale," says one of these old authorities, "giuen to a madde man cureth him." Putrid hedgehog fetched out of a ditch and given as food or medicine to a man! The flesh salted, dried, beaten to a powder and then drank in vinegar was held in high repute as a remedy for dropsy, and for "Leprosie, the Crampe, and all sicknesse in the nerves," and the fat beaten up with honey was deemed an excellent strengthener for a weak voice.

Topsell states that "the left eie of a Hedgehog being fried with oyle, yealdeth a liquor which causeth sleep, if it bee infused into the eares with a quill. Warts of al sorts are likewise taken away by the same. If the right eie be fryed with the oile of lineseed and put in a vessell of red brasse, and afterward anoint his eies therewith, as with an eie-salue, he shal see as well in the darke as in the light." The distinction is often a very important one in these old recipes.

between left or right, hind leg or front, male or female, and the like, and an error in any of these details completely upsets all hope of any benefit being derived ; thus we see in this last receipt that a man might fry the left eye for ever, and never get any nearer the gift of nocturnal vision. In the same way "tenne sprigs of Laurell, seauen graines of Pepper, and the skin of the ribs of an hedgehog dryed and beaten, cast into three cups of water and warmed, so being drunk of one that hath the Collicke, and let rest, he shall be in perfect health ; but with this exception, that for a man it must bee the membrane of a male hedgehog, and for a woman a female."

Porta declares that the ancients made their hair grow by using the ashes of a land-hedgehog. As no one ever heard of a water-hedgehog this stipulation seems almost needlessly precise. In another recipe we are told to " take the body of a hedgehog burnt to powder,* and if you adde thereto Beares-grease it will restore unto a bald man his heade of haire againe, if the place be rubbed vntil it be ready to bleed." Bear's grease pure and simple has long had a reputation amongst hair-dressers, and if this be as potent as they would have us believe, the rest of the

* A mole skinned, dried in the oven, and then powdered, was held in the fen districts to be a specific for ague. It may still be in vogue—it certainly was in use twenty years ago. The mole must be a male. As much of the powder as would lie on a shilling was to be taken every day, for nine days, in gin. Nine days were then to be omitted, and then the remedy was to be resumed for nine days, by which time a cure was supposed to be effected.

prescription can scarcely claim much of the credit. The writer adds that "some mingle red Snailes," but this is clearly optional, and we should certainly avail ourselves of the option.

Epilepsy was to be cured by wearing a ring in which a portion of the hoof of a deer was enclosed. It may interest anyone with a partiality for venison to know that "Deer's flesh that is catcht in Summer is poyson; because then they feed on Adders and serpents: these are venemous creatures, and by eating of them they grow thirsty; and this they know naturally, for if they drink before they have digested them they are killed by them; wherefore they will abstain from water, though they burn with thirst. Wherefore Stag's flesh eaten at that time is venemous and very dangerous." Shakespeare refers to the weeping of the deer, and tells how

> "The big round tears
> Cours'd one another down his innocent nose
> In piteous chace."

It was an old belief that the deer wept every year for the loss of their horns, "a likeness of those who grieve for the loss of their worldly possessions. So, too, should a penitent and watchful sinner not cease to weep when he is overtaken." This straining after a moral, as we have already seen, is a very marked feature amongst the old writers. Sometimes the moral sentiment flows fairly naturally, but more often it is terribly laboured. Thus, for example, we read that "the ferret is a bold and audacious beast (though little), and an enemie to all other, and when they take a prey their custome and manner is onely to suck the bloud as they bite it, and not to eat the flesh ; and if at any time their prey shall be taken from them they fall a squeaking and crying. Such are the rich men of this world, who yell and crie out when they part with their riches, weeping and wailing for the losse of such things as they have hunted after with as much greedinesse as want of pitie."

In like manner we learn that "when the Squirrell is hunted she cannot be driven to the ground, unlesse extremitie of faintnesse cause her to do so through an unwilling compulsion, for such is the stately mind of this little beast that while her limbes and strength lasteth she tarrieth and saveth herself in the tops of tall trees, disdaining to come down for every harm or hurt which she feeleth ; knowing, indeed, her greatest danger to rest below amongst the dogs and busie hunters. From whence may be gathered a perfect pattern for us, to be secured from all the wiles and hungrie chasings of the treacherous devil : namely, that we keep above in the loftie palaces of heavenlie meditations, for there is small securitie in things on earth ; and greatest ought to be our fear of danger, when we leave to look and think of heaven."

The fabulists and moralists of ancient and mediæval days regarded animals as so much raw material to be modelled into whatever form best suited their ends. They were little, if at all, concerned in giving a true picture of animal life, but used the various creatures in such conventional and allegorical way as most readily adapted itself to the moral or political end in view in their writings. Art has often pursued much the same course, and instead of giving us the real animal nature has introduced an entirely foreign element, and represented the creatures as swayed by purely human considerations. Æsop and La Fontaine make the animals speak as though they were influenced by human feelings and motives, while Landseer, for example, in some of his noble pictures employs his dogs and other animals to simulate humanity, as in "Laying Down the Law," "Alexander and Diogenes," and other well-known works of the master. The result is quaint, grotesque, delicious, humorous; but these law-givers, philosophers, and so forth, are canine in form alone, and are but puppets acting a part that is a good-natured satire on humanity.

It was a very old belief that when the wild boar was hunted its tusks grew so hot in its rage and excitement as to actually burn the dogs if they came within the terrible sweep of them. Xenophon tells us in his description of the chase of the boar that hairs laid upon the tusks shrivel up even after the brute is slain. This belief has been handed down from generation to generation of writers on so-called natural history, and even in a book in our possession, published in London in 1786, we find the statement only very slightly qualified by a preliminary "it is said." "It is said that when this creature is hunted down his tusks are so inflamed that they will burn and singe the hair of the dogs." Shakespeare says that the "ireful boar" does not even fear the lion, and Guillim says that "he is counted the most absolute Champion amongst Beasts, for that he hath weapons to wound his foe, which are his strong and sharp Tusks, and also his Target to defend himself: for which he useth oft to rub his shoulders and sides against Trees, wherewith to harden them against the stroke of his Adversary."

Herbert states in his book of travels that there are on the African coast, opposite Madagascar, vast herds of wild swine that are greatly esteemed by the natives of those parts, not only for their flesh, but more especially for a stone that is found often within them, which is "very soveraign against poison." The Spaniards, he tells us, call it Pietro del Porco. The virtue of this stone is supposed to arise from their feeding upon certain medical herbs.

The ermine was believed to prefer death to defilement, and if placed within a wall or ring of mud, would kill itself rather than contaminate its spotless fur. It is on this account that ermine is selected as the robe of prince and judge—an emblem of unspotted purity. Beaumont and Fletcher, in their "Knight of Malta," refer to this in the line :—

"Whose honour, ermine-like, can never suffer spot."

In a portrait of Queen Elizabeth at Hatfield, an ermine is represented as running up her arm, as a delicate compliment to the Virgin Queen.

It was reported that goats see as well by night as by day, hence those people who are unable to see after dark can be cured of their infirmity by eating the liver of a goat; while for those who suffered from insomnia no remedy was held in better repute than the horn of a goat: this placed beneath the head of the patient speedily brought refreshing sleep. Porta affirms that "goats, when their eyes are blood-shotten, let out the blood; the she-goat by the point of a bullrush, the he-goat by the pricking of a thorn." Such examples of animal sagacity have a great attraction for this old author, and he gives many instances in support of his contention, that "living creatures, though they have no understanding, yet their senses are quicker than ours, and by their actions they teach us Physick, Husbandry, the art of Building, the disposing of Household Affairs, and almost all Arts and Sciences. The beasts that have no reason, do by their nature strangely shun the eyes of witches and hurtfull things; the Doves, for a preservative against inchantment, first gather some little Bay-tree boughs, and then lay them upon their nests to preserve their young; so do the Kites use brambles, the Turtles swordgrasse, the Crows withy, the Lapwings Venus-hair, the Ravens ivy, the Herns carrot, the Blackbirds myrtle, the Larkes grasse, for the same purpose. In lyke manner they have shewed us preservatives against poysons; the Elephant having by chance eaten a

Chameleon, against the poyson thereof eats of the wilde Olive; the Tortoise, having eaten a Serpent, dispels the poyson by eating the herb Origan. There is a kind of Spider which destroyeth the Harts, except permitting they eat wilde Ivy; and whensoever they light upon any poysonous food they cure themselves with the artichoke; and against Serpents they prepare and arm themselves with wilde Parsneps." We need not further pursue matters with our author. Suffice it to say, that he brings forward an enormous number of examples, and amply proves his case to his satisfaction, as indeed he should have no difficulty in doing, when it is once understood that facts are of secondary importance.

One strange notion of antiquity was that the blood of the goat would dissolve the diamond. The statement is found in Pliny, Solinus, Albertus, Cyprian, Isidore, and many other writers, right away down to comparatively recent days. Legh, for instance, states, without hesitation, "The Diamonde, which neither iron nor fier wil daunt, the bloud of the gote softneth to the breaking." Maundevile, of course, receives it as an undoubted truth; while even Browne writes: "We hear it in every mouth, and in many good Authors reade it, that a Diamond, which is the hardest of stones, not yeelding unto Steele, Emery or any other thing, is yet made soft and broke by the bloud of a Goat."

That things are not always what they seem must have been a mere truism in the Middle Ages. Thus Aubrey in his "Remains of Gentilisme and

Judaism," introduces the goat in an entirely new character. "A conceit there is that ye devil commonly appeareth with a cloven hoof, wherein though it seem excessively ridiculous there may be something of truth, and ye ground at first might be his frequent appearing in the shape of a goat, which answers that description. This was the opinion of ancient Xtians concerning ye apparition of Fauns and Satyrs. The devil most often appears in the shape of a goat, nor did he only assume this shape in olden times, but commonly in later times, especially in ye place of his worship, if there be any truth in the confession of witches. And therefore a goat is not improperly made an hieroglyphic of ye devil."

The shrew-mouse, one of the most inoffensive of creatures, was by our ancestors held to be of terribly poisonous nature. Its bite was thought to be most venomous, and even contact with it in any way was accounted extremely dangerous. Cattle and horses seized with any malady that appeared to cause any numbness of the legs were at once reputed shrew-struck. "It is a ravening beast," quoth Topsell, "feigning itself gentle and tame, but being touched it biteth deep and poysoneth deadly. It beareth a cruel minde, desiring to hunt anything, neither is there any creature that it loveth." On whatever limb it crept was "cruel anguish," often ending in paralysis. These calumnies have prevailed in many countries and for many ages, the Romans being as firmly convinced of the deadly nature of the shrew-mouse, as any British rustic of a century ago. The shrew-mouse, according to the author of the "Speculum Mundi," "hath a long and sharp snout like a mole. In Latine it is called Mus araneus, because it containeth in it poison or venime like a spider, and if at any time it bite either man or beast the truth of this will be too apparent. But commonly it is called a Shrew-mouse, and from the venimous biting of this beast we have an English imprecation, I beshrew thee; in which words we do, indeed, wish some such evil. And again, because a curst scold or brawling wife is esteemed none of the least evils; we, therefore, call such a one a Shrew." Hence Shakespeare, dealing with such a character, entitled one of his plays the Taming of the Shrew.

Happily there was a certain antidote against the evil wrought by this malevolent beast. A large ash-tree being chosen, a deep hole was made in its trunk, and after certain incantations were made a shrew-mouse was thrust alive into the opening, and the hole securely plugged. "A shrew-ash," says Gilbert White in his "Natural History of Selborne," "is an ash whose twigs or branches, when gently applied to the limbs of cattle, will immediately relieve the pain which a beast suffers from the running of a shrew-mouse over the part affected. Against this accident, to which they were continually liable, our provident forefathers always kept a shrew-ash at hand, which when once medicated would maintain its virtue for ever." One of these shrew-ashes, now but a fragment of what was evidently once a massive stately tree, may still be seen near the Sheen

Gate in Richmond Park, and there are those still living who can remember cattle and horses being brought to it for its healing virtues.

The horse does not seem to have so much unnatural history associated with him as we might have anticipated, such stories as that of the feeding of the horses of Diomed with human flesh, or of the milk-white steed, Al Borak, of Mohammed, each of whose strides was equal to the furthest range of human vision, being altogether fabulous and mythical. Diomed, the tyrant of Thrace, seems to have held out very little encouragement to immigrants or wandering tourists, if the legend be true that he utilized them as fodder.

> "Here such dire welcome is for thee prepared
> As Diomed's unhappy strangers shared;
> His hapless guests at silent midnight bled,
> On their torn limbs his snorting coursers fed."*

One meets with many famous steeds in classical and mediæval literature, but these, of course, are individual examples of the race, and anything told of them can scarcely be considered as testifying to the general though erroneous notions entertained on the subject of horses generally. The horse Bayard, for example, the property of the four Sons of Aymon, had a most useful peculiarity in that he grew larger or smaller in fair proportion to his rider, according as the big stalwart brother of six feet high, or the little fellow not yet in his teens got astride him. One of the horses of Achilles is said to

* The "Lusiad"; Camoens.

have announced to his master his impending death. It is sufficiently evident that expanding, contracting, and talkative horses are altogether outside the ordinary pale.

According to a small manuscript of the twelfth century, called "Mappæ clavicula," "if oxen drink first, then there will be enough water for both oxen and horses: but if the horses drink first there will not be sufficient either for horses or oxen." Horses are afraid of elephants until they get used to them, and there is also some little antipathy between camels, bears and horses. Porta declares that "Horses will burst if they tread upon the Wolf's footing. If Drums be made of an Elephant, Camel, or Wolves skin, and one beat them, the Horses will then run away and dare not stand. By the same reason, if you will drive away Bears, a Horse hath a capital hatred with a Bear: he will know his enemy that he never saw before, and presentlie provide himself to fight with him, and I have heard that Bears have been driven away in the Wildernesse by the sound of a Drum, when it was made of Horse's skin."

It has for centuries been a belief in many parts of the country that the hairs from a horse's tail, when dropped in the water, become endued with life, and turn into small eels. A horsehair tied round a wart has been held to be of potent efficacy for its removal; and horsehair spread on bread and butter has been prescribed as a remedy, even in quite recent times, for worms. For sciatica, according to one Dr. Floyer, once on a time one of the shining lights of the medical profession, the finest preparation is " the marrow of a horse (kill'd by chance, not dying of any disease) mixed with some rose-water. Chafe it in with a warme hand for a quarter of an houre, then putt on a Scarlett cloth, broad enough to cover ye part affected, and go into a warme Bed." As personal experience is so valuable in all such cases, he adds : " It cured my Aunt Lakes, who went yearly to the Bath for ye Sciatica, but never went after she knew and used this medicine."

In Winstanley's "Book of Knowledge," a book that went through several editions (our copy we see is dated 1685),* he deals with many strange matters, and gives receipts for various extraordinary requirements : to make men seem headless, to make it that men shall not find the door, and so forth; but amongst rather more reasonable items we find, " to make one dance." The *modus operandi* is sufficiently simple, though perhaps a trifle disgusting; it is as follows :— " Cut the Hoof of a Horse in pieces, seethe it with Oyl and anoint the Table or any other

---

* Published therefore in the reign of Charles II., "Our most undoubted and lawful King." We have most of us formed an opinion on the character of this wearer of the spotless ermine; and the fulsome verse of Winstanley, written, not when the reign was commencing and the national hopes were high, but as it neared its end, is somewhat startling :—

"Long may he live who now doth wear the Crown
 To tread all Heresies and Schismes down.
 Great God, let not his prayers e'er return empty,
 But Crown his Head with Years and Years with plenty.'

place, and lay his head thereon, when you would have him to dance." Such is a sample of the best that this storehouse of knowledge could yield to those who sought its help.

Horse-shoes were at one time often nailed on doors as a protection against witches and malignant spirits, and " The horse-shoe nailed, each threshold's guard "* may often still be seen on old country houses. John Aubrey, writing some two hundred years ago, says : " Most houses at the West End of London have a horse-shoe on the threshold." Dwellers in town, however, have not the same dread of the mysterious as the more lonely dwellers in the country, though many a man who is brave enough on the gas-lighted pavement would feel a little " creepy " when the shrill scream of a trapped hare, or the wild cry of the peewit, broke upon the stillness of the night and found him in some country lane or on the open downland. It is a firm article of belief, however, with all who have faith in the efficacy of the horse-shoe that it must be picked up, not bought. Whatever virtue may reside in one that is found is wholly wanting in one that is purchased.

The humble donkey has its share of quaint associations. The conspicuous cross upon its back is popularly supposed to date from the day that our Saviour rode in Jerusalem upon an ass. It is, however, more probable that the ass that brayed and browsed in Eden bore a similar mark.

* Gay's Fables.

Amongst the ancient Egyptians the ass was
dedicated to the evil spirit Typho, and once a
year, if we may believe Plutarch, the people
sacrificed an ass to this foul deity by hurling it
over a precipice. The people of Lycopolis carried
their antipathy so far that they excluded the
trumpet from their festivals and military service
from a fancy that its sound was a little too
suggestive of the asinine vocal performances.
The asses of the East are of a more tawny
colour than those with which we are familiar
in England; as this red tint was associated in
people's minds with a creature devoted to the
Evil One, it was but a step further to ascribe an
evil association to the colour itself; hence
anyone who was so unfortunate as to have an
especially ruddy countenance, or a more than
usually deep shade of red in the hair, was at
once held to be in an uncomfortably close
relationship with Typho. The dun-colour of
our British specimens gave them their name.
Chaucer, for instance, calls the donkey the dun,
as we may see in the "Canterbury Tales"—
"Dun is in the mire."

According to De Thaun, "The wild Ass, when
March in its course has completed twenty-five
days, brays twelve times, and also in the night,
for this reason, that that season is the equinox—
days and nights are of equal length. By the
twelve times that it makes its braying and
crying it shows that night and day have twelve
hours in their circuit. The ass is grieved when
he makes his cry that the night and the day have

equal length, for he likes better the length of the night than of the day." One can only read such an extract as this with a feeling of utter wonder; in the first place, how De Thaun could believe such a thing himself, and in the second place, how he could expect anyone else to do so. The exact accuracy of the wild ass as to the day of the month, and his twelvefold bray of regret as each recurring year brings it round again, are triumphs of the imaginative faculty. We may probably infer that when the twenty-ninth day of September has come round again the balance is redressed, hope springs again, and the twelve brays this time are of a peculiarly jubilant and sonorous character.

Asses' hair was in the Middle Ages held to be a sterling remedy for ague, though one must have been credulous indeed to try it. It is interesting more especially perhaps as a foreshadowing of that doctrine of homœopathy which deals with the cure of like by like. Great healing powers are attributed to the hairs from the cross on the donkey's back: hairs cut from it and suspended in a bag round a child's neck were a potent influence in the prevention of fits and convulsions. Another famous remedy was the cure of whooping cough by passing the sufferer three times under the belly and three times over the back of a donkey. In Sussex a standard remedy for the same distressing complaint was procured by cutting some of the hair out of the cross, chopping it up finely, and spreading it on bread and butter for the breakfast of the patient; while in Dorsetshire prevention was rightly considered better than cure, and though the rustics may have doubted the efficacy of vaccination as a remedy against small-pox, they had no hesitation whatever in getting their children astride on the donkey's back as early as possible as a preventative to their ever catching whooping cough. One meets with remedy after remedy of the same general nature, and all owing their efficacy to some mysterious connection between this particular complaint and donkey-hair, but what this occult influence can be is wholly unknown to us.

The old herald, Legh, says of the ass—" As he is not the wisest so is he the least sumptuous, especially in his diet, for his feeding is on Thistles, Nettles, and Briers, and therefore small birdes hate him, especially the Sparrowe is most enemie unto him," as they see him stolidly devouring the plants that they visit for their own sustenance. The ancient author with ponderous humour finishes his account of the ass by saying, "I could write much of this beast, but that it wolde be thought it were to mine owne glorie."

The dog, the friend and companion of man, was said to see ghosts, and their howling at untoward times portended death or conflagration or some such grave event, and has, therefore, for many centuries been held of evil omen, and no doubt in remote country districts the feeling still remains. The cries were said to be often in terror of sights invisible to man. Rabbi Menachem declares in his exposition of the Pentateuch that "when the Angel of Death enters into a city the dogs do howl,"* and he records an instance of a dog that fled in terror from before the angel, and that someone kicked it back and it died, but whether from the effects of a too vigorous kick, or from being thrust into the path of the destroying angel, he does not venture to pronounce.

If a child has whooping cough some of its hair must be placed between slices of bread and given to a dog. Should the dog cough, as he most probably will, it is an indication that the disease has passed from the child to the dog. The same idea may be seen in the old custom of giving some of the hair of anyone attacked with scarlet fever to a donkey. Should the animal swallow it the disease was supposed then and there to pass from the one ass to the other.

Coles, in his "Art of Simpling," says that "the herb called Hound's tongue will tye the Tongues of Houndes, so that they shall not bark at you, if it be laid under the bottom of your foot." A little hare's fur somewhere about the person was held to be equally valuable, and no doubt it was. One authority hath it that a dog will not bark if another dog's tongue be carried under the great toe, and the carrying of a dog's heart in one's pocket is another capital idea to the same end. "The tail of a young Wheezel put under your foot is also

---

* "In the Rabbinical book it saith the dogs howl when with icy breath Great Sammael, the Angel of Death, takes through the town his flight."—LONGFELLOW, *Golden Legend*.

recommended," and if none of these methods are available, the dog may be equally well silenced by giving him a frog to eat, artfully secreted in a piece of meat.

During the Middle Ages it was held that the head of a mad dog pounded up and drank in wine was a specific for jaundice. If, on the other hand, the head was burnt and the powdered ashes put to a cancer, it was held a sure remedy, and, naturally, on the homœopathic principle of like to like, these ashes, if given to a man who had been bitten by a rabid dog, "casteth out all the venom and the foulness, and healeth the maddening bites." The liver of the dog was equally efficacious. A gipsy preventative of hydrophobia was to take some hairs from the dog that gave the bite, a very risky operation by the way, and fry them in oil, applying them with a little green rosemary to the wound. To eat churchyard grass* was esteemed also a good thing in the case of anyone bitten by a rabid dog. So lately as the year 1866 it came out at the inquest held on the body of a child that had died of hydrophobia, that one of the relatives fished up out of the river the dead body of the dog that had done the mischief, in order that its liver might be cooked and eaten by the child. In spite of this the patient died.

It was held that if a cat were in a cart, a state of things that need rarely happen one would imagine, the horses would soon tire if the wind

---

* The butter made from the milk of a cow fed in a churchyard was held to be a potent remedy for consumption.

blew from Pussy to them, and that in like manner the steed would soon flag that was ridden by a man who had any cat's fur in his dress, and that anyone swallowing the hair of a cat would be subject to fainting fits. On the other hand, it was believed that nothing was better as a cure for whitlow than to put the ailing finger for a quarter of an hour each day into the ear of a cat. Anything that touches a cat's ear is received with such marked disfavour that we imagine this remedy is simply unworkable, as the cat would never be a consenting party. Three drops of blood from a cat's tail were held to be a cure for epilepsy, while a sovereign remedy for those who would preserve their sight was to burn the head of a black cat to ashes, and then blow a little of the dust three times a day into the eyes. This, we imagine, should rather be classed amongst the methods of injuring the sight.

To cure a stye our forefathers had great faith in rubbing it with hairs from a cat's tail,* two essential points being that the cat should be a black one, and that the operation should take place on the first night of the new moon; but to cure warts the hairs must be taken from the tail of a tortoiseshell cat, and even then the remedy is only efficacious during the month of May. Another strange belief was that a cat having three colours in its fur was a great protection against fire. It is an old idea that the brains

* As this led to vigorous protests from the cat, and very possibly a good scratching, a gold ring or coin was often substituted, and found to be equally beneficial.

of cats are of destructive malignity, and that anyone desiring to quietly get rid of an enemy has only to invite him to a repast in which some of the delicacies have an imperceptible fragment of this poison added.

Cats see well by night, and were often, and especially black ones, believed to be the witches' familiars, and therefore regarded with fear and aversion. It was held that they had power to raise a gale, and on board ship the malevolent disposition with which they were credited has made them in an especial degree unpopular shipmates. Pussy was thought to particularly provoke a storm by playing with any article of wearing apparel, by rubbing her face, or by licking her fur the wrong way; she was sheltered from rough usage however by the belief that provoking her would bring a gale, while drowning her would cause a regular tempest. In Germany there is a belief that anyone who makes a cat his enemy will be attended at his funeral by rats and heavy rain. As cats see well by night, and are given to wandering abroad at unholy hours, they were connected with the baleful influences of the moon. Freye, the Norse goddess, was attended by cats, and Friday, her especial day, was always considered unlucky. The ruffling of the water by the rising wind is called a cat's paw, and cats are said to smell a coming gale, while all must be familiar with that tempestuous state of affairs known as "raining cats and dogs." In Cornwall, and on some other parts of the coast, the people say that a spectral dog, called Shony, is sometimes seen, and that this always predicts a storm.

Some persons have a marked antipathy to cats. Henry III. of France fainted if he caught sight of one, and Napoleon I. had almost as strong a feeling and failing. Shylock, in the Merchant of Venice it will be remembered, says :—

> "Some men there are that love not a gaping pig,
> Some that are mad if they behold a cat."

It is well known that cats have a wonderful knack of falling on their feet, and they are so tenacious of life that they are ordinarily credited with having nine lives, though it is proverbially held that care will kill even a cat. Not only does Shakespeare refer to cat-lore in Macbeth in "the poor cat i' the adage," but in Romeo and Juliet this old belief in the strong hold that Pussy has on life is distinctly referred to in the first scene of the third act:—

> "What would'st thou have with me?
> Good king of cats, nothing but one of your nine lives."

The cat again appears in the legend of the indomitable cats of Kilkenny that fought till a little fluff was all the record of that sanguinary struggle, and we have all of us heard of the special power of facial expression of the cats of Cheshire.

The Grimalkin of Shakespeare's Macbeth was one of the witch's familiar spirits, and the cat, the reputed companion of these unlovely and unloved personages, often therefore receives this name.

Aubrey, writing in 1686, tells a story that smacks strongly of witchcraft and the black cat. "Mrs. Clarke, a Herefordshire woman, told me," he says, "to bury the head of a black Catt with a Jacobus or a piece of gold in it, and put into the eies two black beanes (what was to be done with the beanes she hath forgott), but it must be done on a Tuesday at twelve o'clock at night, and that time nine nights after the piece of gold must be taken out, and whatsoever you buy with it (always reserving some part of the money) you will have money brought into your pockett, perhaps the same piece of gold again." Unfortunately, he does not seem to have tried it, so we never learn what success might have attended the experiment.

The description of pussy by Bartholomew Anglicus is most graphic, and is an evident study from the life. "He is a full lecherous beast in youth," saith he, " swift, pliant, and merry, and leapeth and reseth on everything that is afore him, and is led by a straw and played therewith, and is a right heavy beast in age and full sleepy, and lieth slyly in wait for mice, and is aware where they be more by smell than by sight, and hunteth and reseth on them in privy places, and when he taketh a mouse he playeth therewith, and eateth him after the play. In time of love is hard fighting for wives, and one scratcheth and rendeth the other grievously with biting and with claws; and he maketh a rueful noyse and ghastful when one proffereth to fight with another, and hardly is he hurt when he is thrown down off an high place.* And when he hath a fair skin he is, as it were, proud thereof, and goeth fast about, and is oft for his fair skin taken of the skinner and slain and flayed."† This is clearly the description of a close and accurate observer.

The description in the "Speculum Mundi," though much shorter, is almost equally happy. "The common or vulgar Cat is a creature well known, and being young it is very wanton and sportfull: but waxing older is very sad and melancholy. It is called a Cat from the Latine word signifying wary, for a Cat is a watchfull and warie beast, seldome overtaken, and most attendant to her sport and prey." John Bossewell says of the cat that "he is slie and wittie and seeth so sharply that he overcommeth darknesse of the nyghte by the shynynge lyghte of his eyne. He doth delighte that he enjoyeth his libertie." Men may come and men may go, but cat-nature is evidently unchanging.

Cats naturally suggest rats and mice. It was an ancient belief that these sprang spontaneously from any mass of putrefaction. "Mice excell

---

* "It is also watchful, dextrous, swift, pliable, and has such good nerves that if it falls from never so high it still lights upon its feet, and therefore may denote those that have so much foresight that whatever befalls them they are still upon their guard."—*Coats*, A.D. 1747.

† The skin of the cat is the only portion of the animal that can be turned to any use. According to mediæval belief, Satan once thought he could make a man, but only succeeded in turning out a skinless cat. St. Peter, filled with compassion for the miserable object, bestowed on it a fur coat, its only valuable possession, and a queer-tempered beast it has turned out.

all living creatures," writes one of the ancient authorities, "in the knowledge and experience of things to come: for when any old house, habitation, tenement, or other dwelling place waxeth ruinous and ready to fall, they perceive it first, and out of that their foresight they make present avoidance from their holes, and betake themselves to flight even as fast as their little legs will give them leave, and so they seek some other place wherein they may dwell with more securitie." Our readers will naturally recall the proverbial belief that rats desert the sinking ship. Swift, in his epistle to Mr. Nugent, writes of those that "fly like rats from sinking ships," and the desertion of the losing side has received the opprobrious name of "ratting" on this account.

Maundevile, amongst many other wonderful things that he saw or heard of in his travels, came to a place where the rats were as large as dogs;* requiring great mastiffs for their capture, as they were altogether beyond the power of the cats of the place to deal with. "And ther ben Myse als grete as Houndes, and yalowe Myse als grete as Ravennes." If the rats and mice kept the proportion between their respective sizes that we are familiar with, and the mice were as big as hounds, we can readily understand that the rats must have been

---

* He does not specify what dogs—
"Mastiff, greyhound, mongrel, grim,
Hound, or spaniel, black, or lym,
Or bob-tail tike, or trundle tail,"
though this is clearly not an unimportant detail.

very formidable creatures indeed, and quite beyond the power of ordinary terrier or pussy to cope with.

Jordanus brought home a story of rats in India as large as foxes. The creatures he saw were probably bandicoots,* very rat-like animals, though not quite so big as foxes, even though the Indian foxes are much smaller than the species we have in England. A bandicoot is about twenty-one inches long, full measure, about five inches of this being tail. According to Herodotus, it was not the rats that were equal in size to foxes in India, but the ants. We can recall an absurd picture of these in one of the mediæval natural history books, where a couple of Europeans stand at a very respectful distance from a large mound that is covered with ants as big as cats, the effect of the ant-form when thus magnified being very quaint.

It was a very ancient belief that oysters, mussels, cockles, and all shell fishes grew or diminished according to the phases of the moon. "Some have found it out by diligent search that the fibres in the livers of rats and mice answer in number to the days of the month's age." This was really a very curious discovery to make, or shall we rather say—a very curious assertion to be responsible for?

It is impossible to mention a tithe of the strange facts got together by the industry of

* The name is said by Sir E. Tennent, in his "Natural History of Ceylon," to be from the Telegu words: Pandi-koku, the pig-rat.

the men of science of the past; sometimes introducing to our notice the most extraordinary creatures, at others presenting the most ordinary creatures in an extraordinary way. What can we say, for instance, of the Catoblepas, a beast bred in Lybia, "a fearful and terrible beast to look upon"? His eyes "very fierie, as it were of a bloudie colour, and he never useth to look directly forward, nor upward, but always down to the earth." He has a long mane and cloven feet, and his body covered with scales. "As for his meat, it is deadly and poysonfull herbes, and he sendeth forth a horrible breath which poysoneth the aire over his head and about him, inasmuch that such creatures as draw in the breath of that aire are grievously afflicted, and losing both voice and sight, they fall into deadly convulsions." What shall we say of the Oryges, the only beast in creation that has his hair growing reversed and turning towards the head? Or of the Lomie in the forests of Bohemia, "which hath hanging under its neck a Bladder always full of scalding water, with which, when she is hunted, she so tortureth the Dogs that she thereby maketh her escape"? Or of the wonderful Eale of Ethiopia as large as a hippopotamus, and having horns that he can incline backwards or forwards at any angle to suit the exigencies of conflict? Or of the Manticora, having the face of a man and the body of a lion, and voice like the blending of flute and of trumpet? Or of fifty other creatures equally extraordinary? It is painful to think that such stories were deliberate inventions, and that knaves devised them and fools accepted them; and we must, we believe, conclude that almost every story had a grain of truth in it, but that the love of the marvellous, the tendency to exaggeration, the change that took place as the story travelled, and received almost unconsciously here an additional graphic touch and there a little more fully developed detail, made the fully matured statement an entirely different thing to the modest seed from which it sprang.

We have already encountered many instances of how the most ordinary creatures are described in a way that leads one to suppose that the two great virtues in a naturalist, observation and experiment, were almost entirely wanting at any period for the last two thousand years or more. How else could such a belief as that the badger has his two legs on one side shorter than the other two have ever gained credence? or that the ram "when he slepeth, from spring-time till harvest he lyeth on the one side, and from harvest till spring-time againe on the other side"? Or, to travel a little further afield, that the whiskers of a tiger are mortal poison, causing men to die mad if given to them in meat? Or that the camel is so ashamed of its ugliness that before drinking in a stream it always fouls the water so that it may not see the reflection of itself? Or fifty other statements equally at variance with the facts? The respect for those who by the vigour and uncompromising directness of their assertions became regarded as great authorities was so tremendous and all-embracing that no one seemed to dare to challenge statements made by them, while the ease and comfort to subsequent writers of having all responsibility taken off their own shoulders by merely copying instead of testing had a fatal fascination, the result being that many assertions have had a vigorous vitality for centuries that could have been readily disproved in a week or even an hour of honest personal investigation.

CHAPTER IV.

The phœnix—Various ancient and mediæval writers thereon—The Bird of Paradise—The Museum of Tradescant—The roc—The barnacle goose—The eagle—Its power of gazing upon the sun—Its keenness of vision—The pelican—The swan and its death song—A favourite idea with the poets—Hostility between the swan and the eagle—The ostrich—Its digestive powers—How its eggs are hatched—The cock—Antipathy between lion and cock—Cock-broth and cock-ale for invalids—Incorporation in man of various valued animal characteristics—The stone alectorius—Animals haled before the judges for offences against man—The deadly cockatrice—Cock-crow—The "Armonye of Byrdes"—The raven—How it became black—The ravenstone—The owl—The swallow—Sight to the blind—Oil of swallows as a remedy—The robin and the wren—Their pious care of the dead—The nightingale—The doctrine of signatures—Thorn-pierced breast—Philomela—The cuckoo—His voice-restorer—The peacock—Its pride and its shame—The kingfisher—As a weathercock—Sir Thomas Browne thereon—Halcyone—Halcyon days—The filial stork—The cautious cranes.

Though a belief in the phœnix has long since died away it was for a thousand years or more as much an article of credence as a swan or an eagle. As far as we are aware, the first reference to it is found in the pages of Herodotus, and the story, as he tells it in the seventy-third chapter of the second book of his history, was the basis upon which for centuries a vast superstructure of fabledom was reared.

Even Tacitus, one of the most cautious and reliable of authors, seems to have felt no difficulty in believing in the existence of the phœnix. Erroneous as his account is, we feel at once on reading it that we have the opinions of one honestly seeking the truth, a very different sort of man to such a credulous old fellow, for example, as Maundevile. Tacitus writes that " in the course of the year* the miraculous bird known to the world by the name of the phœnix, after disappearing for a series of ages, revisited Egypt. A phenomenon so very extraordinary could not fail to produce abundance of speculation. The facts, about which there seems to be a concurrence of opinions, with other circumstances in their nature doubtful, yet worthy of notice, will not be unwelcome to the reader. That the phœnix is sacred to the Sun, and differs from the rest of the feathered species in the form of its head and the tincture of its plumage, are points settled by the naturalist. Of its longevity the accounts are various. The common persuasion is that it lives five hundred years, though by some writers the date is extended to fourteen hundred and sixty-one. It is the custom of the phœnix when its course of years is finished, and the approach of death is felt, to build a nest in its native clime, Arabia, and there deposit the principles of life, from which a new progeny arises. The first care of the young bird, as soon as fledged and able to trust to its wings, is to perform the obsequies of its father. But this duty is not undertaken rashly. He collects a great quantity of myrrh, and to try his strength, makes frequent excur-

* A.U.C. 787, equivalent to A.D. 34.

sions with a load on his back. When he has made his experiment through a great tract of air, and gains sufficient confidence in his own vigour, he takes up the body of his father and flies with it to the Altar of the Sun, where he leaves it to be consumed in flames of fragrance. Such is the account of this wonderful bird. It has, no doubt, a mixture of fable; but that the phœnix from time to time appears in Egypt seems to be a fact satisfactorily ascertained."

Pliny feels no difficulty in describing the phœnix, declaring that it is about the size of an eagle, the neck being of a golden sheen, the body purple, and the tail of an azure blue, though he admits feeling a doubt as to whether it can be true that only one is in existence at one time. According to Maundevile, "he hathe a Crest of Fedres upon his Hed more gret than the Poocok hathe, and his Nekke is yalowe aftre colour of an Orielle, that is a Ston well schynynge, and his Bek is coloured Blew, and his Wenges ben of purpre colour, and the Taylle is yelow and red. And he is a fulle fair Brid to loken upon, for he schynethe full nobely." One wonders at first how this old writer is able to give such very precise details, but as he tells us that "this Bryd men sene often tyme fleen in the Countrees," he would have no difficulty in getting a full description of it from some of these countrymen to whom it was a familiar sight.

Maundevile does not fail in his book of "Voiage and Travaile" to recite the whole wonderful story. He tells us that "in Egypt is the Cytee of Elyople,* that is to seyne, the Cytee of the Sonne. In that Cytee there is a Temple made round, after the schappe of the Temple of Jerusalem. The Prestes of that Temple have alle here Wrytynges, under the Date of the Foul that is clept Fenix, and there is non but one in alle the Worlde. And he comethe to brenne him selfe upon the Awtre of the Temple at the end of five hundred Yeer: for so longe he lyvethe. And at the five hundred Yeres ende the Prestes arrayen here Awtere honestly and putten there upon Spices and Vif Sulphur and other thinges that wolm brenne lightly. And then the Bryd Fenix comethe and brenneth him self to Ashes. And the first Day aftre Men fynden in the Ashes a Worm; and the seconde Day next aftre Men finden a Brid quyk and perfyt; and the thridde Day next aftre he fleethe his wey. And so there is no more Briddes of that Kynde in alle the World but it alone."

This belief in the phœnix is found not only through heathen and mediæval literature, but in the Rabbinical writings, and those of the early Fathers of the Christian Church. By these latter it was accepted as a symbol of the resurrection of the dead, and it may not unfrequently be found figured in the mosaics that adorn the basilicas of the primitive Church. The Rabbins tell us that all the birds, save the phœnix, shared in the sin of Eve, and eat of the forbidden fruit; hence the phœnix, as a reward,

* Heliopolis.

obtained this modified form of immutability. Philippe de Thaun, in his "Bestiary," writes of the mystic bird : " Know this is its lot ; it comes to death of its own will, and from death it comes to life : hear what it signifies. Phœnix signifies Jesus, Son of Mary, that he had power to die of his own will, and from death came to life. Phœnix signifies that to save his people he chose to suffer upon the cross." "God knew men's unbelief," writes St. Cyril, "and therefore provided this bird as evidence of the Resurrection." St. Ambrose says, too, that "the bird of Arabia teaches us, by its example, to believe in the Resurrection." Other passages of like tenour could be quoted from Tertullian and others of the writers of the early Christian Church, and all alike show the most unquestionable belief in the existence of the bird.*

It was suggested by Cuvier that at remote intervals a golden pheasant from China might have strayed as far west as Arabia or Egypt, and given rise to the legend ; but gorgeous as the bird is, and fully capable of making a considerable sensation on its appearance in a land where it was previously unknown, one feels that such an appearance goes but a very little way indeed towards clearing up the mass of myth that still remains to be some way accounted for.

* Even so comparatively recently as the time of Maundevile we meet with the same symbolic significance, as we find this author declaring that " men may well lykne that Brid unto God : because that there hys no God but on ; and also that oure Lord aroos fro Dethe to Lyve the thridde Day."

Browne, in his excellent dissection of the vulgar errors of his day, approaches the Phœnix story tenderly, but feels bound to declare against it, though he rather takes refuge in the Scottish verdict of "not proven" than slaughters it in cold blood. "That there is but one Phœnix in the world," saith he, "which after many hundred yeares burneth itself, and from the ashes thereof ariseth up another, is a conceit not new or altogether popular, but of great Antiquity: not only delivered by humane Authors, but frequently expressed by holy Writers; by Cyril, Epiphanius, and others. All which, notwithstanding, we cannot presume the existence of this Animall, nor dare we affirm there is any Phœnix in Nature. For, first, there wants herein the definite test of things uncertain—that is, the sense of man. For though many writers have much enlarged hereon, there is not any ocular describer, or such as presumeth to confirm it upon aspection. Primitive Authors, from whom the stream of relations is derivative, deliver themselves dubiously, and either by a doubtful parenthesis, or a timorous conclusion, overthrow the whole relation. As for its unity or conceit that there should be but one in Nature, it seemeth not only repugnant unto Philosophy, but also Holy Scripture, which plainly affirmes there went of every sort two at least into the Ark of Noah. Every fowle after his kinde, every bird of every sort, they went into the Ark, two and two of all flesh wherein there is the breath of life. It infringeth the Benediction of God concerning multiplication. God blessed them, saying Be fruitfull and multiply and let fowls multiply in the earth, which terms are not applicable unto the Phœnix, whereof there is but one in the world, and no more now living than at the first benediction. As for longevity that it liveth a thousand years or more, besides that from imperfect observations and rarity of appearance no confirmation can be made, there may probably be a mistake in the compute. For the tradition being very ancient the conceit might have its originall in times of shorter compute. For if we suppose our present calculation, the Phœnix now in nature will be the sixt from the Creation, and but in the middle of its years, and, if the Rabbine's prophecy succeed, it shall conclude its daies not in its own, but in the last and generall flames."

Some medical enthusiasts held that a bird of such singular and noble properties must be of sovereign virtue for the ills of mankind, and did not hesitate to assign its several healing properties. On these mistaken individuals Browne descends heavily. "Surely," quoth he, "they were not wel-wishers unto Physick or remedies easily acquired, who derived Medicines from the Phœnix, as some have done. It is a folly to finde out remedies that are not recoverable under a thousand years, or propose the prolonging of life by that which the twentieth generation may never behold. More veniable is a dependence upon the Philosopher's stone, potable gold, or any of those Arcanas whereby Paracelsus, that died himself at fourty seven, gloried that he could make men immortall, which, although exceedingly difficult, yet they are not impossible : nor doe they (rightly understood) impose any violence on Nature. And, therefore, if strictly taken for the Phœnix, very strange is that which is delivered by Plutarch, that the brain thereof is a pleasant morsel, but that it causeth the headach." The amount of headache caused by too free an indulgence in Phœnix must have been infinitesimal.

The Phœnix may still be considered to have a literary existence, and remains part of the stock-in-trade of the orator and poet as an emblem of something especially choice and rare. Fletcher writes of

"That lone bird in fruitful Arabie,
When now her strength and waning life decays,
Upon some airy rock or mountain high,
In spicy bed (fir'd by near Phœbus' rays)
Herself and all her crooked age consumes :
Straight from her ashes, and those rich perfumes,
A newborn Phœnix flies, and widow'd place resumes."

Ariosto, in his "Orlando Furioso," refers to the bird in the Voyage of Astolfo in the following lines :—

"Arabia, nam'd the happy, now he gains,
Incense and myrrh perfume her grateful plains :
The Virgin Phœnix there in search of rest
Selects from all the world her balmy nest."

In the two foregoing extracts the Phœnix has been represented as maiden and as widow, and in the first line of Ariosto the pronoun is masculine, and in the fourth line feminine. Ovid, and many other writers, in describing him, her, or it, select the masculine as the most appropriate. Thus Ovid, in the translation of Dryden, sings :—

> "All these receive their birth from other things,
> But from himself the Phœnix only springs:
> Self-born, begotten by the parent flame
> In which he burn'd, another and the same."

It is needless to give the rest of the reference, as the ancient poet naturally follows in the lines of the recognized tradition : the funeral pyre, the infant Phœnix rising from the ashes, the dutiful removal of the paternal remains to Heliopolis, all taking their proper and accustomed place in the narrative.

Shakespeare frequently refers to the mythical bird in his writings, and seems to have thoroughly mastered all that could be said on the subject. Some half-dozen passages naturally rise to one's mind as illustrations of this : thus Rosalind says in As You Like It :—

> "She calls me proud; and that she could not love me,
> Were man as rare as Phœnix."

And the idea of its unique character is again brought out in Cymbeline, in the passage "If she be furnished with a mind so rare, she is alone the Arabian bird." The destruction of the bird on its own funeral pyre, and the resurrection of its successor therefrom, are several times referred to. Thus in 1 Henry VI. we read : "But from their ashes shall be reared a Phœnix that shall make all France afeared," and in 3 Henry VI.: "My ashes, as the Phœnix, may bring forth a bird that will revenge upon you all." Some little doubt of its existence at all is suggested by the words of Sebastian in the Tempest. Now I will believe

> "That there are unicorns : that in Arabia
> There is one tree, the Phœnix throne; one Phœnix
> At this time reigning there."

Notwithstanding the doubts as to the reality of this creature that were freely expressed in the seventeenth century, two feathers that were said to be from the tail of a Phœnix were amongst the treasures of Tradescant's Museum.*

It was held a firm article of belief during the Middle Ages that the Bird of Paradise fed upon nothing more gross than the dew of Heaven and the odours of flowers, and that it had no feet, nor ever rested on earth at all.

> "Thou art still that Bird of Paradise
> Which hath no feet, and ever nobly flies."

It is a sadly prosaic explanation of this to recall that its footless condition simply arose from the fact that the natives of Molucca in sending the skins to Europe removed the legs

---

* " I know," writes Izaak Walton, in his "Complete Angler," " we islanders are averse to the belief of wonders, but there be so many strange creatures to be now seen, collected by John Tradescant, who keeps them carefully and methodically at his house near to Lambeth. I will tell you some of the wonders you may now see, and not till then believe, unless you think fit. You may see there the hog-fish, the dogfish, the dolphin, the coney fish, the parrot fish, the shark, the poison fish, the sword-fish; and not only other incredible fish, but you may there see the salamander, several sorts of barnacles, of Solan geese, and the bird of paradise; such sorts of snakes, and such birds' nests, and of so various forms, and so wonderfully made, as may beget

and feet as needless additions, seeing that the beauty of the plumage was the reason for their export.

Tavernier relates that "the Birds of Paradise come in flocks during the nutmeg season to the South of India. The strength of the nutmeg odour intoxicates them, and while they lie in this state on the earth, the ants eat off their legs." Saving the last terrible detail and shocking instance of what may befall those who stray from the paths of temperance, Moore evidently adopts this account in Lalla Rookh in the lines :—

> " Those golden birds that in the spicetime drop
> About the gardens, drunk with that sweet fruit
> Whose scent hath lured them o'er the summer flood."

Literary allusions to the Bird of Paradise are not unfrequent, and testify to the general acceptance of the myth that has grown up around the prosaic facts of the case. Francis Thynne, in his "Emblemes and Epigrames," A.D. 1600,

wonder and amazement in any beholder." Walton, as an enthusiastic angler naturally, it will be noted, dwells most upon the strange fish. Charles I. and his queen, together with Archbishop Laud, and many others of rank and influence, visited the museum and assisted by contributing to its stores, and we find in Evelyn's Diary, September 17th, 1657, that he, too, visited it. The brothers Tradescant were the first well-known collectors of natural curiosities in England, and portraits of them may be seen in the Ashmolean Museum at Oxford. The Tradescant collection was on December 15th transferred to Elias Ashmole. The botanical genus, *Tradescantia*, is so called in honour of John Tradescant.

takes the somewhat exceptional view that the bird is to be pitied :—

"There is a birde which takes the name of Paradise the fair,
Which allwaies lives beatinge the winde and flienge in the Ayre,
For envious Nature him denies the helpe of resting feete
Wherby hee forced is in th'ayre incessantlie to fleete."

The Roc or Rukh, though associated nowadays in our minds with the "Thousand and One Nights," and regarded as simply an illustration of the lengths that the Eastern love of the wonderful can be carried to, was an article of faith with our ancestors. Marco Polo, in his wonderfully interesting book on his travels in Eastern lands, refers to this remarkable bird; but it will be noted that he merely gives the account as hearsay, and protects himself more than once from any admission of personal belief in the creature. He states respecting it as follows: "The people of the island* report that at a certain season of the year an extraordinary kind of bird, which they call a rukh, makes its appearance from the southern region. In form it is said to resemble the eagle, but it is incomparably greater in size; being so large and strong as to seize an elephant with its talons, and to lift it into the air, from whence it lets it fall to the ground, in order that when dead it may prey upon the carcase. Persons who have seen this bird assert that when the wings are spread they measure sixteen paces in extent from point to point, and that the feathers are eight paces in length and thick in proportion. The Grand

---

* Madagascar.

Khan, having heard this extraordinary relation, sent messengers to the island on the pretext of demanding the release of one of his servants who had been detained there, but in reality to examine into the circumstances of the country, and the truth of the wonderful things told of it. When they returned to the presence of his Majesty they brought with them (as I have heard) a feather of the Rukh, positively affirmed to have measured ninety spans. This surprising exhibition afforded his Majesty extreme pleasure, and upon those to whom it was presented he bestowed valuable gifts."

The existence of such a bird seems to have been universally credited in the East. While the tale passes all belief as it stands, or rather as it lies, it may possibly be that it is grossly exaggerated rather than entirely fabulous, as it may have originated from the occasional sight of some bird of vast, though not miraculous, dimensions, such as the albatross, birds of fierce aspect, measuring many feet from tip to tip of their wings, though with strength and power of grip considerably short of transporting elephants from their umbrageous retreats to mid-air. The sixteen paces that are given by the informants of Marco Polo as the measurement of the wings would be about forty feet, while the wing-measurement of the albatross would not exceed fifteen or sixteen feet, thus leaving a handsome balance to be put to the credit of the love of the marvellous.

Jordanus brought back from India the story of

"certain birds which are called Roc, that are so big that they easily carry an elephant into the air." He did not himself see one of these, the nearest he is able to approach to this being, "I have seen a certain person who said that he had seen one of these birds." The Roc was said to lay an egg equal in bulk to one hundred and forty-eight hen's eggs. The precision of this estimate should disarm criticism: one feels in face of it that to have said one hundred and fifty would have been a fatal yielding to the charm of round numbers and a palpable exaggeration.

Mr. Lane refers to an Arab, one Ibou el Wardee, for authority for the statement that Rocs are found in an island in the Chinese Sea that have each wing ten thousand fathoms long.*

* The Eastern love of the wonderful may be readily seen in the well-known "Arabian Nights," in the Koran, and in Oriental literature generally. Mohammed tells us, in his sacred book, that he saw in Heaven infinite companies of angels, each a thousand times bigger than the globe of the earth: each had ten thousand heads; every head threescore and ten thousand tongues; and every one of those tongues praised God in seven hundred thousand languages. The throne of Allah was supported by seven angels, each so great that a falcon, if he were to fly a thousand years, could not get so far as the distance from one of their eyes to the other. Gabriel, the doorkeeper of Paradise, has seventy thousand keys which pertain to his office, every key being seven thousand miles long. This exaggerated balderdash is but childish stuff; it contains no element of grandeur or sublimity; and, in reading it, one only wonders, when astonishment and awe were to be excited by an artifice so commonplace, that, while he was about it, all the numbers were not doubled, quadrupled, multiplied ten or a hundred fold; so that we finally come to the conclusion that, with all the arithmetical possibilities open to him, he was but a poor bungler at his business after all.

These birds find no difficulty in carrying an eagle in their beak, plus two others in their talons. Wardee also knew of a Roc's egg, or said he did—which is, perhaps, not quite the same thing—on one of these islands that looked like an enormous white dome over a hundred cubits high and as firm as a mountain.

Many of the beliefs of our forefathers had a refreshing quaintness about them, and one of the quaintest, perhaps, of these was the notion that a particular kind of goose sprang from the barnacles that cluster in salt water on submerged wood. Butler, in his "Hudibras," tells of those

> "Who from the most refined of saints
> As naturally turn miscreants
> As barnacles turn Soland geese
> In the islands of the Orcades."

Gerarde, in 1597, in his "Historie of Plants," of which there are many editions—our own copy, we see, being dated 1633,—gives in all good faith a description and an illustration of the barnacle-goose tree. The former Gerarde shall give in his own words, the latter we have reproduced in fig. 15 in facsimile from his book. We see in it the branch bearing barnacles, and by its side a bird, which stands for the resulting goose. This "wonder of England, for the which God's name be ever honoured and praised," he thus discourses upon—"Hauing trauelled from the grasses growing in the bottom of the fenny waters, the woods and mountaines, euen unto Libanus it selfe, and also the sea and bowels of the same, wee are arriued at the end of our Historie;

The Goose-bearing Tree.

thinking it not impertinent to the conclusion of the same, to end with one of the maruells of this land, we may say of the world. The historie wherof to set forth according to the worthinesse and ranke therof would not only require a large and peculiar volume, but also a deeper search into the bowels of Nature than mine intended purpose will suffer me to wade into, my sufficience also considered, leauing the historie therof

FIG. 15.

rough hewn unto some excellent men learned in the secrets of Nature, to be both fined and refined; in the meantime, take it as it falleth out, the naked and bare truth, though vnpolished. There are found in the North parts of Scotland and the islands adiacent, called Orchades, certaine trees whereon do grow certaine shells of a white colour tending to russett, wherein are contained little liuing things, which shells in time of maturitie do open, and out of them do grow those little liuing creatures, which falling in the water do become fowles, which we call Barnakles, and in Lancashire tree-geese, but the others that do fall upon the land perish and come to nothing. Thus much by the writings of others, and also from the mouths of people of those parts, which may very well accord with truth.

"But what our eyes haue seene and hands haue touched, we shall declare. There is a small island in Lancashire, called the pile of Foulders, wherein we find the broken pieces of old and bruised ships, some wherof haue been cast thither by shipwracke, and also the trunks and bodies with the branches of old and rotten trees cast up there likewise; whereon is found a certaine spawne or froth that in time breedeth unto certain shels, in shape like those of the muskle, but sharper-pointed, wherein is contained a thing in forme like a lace of silke finely wouen together as it were. One end thereof is fastened into a rude masse or lumpe, which in time commeth to the shape and form of a Birde. When it is perfectly formed the shel gapeth open, and the first thing that appeareth is the foresaid lace or string: next come the legs of the bird hanging out, and as it groweth greater it openeth the shel by degrees til at length it is all come forth and hangeth onely by the bill: in short space after it commeth to ful maturitie, and falleth into the sea, when it gathereth feathers and groweth to a Fowle bigger than a Mallard and lesser than a Goose, hauing blacke legs and bill and beake, and feathers blacke and white, spotted in such manner as is our magpie, which the people of Lancashire call by no other name than a tree-goose : which place therof and all those parts adioining doe so much abound therewith that one of the best is bought for threepence. For the truth wherof, if any doubt, may it please them to repair unto me, and I shall satisfie them by the testimony of good witnesses."

On reading the foregoing one can only wonder what the old fellow really did see on this wild sea shore amidst the wreckage : that he wrote in the most perfect good faith, and in the strongest belief in this "Maruell," is perfectly evident. That he has no desire to practise on our credulity is patent, but it is equally patent that his own credulity got the better of his judgment. He goes on to tell us that on another occasion, near Dover, he found on the sea shore an old tree-trunk covered with "thousands of long crimson bladders, in shape like unto puddings newly filled, and at the nether end therof did grow a shelfish fashioned somewhat like a small muskle." Many of these shells he brought back with him to London, and on opening them he tells us that he found "liuing things that were very naked, shaped like a bird : in others the birds couered with a soft doune, the shel halfe open, and the bird ready to fall out ; which no doubt were the fowles called Barnakles."

Soon after Gerarde's death, Thomas Johnson, "Citizen and Apothecarie of London," brought out another edition of the "Historie of Plants," in which he adds the following note to Gerarde's statement: "The Barnakles, whose fabulous breed my Author here sets downe and diuers others have also deliuered, were found by some Hollanders to haue another originall, and that by egges, as other birds have: for they in their third voyage to find out the North-East passage to China and Mollocos, found little islands, in the one of which they found an abundance of these geese sitting upon their egges, of which they got one goose and tooke away sixty egges." Here again one can only feel that the explanation needs explaining, as it hardly seems necessary to sail for China to find the home of the birds that were to be had retail in any quantity on the Lancashire coast, for the by no means extravagant price of sixpence a brace.

In a description of West Connaught by Roderic O'Flaherty, published in the year 1684, the barnacle is thus mentioned: "There is the bird engendered by the sea, out of timber long lying in the sea. Some call these birds Clakes and Solan'd geese, and some puffins, others barnacles." And in the "Divine Weekes and Workes" of Du Bartas we find another reference:—

> "So Sly Bootes underneath him sees
> In ye cycles, those goslings hatcht of trees,
> Whose fruitfull leaues falling into the water
> Are turn'd, they say, to liuing fowles soon after.

The Goose-bearing Tree.

So rotten sides of broken ships do change
To barnacles! O transformation strange!
'Twas first a greene tree, then a gallant hull,
Lately a mushroom, now a flying gull."

Another version of the barnacle-tree is given in fig. 16. We have extracted it from Parkinson's "Theater of Plants," a book that achieved

FIG. 16.

considerable popularity and ran through several editions. Our own copy, from which we have reproduced the illustration, is dated 1640. Parkinson, we see, classes the barnacle-tree with "Marsh, Water, and Sea Plants, with Mosses and Mushrooms." It seems curious that he should have inserted it at all, as his remarks thereupon are not at all those of a believer. "To finish this treatise of sea-plants," he writes, "let me bring this admirable tale of untruth to your consideration, that whatever hath formerly been related concerning the breeding of these Barnakles to be from shels growing on trees is utterly erroneous, their breeding and hatching being found out by the Dutch and others, in their navigations to the Northward." This second reference to the Dutch shows that the matter had caused some little stir outside England, and we may perhaps not too uncharitably assume that the foreigner did not feel altogether displeased when so great a British wonder was reduced to a very commonplace and everyday affair indeed.

The "Cosmography" of Munster supplies us with the graceful illustration which we have reproduced in facsimile in fig. 17. It is a far more charming representation than either of the others we have given. In the drawing the whole process may be clearly traced, from the immature and unopened fruit to that sufficiently ripe to give some indication of its strange contents in the form of the protruding head of the coming bird, and then on again to the geese actually fallen in the water, and more or less freeing themselves from the encumbering husk, until finally we see them in all respects fit and proper subjects for the ornithologist or the salesman of Leadenhall Market. Munster states in his book that "in Scotland we find trees, the fruit of which appears like a ball of leaves. This fruit, falling at its proper time into the water below,

The Wondrous Goose-Tree.

becomes animated, and **turns to** a bird which they call the tree-goose.

Æneas Sylvius, afterwards better known to the world as Pope Pius II., visited Scotland in the year 1468, and while there made diligent inquiry concerning this wonderful tree, but **found** that no one could point it out **to** him. As the

FIG. 17.

general impression that one gathers on reading his account of his travels is that he appeared in Scotland rather as a seeker after knowledge than as the recipient of a wonderful story till then unknown to him, we must conclude that the myth **had** spread considerably beyond **the** land of its origin. In fact, as we often find even **unto** the present day, in divers matters the intelligent stranger is often able to enlighten the natives on matters in which we might reasonably have expected to find them well informed. Who, for instance, would ever dream of asking the nearest resident to a cathedral anything of its history, or seeking from "the Shepherd of Salisbury Plain" any light on the mysterious origin of Stonehenge?

William Turner, one of the earliest writers on ornithology, described the barnacle-goose as being produced from "something like a fungus growing from old wood lying in the sea," and quotes Giraldus Cambrensis as his authority. "Having uncomfortable misgivings I asked," he writes, " a certain clergyman named Octavianus, by birth an Irishman, whom I knew to be worthy of credit, if he thought the account of Giraldus was to be believed. He, swearing by the Gospel, declared that which Giraldus had written about the bird was most true: that he had himself seen and handled the young unformed birds, and that if I would remain in London a month or two he would bring me some of the brood." Whether Turner was satisfied by the very unsatisfying proof of the production of some dubious ducks in London, or by the solemn declaration and oaths taken on the Gospels by his reverent informant, we have no means of knowing, but as he inserts the wonder in his book, he was evidently relieved from his previous doubt of the veracity of the story.

In a land even beyond far distant Cathay,

according to Maundevile, "growethe a maner of Fruyt as thoughe it weren gowrdes, and whan thei ben rype men kutten hem a to and fynden with inne a lytylle Best in Flessche, in Bon and Blode, as though it were a lytylle Lamb with outen Wolle. And Men eten bothe the Fruyt and the Best, and that is a gret Marveylle. Of that Frut I have eten, alle thoughe it were wondirfulle, but that I knowe wel that God is marveyllous in his Werkes. And nathles I tolde hem that in oure Contree weren Trees that beren a Fruyt that becomen Briddes fleeynge, and tho that fellen in the Water lyven, and thei that fellen on the Erthe dyen anon, and thei ben righte gode to Mannes mete. And here of had thei als gret marvaylle that sume of hem trowed it were an impossible thing to be." One would have thought that people who were quite familiar with the sight of a lamb-tree would have found no great difficulty in believing in a goose-tree. Anyone who can credit the one should feel no hesitation in accepting the other.

Saxo Grammaticus, Lobel, Valcetro, and many other writers, refer to the barnacle-tree, some with full belief in it, others more dubiously, but it is, of course, needless to quote a multiplicity of authors. Should any of our readers themselves feel any doubt in the matter, they may very advantageously pay a visit to a good museum, where probably, even if they fail to find a goose-tree, they may see much else that will be almost equally a wonder and a delight to them.

The ancients thoroughly believed that the eagle proved her young by forcing them to gaze upon the sun, discarding any that failed to face the test, and the belief survived well into the Middle Ages. "Before that her little ones bee feathered she will beat and strike them with her wings, and thereby force them to looke full against the sunne beames. Now if shee see any one of them to winke or their eies to water at the raies of the sunne shee turnes it with the head foremost out of the nest as a bastard and none of hers, but bringeth up and cherisheth that whose eie will abide the light of the sunne as she looketh directly upon him." It will be remembered that Shakespeare, in King Henry VI., refers to this old belief when the Duke of Gloucester addresses the young prince in the words—

> "Nay, if thou be that princely eagle's bird,
> Show thy descent* by gazing 'gainst the sun."

In Ariosto, again, we have the same reference, where he styles the eagle

> "The bird
> That dares with steadfast eyes Apollo's light."

And Dryden exclaims in his "Britannia Rediviva,"

> "Truth, which is light itself, doth darkness shun,
> And the true eaglet safely dares the sun."

The keenness of vision of the eaglet† has been

---

* "She dwelleth and abideth on the rock, upon the crag of the rock, and the strong place. From thence she seeketh the prey and her eyes behold afar off."—*Job* xxxix. 28, 29.

† "The nature of the Eagle is to bend her eyes full into the sunne beams. So strong is her sighte that she can even see into the great and glaring sunne."— FERNE, *The Blazon of Gentrie.*

noted in all ages, and its powers sometimes made even more astonishing than facts can justify. It has been asserted that when the eagle has soared into the air to a height that has rendered it perfectly invisible to human eye, it can discern the motions of the smaller animals upon the earth, and swoop down upon them from the sky, and Homer, in the "Iliad," it will be recalled, describes Menelaus as

> "The field exploring, with an eye
> Keen as the eagle's, keenest eyed of all
> That wing the air, whom, though he soar aloft,
> The lev'ret 'scapes not hid in thickest shades.
> But down he swoops, and at a stroke she dies."

The eastern writers, ever given to hyperbole, have assigned to the eagle powers of vision of a far more astonishing character than this. One of them, Damir, quoted by Burckhardt, declares that the eagle can discern its prey at a distance of four hundred parasangs—more than a thousand miles—and poets of all periods have drawn striking images from the wonderful power of vision of the king of birds. Mediæval naturalists have asserted that this magnificent eyesight was strengthened even beyond its natural powers by a diet on the eagle's part of wild lettuce, in the same way that the linnet cleared its sight by means of the eyebright, the swallow through use of the celandine, and divers other birds through use of some special herb that they had proved to be of value to them.

Our readers will doubtless remember the fine passage in the "Areopagitica" of Milton:

"Methinks I see in my mind a noble and puissant nation rousing herself like a strong man after sleep, and shaking her invincible locks: methinks I see her as an eagle renewing her mighty youth, and kindling her undazzled eyes at the full midday beam." It was one of the beliefs of our forefathers that the eagle had this power of rejuvenescence. The description of the process has a very prosaic sound about it, but the result is highly successful. When the eagle "hathe darknesse and dimnesse in eien and hevinesse in wings against this disadvantage she is taught by kinde to seeke a well of springing water, and then she flyeth up into the aire as farre as she may, till she bee full hot by heat of the aire and by travaile of flight, and so then by heat the pores be opened, and the feathers chafed, and she falleth sideinglye into the well, and there the feathers be chaunged and the dimnesse of her eien is wiped away and purged, and she taketh againe her might and strength."*

It was a strange belief of the writers of antiquity on these natural history topics that the feathers of the eagle, when placed amongst those of other birds, in a short space of time entirely consumed them.

While the king of beasts has been credited with generosity and other royal virtues, the eagle, king of birds, seems not to have developed,

* "As eagle fresh out of the ocean wave
  Where he hath left his plumes, all hoary grey,
  And decks himself with feathers, youthful, gay."
  SPENSER.

either in nature or in fable, any such regal qualities. The most favourable estimate we have encountered is that of the "Speculum Mundi," and even that leaves much to be desired. "The Eagle," writes our authority, "is commended for her faithfulnesse towards other birds in some kinde, though sometimes she show herselfe cruell. They all stand in awe of her; and when she hath gotten meat she useth to communicate it unto such fowls as do accompany with her; onely this some affirme, that when she hath no more to make distribution of, then she will attack some of her guests, and for lack of food, dismember them."

The eagle is often depicted as bearing the thunderbolts of Jove, from an ancient belief that "of all flying fowles the ægle only is not smitten nor killed with lightening."

"Secure from thunder, and unharm'd by Jove." *

A man clothed in the skins of seals, or crowned with bay-leaves, enjoyed like immunity.

The pelican has been pressed into the service of religious symbolism, from a belief that it nourished its young with its own blood, and hence it was made the emblem of loving sacrifice.† "The pelicane, whose sons are nursed with bloude, stabbeth deep her breast,

---

* Dryden.
† Hence Dante terms the Saviour of the World "Nostro pelicano;" and an enthusiastic admirer of Charles I., and an evident believer in the idea that he shed his blood for his people, wrote in the year 1649, a book on that king, entitling him "the Princely Pelican."

self-murdresse through fondnesse to hir broode," and the Shakespearian student will recall the lines in Hamlet:—

> "To his good friends thus wide I'll ope my arms,
> And, like the kind, life-rendering pelican,
> Refresh them with my blood."

The whole myth is based upon a very slender basis indeed, as it is conjectured that it arose from the habit of the bird pressing its breast feathers with its bill, the bill itself having a crimson spot at its extremity that suggested the idea of blood. When the bird is represented in ecclesiastical work, or as a charge in heraldry, it is always shown in this position, and is known technically as "a pelican in her piety." Many of the early writers accept the legend in the most perfect good faith, and no more doubted that the young pelicans were reared on the blood of the mother bird, than that hens would eat barley, or sparrows come for bread-crumbs. Some ecclesiastical writers, whom we cannot quite exonerate from acting on the principle that it is lawful to do ill if good flows from it, added the detail that when the young of the pelican were destroyed by serpents, the mother pelican shed her blood upon them, and brought them to life again, and hence became a striking symbol of the restoration to life of those dead in trespasses and sin by the vivifying blood of the Redeemer of mankind.

It was for many centuries a belief that the swan, mute through life, sang melodiously at its death.

> "Sweet strains he chaunteth out with's dying tongue,
> And is the singer of his funerall song."

"Wherein," writes the author of the "Speculum Mundi," "he is a perfect embleme and pattern to us, that our death ought to be cheerfull, and life not so deare unto us as it is." Martial writes of the swan's "joyful death, and sweet expiring song," and Virgil, Lucretius, Horace, Ovid, and other ancient authors all refer to the belief. Cicero compared the excellent discourse which Crassus made in the senate a few days before his death to the melodious singing of a dying swan, while Socrates declared that good men ought to imitate swans, who, perceiving by a secret instinct what gain there was in death, die singing with joy.

Shakespeare refers frequently to the belief: thus in the Merchant of Venice Portia says: "Then if he lose he makes a swan-like end, fading in music." After King John is poisoned his son, Prince Henry, is told that in his dying frenzy he sang; whereupon the prince replies:—

> " 'Tis strange that death should sing,
> I am the cygnet to this pale faint swan,
> Who chants a doleful hymn to his own death;
> And from the organ-pipes of frailty sings
> His soul and body to their lasting rest."

Many similar passages might be quoted from the poets; it will suffice to give but one example:—

> "Place me on Sunium's marbled steep,
> Where nothing, save the waves and I,
> May hear our mutual murmurs sweep.
> There, swan-like, let me sing and die."*

* Byron.

Though the ordinary swan of our English lakes and rivers would appear to be without a grain of music in its composition, the black swan of Australia,* now naturalized in our midst, has a really very musical note, and one,

FIG. 18.

too, which it very readily utters, not by any means reserving it as a pæan of approaching dissolution.

It was a firm article of belief with the older writers, such as Pliny, Aristotle, and Ælian, that the swan was especially exposed to attack from

* It is curious that until this species was discovered at the Antipodes a black swan was regarded both by ancient and mediæval writers as the very emblem and type of extravagant impossibility, so that those who found no difficulty in believing in centaurs, mermaids, and fifty other extravagances, felt that they really must draw the line at this.

the eagle, and that when thus assailed it fought with extreme determination, and never failed to come off victor in the fray.

To the ostrich was accredited the power of digesting iron. How such an idea could have arisen, it is now impossible to explain. In allusion to this myth the bird, when introduced in blazonry, as in fig. 18, from a mediæval flagon, ordinarily has a horse-shoe in its mouth.* The artist who thus represented the bird was evidently by no means oblivious of the fact that the plumage of the ostrich was another very characteristic feature. Shakespeare, in his Henry VI., makes Jack Cade declare "I'll make thee eat iron like an ostrich, and swallow my sword like a great pin;" while Munster, in his "Cosmography," gravely gives a picture of an ostrich with an immense key in his mouth, and at his feet, as second course, a horse-shoe. Cogan, the author of the very popular "Haven of Health," finds apt simile herein. "The fat of flesh," he says, "alone without leane is unwholesome and cloyeth the stomack and causeth lothsomnes, yet have I knowne a country man that would feed onely of the fat of Bacon or Pork, without leane, but that is not to bee marvelled at, considering that many of them have stomackes like the bird that is called an Ostridge, which can digest hard Iron."

It was held that the ostrich never hatches her

---

* In "Camden" we read that the device of Anne, queen of Richard II., was "an ostrich with a nayle in his beake."

eggs by sitting upon them, but by the rays of warmth and light from her eyes. Southey alludes, it will be remembered, to this old fancy in the lines : —

> " With such a look as fables say,
> The mother ostrich fixes on her eggs,
> Till that intense affection
> Kindle its light of life."*

A considerable body of folklore is associated with the cock. One strange notion that crops up in the books of the mediæval writers is that the lion has a strong antipathy to this bird, and that the crowing of chanticleer will effectually put to the rout the king of beasts. One can readily imagine that the lion, prowling in the darkness round some human habitation, would naturally resent the shrill clarion of the cock, and that this idea might, with the delight in mysticism and symbolism of the Middle Ages, be readily transferred to the roaring lion, seeking whom he may devour, thwarted by the vigilance of which the cock is the emblem. Even so early, however, as the pre-Christian days of Pliny we find this belief in the antagonism between the two creatures in full operation, for this ancient author prescribes the broth from a stewed cock as an excellent outward application for those in peril from wild beasts, declaring confidently that whosoever shall bathe himself in this shall fear no harm from lion or panther.

Gerard Legh, in his " Accedence of Armorie," affirms that " the Cocke is the royallest birde

* Thalaba.

that is, and of himself a king, for Nature hath crowned hime with a perpetuall Diademe, to him and to his posteritie for ever. He is the valiantest in battle of all birdes, for he will rather die than yeelde to his aduersarie." And one old writer goes so far as to declare that the lion, whom we have always been taught to regard as generosity itself, feels his royal title somewhat impaired by the rivalry of the barn-door fowl, and that the pretension to royalty suggested by the scarlet crest is distasteful to the king of beasts, who can brook no idea of a rival.

There was throughout the Middle Ages an idea that one was able to incorporate* any desirable quality by looking around for some creature of which it was a characteristic, and then promptly making some culinary preparation of which this creature's flesh should be a leading ingredient. "If," says one of these sages, "you would have a man talkative give him tongues, and seek out for him water-frogs, wilde geese and ducks, and other such creatures, notorious for their continual noise-making," and thus the sturdy self-assertion and valour of the cock naturally suggested the idea that the weakly and retiring would find in him valuable nutriment.

---

* While actual incorporation was doubtless regarded as the most effectual, mere possession was not by any means to be despised. Thus Porta tells us that "if you would have a man become bold and impudent, let him carry about him the skin or eyes of a Lion or a Cock, and he will be fearlesse of his enemies —nay, he will be very terrible unto them." Scores of equally valuable hints may be gathered from these old authors.

In an old cookery book we find "how to still a cocke for a weak body that is in consumption, through long sicknesse." The cock selected must be a red one,* and not too old. Having cut him into quarters, he must be put into an earthenware pot with "the rootes of Fennell, Parcely and Succory, Corans, whole Mace, Annise seeds, and liquorice scraped and slyced." Half a pint of rosewater and a quart of white wine are then to be added, together with "two or three cleane Dates, a few prunes and raysons," and then all must stew gently for the space of twelve hours. Finally, "streine out the broth into some cleane vessell, and give thereof unto the weak person morning and evening, warmed and spiced as pleaseth the patient." Our ancestors, even when in rude health, quaffed a beverage known as cock-ale, in order that they might preserve their vigour. This drink—strong ale mixed with the broth of a boiled cock—is mentioned in the old plays, such as "Woman turned Bully," written in the year 1675; in Digby's book of receipts—"The Closet Open,"—published in 1648, and divers other medical and culinary works of the Middle Ages.

In these same "good old times," the liver of a male goat, the tail of a shrew-mouse, the brain

---

* In another book we consulted, "Notes for Cookerie, gathered from experienced Cookes," published in 1593, it is equally emphatic that "a Cock to be stewed to renew the weake" must be a red one. There is naturally here a connection suggested between the colour of the bird and the ruddy hue of health that is to be hoped for after such a dietary.

and comb of a cock, the worm under the tongue of a mad dog, pounded ants, cuckoo-broth, were all suggested as remedies for hydrophobia, though, like the fish-brine of Pliny or the pounded crab of Galen, they must have been but sorry reeds to rest upon in the dreadful paroxysms of this terrible malady.

The ancient Romans believed in the existence of a crystalline stone which they called alectorius, as large as a bean, and to be found in the gizzard of a cock, though not by any means discoverable in every fowl cut open. This stone was held to have the wonderful property of rendering the human possessor of it invisible. It may indeed have had the same effect on the original owner, as there could scarcely be an authentic instance of a stone of such peculiar property being found, but if the fowl itself could not be seen it is scarcely to be wondered at that the stone within it should be equally invisible. The belief in some such stone was one of the numerous articles of faith of the Middle Ages, but instead of the property of invisibility being attached to its possessor they sometimes substituted for it the much more prosaic idea that its owner could never feel thirsty, while the way to discover the bird that possessed it was simplicity itself, it being only necessary to discover which fowl at feeding time never drank. The first belief is much the more tenable, and is in fact impossible of refutation, as the world may be full of the owners of alectorius, invisible to us, and therefore unknown.

The cock was at one time supposed to possess the power of laying eggs from which were reared the deadly cockatrice. "When the cock is past seven years old an egg grows within him, whereat he greatly wonders. He seeks privately a warm place, and scratches a hole for a nest, to which he goes ten times daily. A toad privily watches him, and examines the nest every day to see if the egg be yet laid. When the toad finds the egg he rejoices much, and at length hatches it, bringing forth an animal with the head, neck, and breast of a cock, and from thence downward the body of a serpent."* In the year 1474 a cock at Basle was publicly accused of having laid one of these very objectionable eggs, and after a short trial† was sentenced to death and burnt, together with the egg, in the market place, amid a great concourse of the towns-folk, who were right joyfully thankful to feel that a great peril had been averted by the prompt action of their rulers, for a cockatrice was indeed no laughing matter to those who thought it one of the possibilities of life. In England the hens have entirely usurped the egg-laying department, and we are therefore spared the mortification of finding that our hoped-for

* MS. No. 10,074 in the Royal Library, Brussels.
† In the Middle Ages animals were frequently haled before the judges for various offences. In 1266 a pig was burnt at Fontaney, near Paris, for having killed a child, and in 1386, at Falaise, a sow was condemned to death for a similar offence. Horses and cattle were solemnly tried before the magistrates for manslaughter, and either expiated their offence on the gallows or were burned.

chick has assumed the less welcome form of a cockatrice.

The poison of a cockatrice was without cure, and the air was in such a degree affected by it that no creature could live near it. It killed, we are assured, not only by its touch, for even the sight of the cockatrice, like that of the basilisk, was death. We read, for instance, in Romeo and Juliet of "the death-darting eye of cockatrice," and again in King Richard III., "a cockatrice hast thou hatched into the world whose unavoided eye is murtherous;" while in Twelfth Night we find the passage, "this will so fright them both, that they will kill one another by the look like cockatrices." The good people of Basle might therefore, believing all this, very heartily congratulate themselves on their escape from a fearful peril.

The baleful cockatrice is often referred to in literature. Thus in the book entitled "Some Yeares Trauels into Africa and Asia the Great," written by Sir Thomas Herbert, and published in London in the year 1677, the writer says that Mohamed, on finishing his Koran, was "so transported, that to Mecca he goes to have it credited; but therein his predictions fail him, for so soon as the Arabs perceived his design (being formerly acquainted with his birth and breeding) they banish him, and (but for his Wives' relations) there had crushed him and his Cockatrice egg, which was but then hatching."

Legh, in his "Curiosities of Heraldry," gives the usual details of the death-dealing cockatrice, but adds, "Though he be venome withoute remedye whilest he liueth, yet when he is dead and burnt to ashes he loseth all his malice, and the ashes of him are good for alkumistes in turnyng and chaungyng of metall." Practically, therefore all that stands, or shall we say lies, between ourselves and wealth beyond the dreams of avarice is but a cockatrice moribund. Orthography was not a strong point in these old writers, and the word which is now established as cockatrice, may be met with as cocatrice, cokatrice, kokatrice, kocatrice, cockatryse, cocatryse, cocautrice, cockautrice, coccatryse, cocatris, kokatrix, chocatrix, and many other forms.

It has long been a belief in many parts of the country that if a cock crow at midnight the Angel of Death is passing over the house, and that if he delays to strike it is but for a short season. It is evident however that a score or more of different households may hear the same cock-crow, and we can scarcely conclude that it is to be fatal to all, since such wholesale slaughter would quickly depopulate whole hamlets, and we might really almost as well have the dread cockatrice at once.

Cock-crowing in mediæval days received mystical importance from a belief that it was in the dawn of the morning that our Saviour was born; it was regarded, too, as a warning voice telling of the coming of the day of Judgment,* and from its association with St. Peter's

---

* Aubrey tells us that in his younger days people had "some pious ejaculation when the cock did crow, which put them in mind of ye Trumpet at ye Resurrection."

grievous denial of his Master a warning against self-sufficiency and base cowardice. It was thought that during the hours of darkness evil spirits and the souls of the departed were abroad and that these fled at daybreak: hence Shakespeare makes the ghost of Hamlet's father vanish at this season—" It faded on the crowing of the cock." To the belief that on Christmas Eve the night was entirely free from any such spiritual manifestation he refers in the beautiful lines :—

> " Some say that ever 'gainst that season comes
> Wherein our Saviour's birth is celebrated,
> The bird of dawning singeth all night long,
> And then, they say, no spirit dares stir abroad ;
> The nights are wholesome; then no planets strike.
> No fairy takes, nor witch hath power to charm,
> So hallow'd and so gracious in the time."

In the quaint and delightful " Armonye of Byrdes" with its mingled Latin and English:—

> " The Cock dyd say:
> I use alway
> To crow both first and last.
> Lyke a Postle I am,
> For I preache to man
> And tell him the nyght is past.*

---

* " The peasants' trusty clock,
True morning watch, Aurora's trumpeter,
The lion's terror, true astronomer,
Who leaves his bed when Sol begins to rise
And when Sunne sets then to his roost he flies."
Speculum Mundi.

" O chanticleer,
Your clarion blow, the day is near."
LONGFELLOW, Daybreak.

> " I bring new tydyngis
> That the king of kynges
> In tactu profundit chorus:
> Then sang he, mellodious,
> Te Gloriosus,
> Apostolorum chorus."

This poem, of which only one ancient copy is in existence, has been reproduced by the Percy Society. The author is unknown, but is conjectured to be John Skelton. No date appears on it, but the name of the printer, John Wyght, shows that it must have been published somewhere about the year 1550. The poem begins:—

> " Whan Dame Flora
> In die Aurora
> Had covered the meadow with flowers,
> And all the fylde
> Was over dystylde
> With lusty Aprell showers,
> For my desporte
> Me to comforte
> Whan the day began to spring
> Foorth I went
> With a good intent
> To hear the byrdes syng."

The poem then goes on to tell us of the birds all " praisyng Our Lorde without discord, with goodly armony," the popyngay, the mavys, partryge, pecocke, thrusshe, nyghtyngale, larke, egle, dove, phenix, wren, the tyrtle trew, the hawke, the pellycane, the swalowe, all singing in quaint blending of Latin and English the praise of God.

The raven, " the hoarse night-raven, trompe of

doleful drere,"* has been at almost all periods regarded with superstitious awe. Shakespeare, for instance, writes of the raven "that croaks the fatal entrance of Duncan," † and again, in Othello, we find the illustrative passage—

> "It comes o'er my memory
> As doth the raven o'er the infected house,
> Boding to all."

Marlowe, in like spirit, in his "Rich Jew of Malta," dwells on the sad presaging raven

> "That tolls
> The sick man's passport in her hollow beak,
> And in the shadow of the silent night
> Doth shake contagion from her sable wings."

The whole field of literature teems with references of the same ominous character. It will suffice to add but one more illustration, where Gay, in "The Dirge," notices the evil presage in the lines—

> "The boding raven on her cottage sat,
> And with hoarse croakings warned us of our fate."

The raven is sometimes called the devil's bird. It is believed that it was originally white, but that it was changed to black for its disobedience. What this disobedience was appears to be a very moot point. The old Greeks believed that Apollo once sent it to a fountain to fetch water, and the bird on arrival found a fig-tree with very nearly ripe fruit, and determined to wait until they were quite so. As this was a matter of some few days, it became necessary to invent some plausible explanation of the delay, so he took a water-snake out of the fountain and

* Spenser.   † Macbeth.

brought it in the pitcher to the god, and explained that this creature had drunk the reservoir dry. Apollo, declining to accept this explanation, turned the disobedient raven black, condemned it to be always plagued with thirst, and changed its once melodious voice into the monstrous croak* that it has ever since been uttering as token of its punishment. Mediæval writers do not accept this story at all, but declare that the real reason that the raven exchanged its snow-white plumage for the sable garb was the consequence of its disobedience when, instead of returning to the ark to Noah, it stayed to feed on the bodies of the drowned.† It will be seen that in each case disobedience was the offence, and appetite the occasion thereof.

It is rather startling after this to read in the quaint pages of Legh that "the Rauen delighteth so much in her owne bewty that when her birds are hatched she will giue them no meate vntill she see whether they will bee of her

---

* An old writer, one Fulgentius, declares that so far from this croak being monotonous "the Raven hath sixty-four sundry chaunges of her voice." No other observer seems to have detected this.

† A fourteenth-century MS., the "Cursor Mundi," says of the raven's exit from the ark :—

"Than opin Noe his windowe
Let ut a rauen and forth he flow
Dune and vp sought here and thare
A stede to sett upon somequar.
Vpon the water sone he fand
A drinkled best ther flotand.
Of that fless was he so fain
To schip came he neuer again."

owne colour or no." Guillim, another writer, like Legh, on matters heraldic, entirely supports this statement, declaring that "it hath bene an ancient received opinion, and the same also grounded vpon the warrant of the Holy Scriptures that such is the property of the Raven, that from the time his young ones are hatched or disclosed, untill he seeth what colour they will be of, he never careth of them nor ministereth any food unto them, therefore it is thought that they are in the meane space nourished with the heavenly dew. And so muche also doth the kingly prophet, David, affirme, 'which giveth fodder unto the catell and feedeth the young Ravens that call upon him.' The Raven is of colour blacke, and when he perceiveth his young ones to be pennefeathered and black like himself, then doth he labour by all means to foster and cherish them from thence forward."

Surprising as it is to find that the sable plumage that we regard as the mark of disgrace is to the bird himself or herself (for Legh refers to the maternal pride and Guillim to the paternal) a beauty that no bastard brood can attain to, it is still more surprising to find that this "devil's bird" and messenger of woe is really not by any means so black as he is painted, and is, indeed, possessed of deep religious feeling. Maundevile in his pilgrimage to Mount Sinai saw and heard of many wonderful things, and certainly what he heard in that sacred spot of the ravens must have greatly astonished him. He tells us that at the shrine of St. Catherine he found many lamps

16 *

burning, and the monks rejoicing in an abundance of "Oyle of Olyves both for to brenne in here Lampes and to ete also, and that plentee have thei of the Myracle of God, for the Ravennes and the Crowes and the Choughes and other Fowles of the Countree assemble hem there ones every yeer, and fleen thider as in pilgrymage, and everyche of hem bringethe a Braunche of the Olyve in here Bekes in stade of offryng and leven hem there: of the whyche the monkes maken gret plentee of Oyle, and this is a gret marvaylle." The monkish moral to the story is obvious—that if "Foules that han no kyndely wytt ne Resoun" thus willingly offer to the maintenance of the church how much more should the sons of men give of their substance to so excellent a cause. One can indeed only feel that it is more probable that the story was made to fit the moral than the moral to fit the story.

Like most other things in mediæval days the raven found a place in the pharmacopœa, for it would appear that there was scarely anything better "for ye Gowte" than raven-broth, but to make it effectually one or two points that appear in themselves of little importance had to be scrupulously observed. For those who care to make trial of it we append the recipe: "Take Rauynys bryddys all quyke owte of here neste and loke yat yei towche not the erth nor yat yei comy in non hows, and brene hem in a new potte all to powdir and gif it ye seke man to drynkeyn."

The talisman known as the raven-stone was

held to confer on its holder invisibility, and we may remark in passing on the curious attraction that in the Middle Ages this gift of invisibility possessed, whether used as a means of shielding one's self from dangers, as a means of inflicting without detection injuries on others, or the dishonourable desire of secretly spying upon their proceedings. It appears to point to a somewhat unwholesome state of things, too suggestive of cowardice and treachery to be at all an object to be sought after. There were many such kinds of talisman, all doubtless of equal efficacy, and all of them, naturally, presenting considerable difficulties in acquisition. The raven-stone was no exception. It was necessary first to discover a nest, then to climb the tree and to take from the brood one of the nestlings and kill it. The victim must be a male bird and not more than six weeks old. So far, with reasonable powers of observation, a fair amount of agility, and sufficient sense to visit the nest at a time when one might reasonably expect to find young birds therein, there would appear to be no great difficulty ; but unless the parent birds were at least a hundred years old, all this preliminary trouble was of no avail. Having descended the tree in safety, the slaughtered nestling had to be placed at its foot, and watch kept for the return of the parent raven. On its return it will be observed to place a stone in the throat of its offspring, whereupon nothing remains but to secure the treasure and proceed to exercise its mystic power. How many persons actually put the matter to the test it is of course impossible to say, but full belief in its efficacy was for generations an article of faith to thousands.

The owl, like the raven, was regarded by our forefathers with great awe as an omen of misfortune and death; thus in Shakespeare we find several allusions to this superstitious belief—

> "Out on ye owls! nothing but songs of death,"

and the "boding scritch owl," as he is called in Henry VI., reappears in Macbeth in the passage:—

> "It was the owl that shriek'd; that fatal bellman
> Which giv'st the stern'st good night."

The idea dates from time immemorial. Pliny says, in the tenth book of his "Natural History," that "the scritch-owle betokeneth alwaies some heavie newes, and is most execrable and accursed. He keepeth ever in the deserts, and loveth not only such unpeopled places, but also those that are horrible hard of accesse. In summer, he is the verie monster of the night, neither crying, nor singing out cleare, but uttering a certaine heavie grone of dolefull moning. And, therefore, if he be seene within citties or otherwise abroad in any place it is not for good, but prognosticateth some fearfull misfortune."

Raven-like again, the owl is a specific for the gout, all that is necessary being to "take an owl, pull off her feathers, salt her well for a weak, then put her into a pot and stop it close, and put her into an oven, that so she may be brought into a mummy." This has then to be beaten into a powder and mixed with boar's grease, and "the grieved place" well anointed with this preparation. Owl-broth has in many rural districts of England been regarded as invaluable in whooping cough.

The notion of stones of mystic virtue being found in divers animals is a very common one in ancient and mediæval lore. We have already referred to the raven-stone, and many others were sought after. The interior of a fowl was said to yield a precious stone called alectorius; the chelidonius came from a swallow, geranites from a crane, and draconites from a dragon; while corvia was the name of the stone obtained from the crow. Anyone who cares to penetrate farther into this mass of rubbish will find plenty of it in the "Mirror of Stones" of Camillus. A stone from the hoopoe, when laid upon the breast of a sleeping man, forced him to reveal any rogueries he might have committed. The swallow was believed by some people to have two of these precious stones stowed away somewhere in its interior; one of these was a red one, and cured insanity; while the other, a black one, brought good fortune. Others said that the swallow found by some inspiration a particular kind of stone on the seashore, and that this stone restored sight to the blind. It will be remembered that Longfellow, in his "Evangeline," refers to this fancy in the lines:—

"Seeking with eager eyes that wondrous stone which the swallow
Brings from the shore of the sea, to restore the sight of her fledglings."*

* This notion of the sightlessness of the young swallow

Hence people assumed, not unreasonably, that what the bird found of such value to its young ones could scarcely fail to be of equal value for suffering humanity. Sometimes the association of the swallow with blindness is much more recondite. Thus Marcellus, writing in the year of our era, 480 A.D., advises one who fears that he is going blind to "look out for the first swallow, then run silently to the nearest spring, wash your eyes, and pray God that you may be free from it that year;" and then, with the callousness that is so characteristic of so many of these folk-lore remedies, very needlessly adds, "and that all the pain may pass into the swallow."

On referring to our copy of Winstanley's "Book of Knowledge," edition of 1685, to find out how far he confirms these wondrous cures of insanity, impecuniosity, and ophthalmia, we find that he does not even recognize their existence, but supplies in their place other facts equally striking. "Take a Swallow on the Wednesday," he writes, "and bind him with a silken thread by the foot, then cut him in the midst, and thou shalt find three stones, a white, a red, and a green; take the white and put it into thy mouth, and it shall make thee fair; put

was a very popular one. The chelidonium, or swallow wort, according to Aristotle and Dioscorides was so called because the swallows use it to give sight to their young. Goldfinches, linnets, and other birds, in like manner were believed to use the eye-bright; while the hawks strengthened their vision, we are told, by means of the plant that was hence called the hawk-weed, and still retains that name.

into thy mouth the red, and thou shalt have favour from her thou lovest ; put the green into thy mouth, and thou shalt never be in peril." If none of these inducements prevail or appeal to the reader, the author can supply another recipe of equal value. " Take a swallow in the moneth of August, look in her breast, and you shall find there a stone of the bignesse of a pease : take it and put it under your tongue, and you shall have such eloquence that no man shall have power to deny thy request." Such a gift would often be invaluable, and it seems distinctly unfortunate for the legal profession that it can only be utilised during the Long Vacation, unless, indeed, this wondrous stone can be in some way preserved without losing its efficacy; but of this the recipe gives no hint. In an old receipt book before us oil of swallows is pronounced "exceeding soveraign " for broken bones, or " any grief in the sinews." It is procured by pounding the swallows in a mortar, and adding thereto divers herbs.

For one that is, or will be, drunken, it is well to have at hand some preparation that may be deterrent, and here is the very thing! "Take swallowes and burne them, and make a powder of them ; and give the dronken man thereof to drinke, and he shall never be dronken hereafter." There is a certain sense of incompleteness here, as one does not quite realize how this powder becomes drinkable.

The ill-luck that attended those who hurt the robin or the wren was an article of faith with our forefathers, and probably still remains so in rural districts. In the "Six Pastorals," written in the year 1770, we find the belief very clearly expressed in the lines :—

> "I found a robin's nest within our shed,
> And in the barn a wren has young ones bred :
> I never take away their nest, nor try
> To catch the old ones, lest a friend should die.
> Dick took a wren's nest from the cottage side,
> And ere a twelvemonth pass'd his mother dy'd."

The belief that they, "with leaves and flowers, do cover the friendless bodies of unburied men" has no doubt had much to do with the kindly feeling extended to them. As Drayton hath it :—

> "Covering with moss the dead's unclosed eye
> The little red-breast teacheth charity."

Its fearless confidence, too, in visiting the habitations of men has begotten a kindly feeling for it, while one ancient legend tells us that when our Saviour hung forsaken on the cross the robin strove to draw out the cruel nails, and thus imbrued its breast in the Sacred Blood, an act of piety of which from thenceforth it bore the token in its ruddy feathers.

Though there are divers quaint beliefs associated with the wren which we need not here particularize, we may perhaps assume that the main reason for its association with the robin lies in the love of alliteration, for though the actual spelling of the words is against this theory, the sound to the ear favours it, and the two R's of the Robin and the 'Ren are certainly not more far-fetched than the three R's that were once held to cover the whole field of rustic scholarship, Reading, Riting and Rithmetic.

"The eyes and heart of a nightingale laid about men in bed," according to the "Magick of Kirani," serve to "keep them awake, and to make one die for sleep. If anyone dissolve them and give them secretly to anyone in drink, he will never sleep, but will so die, and it admits of no cure." It was a belief in the Middle Ages, and termed the doctrine of signatures, that every plant bore stamped upon itself, though men's eyes were in some cases too blind to detect it, an indication of its value to humanity, thus the spots in the inside of a foxglove flower were a sign that this plant was of value for ulcerated sore-throat; the buds of the forget-me-not bent round in a spiral somewhat suggestive possibly of the tail of a scorpion, gave the plant its mediæval name of scorpion-grass, and were held a clear indication that anyone stung by a scorpion would find in this herb his remedy. In a like spirit we see that the eyes and heart of the nightingale, a bird awake when most other creatures are sleeping, were held to be, on application, a cause of wakefulness to anyone coming within their subtle influence.

It was a very common and widespread belief that the nightingale when singing pierced its breast with a thorn, but whether this was to keep it awake, or to give its song the sad character that the poets will insist most wrongfully in attributing to it, seems an open question. Sir

Philip Sidney in one of his sonnets appears to reflect the popular belief—

> "The nightingale, as soon as April bringeth
> Unto her rested sense a perfect waking,
> While late bare earth, proud of her clothing, springeth,
> Sings out her woes, a thorn her song book making:
> And mournfully bewailing
> Her throat in times expresseth,
> While grief her heart oppresseth."

The author of the "Speculum Mundi" also refers to "the nightingale sitting all the night singing upon a bough, with the sharp end of a thorn against her breast," assigning, as the reason, "to keep her waking." The bird is a great favourite with the poets, but in most cases their invocations are somewhat misplaced: it is not the "sweet songstress" that so delights us, for though her notes are sweet, the real flood of melody wells from the heart of her lord. 'Tis he, to quote the words of Coleridge—

> "That crowds, and hurries, and precipitates
> With thick fast warble his delicious notes,
> As he were fearful that an April night
> Would be too short for him to utter forth
> His love-chant, and disburden his full soul
> Of all its music."

The error as to sex, and the error as to the pensive character of the song, have a common origin and date back from the ancient time when Ovid declared that Philomela, the daughter of Pandion, King of Athens, mourning for her children, was turned into a nightingale: hence Virgil uses the word "Philomela" when speaking of the bird, and the mediæval and modern poets have continued the usage; and on this same account, the song of the nightingale has by poetic fiction been deemed pensive and melancholy. Thus Shelley refers to "the nightingale's complaint," and Drayton writes of "our mournful Philomela," while Milton calls the bird "most musical, most melancholy." Coleridge, Clare, and others refuse however to follow this precedent.

When the peasant of mediæval days heard the cuckoo for the first time in each year, he rolled himself vigorously on the grass, and thus secured himself for the rest of the year from pains in the back. Much of the virtue of this remedy, we should imagine, would depend upon how damp the grass might be. We could easily imagine a state of things when this rolling process would be provocative rather than preventative. It was generally believed that the cuckoo sucked the eggs of other birds.

"The cuckoo, he sings in the spring of the year,
And he sucks little birds' eggs to make his voice clear."

Hence so soon as the general nesting season is over, and this selfish ovisuction fails him, the cuckoo to a great extent loses his song.* It was a generally accepted belief, too, that the cuckoo repaid the care of his foster parents, when he had no further occasion for it, by swallowing them. This belief dates from very early times.

* "He was but as a cuckoo is in June," says Shakespeare in reference to Richard II., that is to say, he had lost the power to attract, his utterances no longer commanded attention.

Aristotle refers to it, for instance, while in later days it crops up in the various books on so-called Natural History. On turning again to Shakespeare, who rarely fails us when any quaint folk-lore has to be illustrated, we find an interesting reference to it in King Lear : "The hedge-sparrow fed the cuckoo so long that it had its head bit off by its young"—and again in the first part of King Henry IV., where Worcester, reminding the king of his broken word, says :—

> "And being fed by us, you used us so,
> As that ungentle gull, the cuckoo's bird,
> Useth the sparrow; did oppress our nest;
> Grew by our feeding to so great a bulk,
> That even our love durst not come near your sight
> For fear of swallowing."

Those, it was believed, who turned their money over in their pockets when they each year first heard the cuckoo, would have good fortune throughout the rest of the year, and keep their pockets well supplied until the recurring spring necessitated a re-turning of the contents.

It was a curious fancy of many of the old writers on such matters, that the peacock, though arrayed in such splendour, was ashamed of his feet, the mortification at the latter being more than a set-off to his pride in his plumage. "The peacock," says, for instance, one of these ancient authorities, "is a bird well-known and much admired for his daintie coloured feathers, which, when he spreads them against the sunne, have a curious lustre, and look like gemmes. Howbeit his black feet make him ashamed of his fair tail: and therefore when he seeth them, (as angrie with nature, or grieved for that deformitie) he hangeth down his starrie plumes, and walketh slowly in a discontented fit of solitary sadnesse, like one possest with dull melancholy." The peacock was throughout the Middle Ages the symbol of pride, and doubtless those who started and those who accepted such a story as this saw in it a happy illustration of the haughty spirit that goeth before a fall, and very gladly added it to the great body of moral teaching that the works of creation were required to furnish.

A large mass of legend and folk-lore is associated with the halcyon or kingfisher. One curious old superstition is that if a dead kingfisher is suspended from the roof it will always turn its breast in the direction from which the wind blows.* On looking over any old works on natural history one is repeatedly struck by the way in which the writers all copy each other, and reproduce the most outrageous statements, without ever seeming to care to bring the matters they deal with to the easy test of actual proof. It is, therefore, the more refreshing to find the old writer, Sir Thomas Browne, the author of the "Enquiry into Vulgar Errors," very wisely declining to accept the statement without

* Thus Christopher Marlowe enshrines the old belief in the lines:—
"But how now stands the wind?
Into what corner peers my halcyon's bill?"
While Shakespeare, in King Lear, refers to the time-servers who "turn their halcyon beaks with every gale and vary of their masters."

proof, but actually getting a kingfisher for himself, and seeing what would befall. His reflections and experience are so graphically and quaintly given in his book that we make no apology for transferring them to our own pages. He says "that a Kingfisher hanged by the bill, sheweth in what quarter the winde is by an occult and secret property, converting the breast to that point of the horizon from whence the winde doth blow, is a received opinion and very strange, introducing naturall Weathercocks, and extending magneticall positions as far as animall natures: a conceit supported chiefly by present practice, yet not made out by reason or experience. Unto reason it seemeth very repugnant that a carcasse or body disanimated should be so affected by every winde as to carry a conformable respect and constant habitude thereto. For although in sundry animals we deny not a kinde of naturall Meteorology or innate præsention bothe of winde and weather, yet that proceeding from sense receiving impressions from the first mutations of the air, they cannot in reason retain their apprehension after death: as being affections which depend upon life and depart upon disanimation. And therefore with more favourable reason may we draw the same effect or sympathie upon the Hedgehog, whose præsention of windes is so exact that it stoppeth the North or Southern hole of its nest, according to prenotion of these windes ensuing; which some men observing, have been able to make predictions whiche way the winde should turn, and been esteemed hereby wise men in point of weather. Now this proceeding from sense in the creature alive, it were not reasonable to hang up an Hedgehog dead and to expect a conformable motion unto its living conversion. Thus Glowewormes alive project a lustre in the dark, which fulgour notwithstanding ceaseth after death; and thus the Torpedo, which being alive stupifies at a distance, applied after death produceth no such result."

"As for experiment we cannot make it out by any we have attempted, for if a single Kingfisher be hanged up with silk in an open room and where the aire is free, it observes not a constant respect unto the winde, but vainly converting doth seldome breast it right. If two be suspended in the same room they will not regularly conform their breasts, but oftimes respect the opposite points of heaven. And if we conceive that for exact exploration they should be suspended where the air is quiet and unmoved, that clear of impediment they may more freely convert upon this naturall verticity, we have also made this way of inquisition, suspending them in large and spacious glasses closely stopped; wherein, neverthelesse, we observed a casuall station, and that they rested irregularly upon conversion."

It was formerly held that if the dead bodies of these birds were put away in chests they protected garments from the ravages of moths, and it was believed that the feathers of a dead kingfisher were renewed in all their splendour every year. It was an article of faith, too, that the plumage of the kingfisher was injurious to the eyes of those who gazed too long and too intently upon it, while the possession of even a feather was a protection against lightning.

According to the old Greek myth, Halcyone was the daughter of Æolus. Her husband, Ceyx, king of Trachyn, was drowned in the Ægean Sea, and the widowed Halcyone, wandering on the shore, saw afar the dead body of her husband. The gods, in pity, turned her into a bird, which with eager wings bore her spirit across the waste of waters, and that Ceyx might be able to return the love she lavished upon him, he, too, was permitted the same transformation.

It was an old belief that during the space of fourteen days, while the young kingfishers were being hatched, a great calm fell upon all things, and this period of quietness and security is referred to by many of our writers.* A very beautiful illustration may be found in Milton's "Hymn on the Nativity," where he describes how :—

"Peaceful was the night
 Wherein the Prince of Light
  His reign of peace upon the earth began ;

---

* The idea is at least as old as Pliny, as he mentions it in his "Natural History" as a recognized fact too well-known to need any apology or explanation. Theocritus in his seventh idyll dwells on it, and it is found in the writings of Pliny and many other ancient authors.

> The winds with wonder whist,
> Smoothly the waters kiss'd,
>   Whispering new joys to the wild ocean,
> Which now hath quite forgot to rave,
> While birds of calm sit brooding on the charmed wave."

The word halcyon is Greek and signifies brooding on the sea, as it was formerly believed that the kingfisher laid its eggs in a floating nest upon the sea. Drayton writes, for example, of

> "The halcyon, whom the sea obeys
>   When she her nest upon the water lays."

While Dryden, to quote one more instance, says:

> "Amidst our arms as quiet you shall be
>   As halcyon brooding on a winter's sea."

This exceptional favour fair Halcyone owes to her close relationship with Æolus, since with him rested the power to lash the waves to fury or to soothe them to rest. This beautiful Greek myth doubtless underlies the superstition as to the dead body of the kingfisher indicating the direction of the wind, though probably it never occurs to the rustic meteorologist as he watches his revolving kingfisher that any idea of the loving Halcyone turning to greet the coming Æolus enters into the philosophy of his test.

It was for centuries a belief that storks fed with filial care their aged parents. Thus Heywood, writing in the year 1635, asserts in "The Hierachie of the Blessed Angells" that

> "The indulgent storke, who builds her nest on hye
>   (Observ'd for her alternat pietie),
> Doth cherish her unfeather'd young and feed them,
> And looks from them the like, when she should need them.

(That's when she grows decrepit, old, and weake)
Nor doth her pious Issue cov'nant breeke:
For unto her, being hungry, food she brings,
And being weake, supports her on her wings."

One meets with the same notion again in Beaumont, where he asserts that

" The stork's an emblem of true piety:
Because, when age has seized and made his dam
Unfit for flight, the grateful young one takes
His mother on his back, provides her food,
Repaying thus her tender care for him,
Ere he was fit to fly."

The extraordinary idea that storks were found only in countries having a republican form of government held its ground for a considerable time, though it would appear as though nothing could have been simpler than its prompt disproof.

Cranes, it was believed, bore stones with them when they were migrating, in order that they might not be swept out of their course by the wind. A somewhat parallel notion was that swallows in their annual migrations carried in their bills, when about to cross the sea, a piece of stick, to be laid upon the water from time to time as a convenient resting place. The idea of the cranes steadying themselves in flight by a ballasting of small rock was too quaintly happy a conception not to bear amplification, so we find that the bees, the never-failing emblems of industry and wisdom, were equally ready to avail themselves of the notion. "Bees that are emploied in carrying of honie chuse alwaies to have the wind with them if they can. If haply there do arise a tempest whiles they bee abroad they catch up some little stonie greet to ballaise and poise themselves against the wind. Some say that they take it and lay it upon their shoulders." How the little stony grit maintains this latter position the old authors do not stop to explain. In the Georgics of Virgil we find a reference to this, which evidently even then was an old and unchallenged belief, in the lines :—

> " And oft with pebbles, like a balanced boat,
> Poised through the air on even pinions float "—

and the idea reappears from time to time as a fact in natural history. There is so much that is legitimately wonderful in bee-arrangements that it is scarcely strange that some of the details given by ancient and mediæval naturalists in praise of their sagacity, and other estimable qualities, should overreach the possibilities, and fail in the not unimportant element of truth.*

The sagacious cranes seem to have found several valuable uses for their pieces of rock. We are told that while the main body are resting at night, sentinels are posted to guard against surprise, so that the flock or covey, or whatever else may be the proper technical term to use, rest in full assurance of safety. To

---

* A quaint little octavo on this subject is that of Dr. Warder, "The true Amazons or the Monarchy of Bees," being a new discovery and Improvement of those wonderful creatures. The book went through several editions. The one that came under our notice is the third ; it is dated 1716.

insure the necessary vigilance, these sentinels stand upon one foot, and hold in the other a large stone.* Should they inadvertently nod, the muscles relax and the stone drops, and by the slight noise it makes awakens them to a proper sense of their duty and their temporary lapse from it.

A third valuable use that the cranes seem to have found for stones was to put them in their mouths when migrating, so that thus gagged they might not make a noise, and by their cries bring the eagles and other birds of prey upon themselves.† In the "Euphues," we find a passage that admirably illustrates the belief in these two latter uses of the stone, as the author

---

* Ammianus Marcellinus has put it upon record that in imitation of the ingenuity of the crane in assuring vigilance, Alexander the Great was accustomed to rest with a silver ball in his hand, so that on the slightest movement it might fall and wake him. This is certainly heroic treatment, since even such an one as Alexander might fairly claim the necessity that other mortals feel of uninterrupted rest. It reminds one of the dictum of the great Duke of Wellington in defence of his camp-bedstead, accommodation so confined that one could scarcely turn round in it, that directly a man begins to think of turning round it is time to turn out.

† In "A Mirror for Mathematics, a Golden Gem for Geometricians, a sure Safety for Saylers, and an auncient Antiquary for Astronomers and Astrologians," by Robert Tanner, Gent, Practitioner in Astrologie and Physic, a book published in the year 1587, we find an " Epistle dedicatourie " to Lord Howard of Effingham, commencing:—"The Cranes when they fly out of Cilicia, over the mountain Taurus, carrie in their mouths a pebble stone, lest by their chattering they should be ceased upon by the eagles, which birds, Right Honourable, might teach me silence," &c., &c.

would naturally not use similes that would be unfamiliar to his readers. "What I haue done," he writes, "was onely to keep myselfe from sleepe, as the Crane doth the stone in hir foote; and I would also, with the same Crane, that I had been silent, holding a stone in my mouth."

It will be sufficiently evident that the birds we have mentioned are but few in number. It would be extremely difficult to make our treatment exhaustive, extremely easy to make it exhausting; we would desire in pity to our readers to avoid either of these alternatives. We would therefore steer straight for the proverbial third course, and trust that it may be held that we have found a happy medium in resting satisfied with the comparatively few species of birds that are here brought under notice.

CHAPTER V.

Forms reptilian and piscine—The basilisk—Shakespeare and Spenser thereupon—King of serpents—The dragon—Aldrovandus thereon—The dragon-stone—The griffin—The scorpion—The "Newe Jewell of Healthe"—Toads—Antipathy between toad and spider—The toadstone—How to procure it—The weeping crocodile—Cockeram's Dictionary—The treacherous seal—The salamander—Its potent venom—Its home in fire—Prester John and his kingdom—Pyragones—The chamæleon—Its changing colour—Serpents from air—The gift of invisibility—The serpent-stone—Theriaca—Viper-broth—Antidotal herbs—The soil of Malta—The deaf adder—The two-headed Amphisbæna—Aldrovandus on serpents—Hairy serpents—The deadly asp—Monstrous snails—Snail and spider remedies—Bees—Virgil on their production—Glowworm ink—Marine forms the counterparts of those on land—The sea-monk—The sea-bishop—The sus marinus—The brewers of the storm—The hog-fish—The sea-elephant—The sea-horse—The sea-unicorn—The remora—The dolphin, its special fondness for man—Its love of music—Its changeful colouring—The acipenser—The loving ray—The sargon—The friendship between the oyster and the prawn—The voracious swam-fish—Leviathan—Cause of the crooked mouth of the flounder—The healing tench—Fish medicaments—The vain cuttle-fish—The fish that came to be eaten—Conclusion.

We turn in conclusion to forms reptilian and piscine, and to "such small deer" as may call for a parting word or two in drawing our labours to a close; and here we find no great amount of material to deal with, for though our section includes such fabulous monsters as the basilisk and the dragon, the general knowledge of reptiles and fish was naturally by no means so extensive as that of the more readily visible beasts and birds.

The basilisk, a wingless dragon, according to some authorities—a serpent, if we may credit others—was a peculiarly objectionable creation, not of nature, but of man. Like all such creatures, it is extremely difficult to get a very definite idea of it, since imagination has run rampant in dealing with it. It was but twelve fingers' breadth long, according to some writers; this we may take to mean some eight or nine inches long,* but, unfortunately, its powers of mischief were out of all proportion to its size. It wore a diadem upon its head, as a sign of its kingship over all other serpents, and its poison was death without remedy. Pliny, however, shall be allowed to describe the venomous little monster in his own way, as he does so with a vivid force that it is impossible to surpass:—
"With his hies he driveth away other serpents; he moveth his body forward not by multiplied windings like other serpents, but he goeth with half his body upright and aloft from the ground; he killeth all shrubs not only that he toucheth, but that he breatheth upon; he burns up herbs and breaketh the stones, so great is his power for mischief. It is received of a truth that one of them being killed with a lance by a man on horseback, the poison was so strong that it

* "This creature is in thicknesse as big as a man's wrist, and of length proportionable to that thicknesse."—*Speculum Mundi.*

passed along the staff and destroyed both horse and man." Its touch caused the flesh to fall from the bones of the animal with which it came in contact, and even the glance of its eye was death upon whomsoever it fell. It will be remembered that Shakespeare refers to this belief in the utterance of the Lady Ann in response to Richard's observation on her eyes—

"Would that they were basilisk's to strike thee dead."

In 2 Henry VI. (act iii. sc. 6) the king exclaims,

"Come, basilisk, and kill the innocent gazer with thy sight,"

—while in Henry V. (act iii. sc. 2) Queen Isabel says—

"Your eyes, which hitherto have borne in them
  Against the French, that met them in their bent
  The fatal balls of murthering basilisks."

Suffolk in cursing his enemies invokes against them the deadly basilisk, while Gloster boasts that he will "slay more gazers than the basilisk." Spenser in like manner mentions one who—

"Secretly his enemies did slay
  Like as the Basilisk, of serpent's seede
  From powerful eyes close venim did convey
  Into the looker's hart, and killed farre away."

The writer of the "Speculum Mundi" hath it that "the Basilisk is the King of Serpents, not for his magnitude nor greatnesse, but for his stately pace and magnanimous minde." Of this magnanimity, however, he gives no illustration or proof, but simply goes on to give the creature as black a character as all other writers do. "His eyes are red in a kinde of cloudy thicknesse, as if fire were mixt with smoke. His poyson is a very hot and venimous poyson, drying up and scorching the grasse as if it were burned, infecting the aire round about him, so as no other creature can live near him. His hissing, likewise, is said to be as bad, in regard that it blasteth trees, killeth birds, &c., by poysoning of the aire, and if anything be slaine by it the same also proueth venimous to such as touch it," —an altogether unloving and unlovely brute. It must be borne in mind that whilst we in this nineteenth century simply regard such a creature as a weird fancy, countless generations of mankind have accepted the basilisk as a very grim reality indeed, that might in all its fearful power some day cross their paths.

Even Sir Thomas Browne, who demolished in his book so many common beliefs, is prepared to accept the Basilisk, for while he declares that "many opinions are passant concerning the basilisk, or little King of Serpents, some affirming, others denying, most doubting the relations made thereof," he, himself, adds "that such an animal there is, if we evade not the testimony of Scripture and humane writers, we cannot safely deny." For his Scriptural proofs he quotes Psalm xci.: "Super aspidem et Basilicum ambulabis," and Jeremiah viii., ver. 17: "For behold I will send serpents, cockatrices among you, which will not be charmed, and they shall bite you." Many of the old writers we may mention in passing, consider the basilisk and the cockatrice the same creature. That by death-dealing glance a basilisk may empoison is not to Browne a thing impossible, "for eies receive offensive impressions from their objects, and may have influences destructive to each other. For the visible species of things strike not our senses immaterially, but streaming in corporall raies doe carry with them the qualities of the object from whence they flow. Thus it is not impossible what is affirmed of this animall; the visible raies of their eies carrying forth the subtilest portion of their poison, which, received by the eie of man or beast, infecteth first the brain, and is thence communicated to the heart." Again he says, "that deleterious it may be at some distance, and destructive without corporall contaction, there is no high improbability," and he proceeds, not by any means without thought or shrewdness, to give reasons for his belief in the possibility of such a thing. "For," says he, "if plagues or pestilentiall Atomes have been conveyed in the air from different Regions, if men at a distance have infected each other, if the shaddowes of some trees be noxious, if Torpedoes deliver their opinion at a distance and stupifie beyond themselves, we cannot reasonably deny that (besides our grosse and restrained poisons requiring contiguity unto their actions) there may proceed from subtiller seeds more agile emanations, which contemn those laws, and invade at distance unexpected."

The belief in the dragon was one of the articles of faith of our ancestors. In another of our books, "Symbolism in Christian Art," we have dwelt at considerable length upon the various legends in which the dragon figures, and the symbolic use made of the monster as representative of the evil principle that all are called upon to combat, but our forefathers had a very real belief in the veritable existence of the dragon, not by any means regarding it as a symbol merely, a figure of speech or apt allegory, but as one of the quite definite perils that the adventurous traveller in distant lands might be called upon to face,* while preparations of the dragon were a recognized feature in the pharmacopœia. "Scale of dragon, tooth of wolf," and many other horrible ingredients are found in the witches' cauldron in Macbeth.

In a mediæval work we are told that "the turning joint in the chine of a dragon doth promise an easy and favourable access into the presence of great lords." One can only wonder why this should be, all clue and thread of connection between the two things being now so hopelessly lost. We must not, however, forget that, smile now as we may at this, there was a time when our ancestors accepted the statement with the fullest faith, and many a man who would fain have pleaded his cause before king or noble, bewailed with hearty regret his want of draconic chine, the "turning-point" of the

* The "Annals of Winchester," for the year 1177, inform us that "in this yeare Dragons were sene of many in England." In 1274 it is recorded that there was an earthquake on the Eve of St. Nicholas' Day, and that there appeared "a fiery dragon which frightened the English."

dragon and of his own fortunes. Another valuable recipe runs as follows: "Take the taile and head of a dragon, the haire growing upon the forehead of a lion, with a little of his marrow also, the froth, moreover, that a horse fomethe at the mouth who hath woon the victorie in running a race, and the nailes besides of a dog's feete; bind all these together with a piece of leather made of red deer's skin, with the sinewes partly of a stag, partly of a fallowe deere, one with another; carry this about with you, and it will work wonders."* It seems almost a pity that the actual benefits to be derived from the possession of this compound are not more clearly defined, as there is no doubt that a considerable amount of trouble would be involved in getting the various materials together, and the zeal and ardour of the seeker after this wonder-working composition would be somewhat damped by doubt as to its actual utility. Mediæval medicine-men surely must have been somewhat chary of adopting the now familiar legend of "prescriptions accurately dispensed" when the onus of making up such a mixture could be laid upon them.

In spite of the familiarity with the appearance

---

* In the "Magick of Kirani," a Persian book that appeared in an English dress in 1685, we find the representation of a dragon employed as a charm. "If therefore any man engrave a woodpecker on the stone dentrites, and a sea-dragon under its feet, every gate will open unto him; savage beasts will also obey him and come to tameness; he shall also be loved and observed of all, and whatever he hath a mind to, he shall perform."

of the creature that the obtaining of its head and tail would suggest, the various authorities differ very widely in describing it. Some writers say that dragons are of "a yellow fierie colour, having sharp backs like saws," and some tell us that "their scales shine like silver." Some dragons are said to have wings and no feet, some again have both feet and wings, others have neither one nor the other, and are only distinguished from the common sort of serpents by the combs growing upon their heads. Father Pigafetta in his book declares that " Mont Atlas hath plentie of dragons, grosse of body, slow of motion, and in byting or touching incurably venomous. In Congo is a kind of dragons like in bygnesse unto rammes with wings, having long tayles and divers jawes of teeth of blue and greene, painted like scales, with two feete, and feede on rawe fleshe." John Leo, in his "History of Africa," says that the dragon is the progeny of the eagle and wolf. Others affirm that it is generated by the great heat of India, or springs from the volcanoes of Ethiopia.

After reading about almost every possible variation of structure that is open to a dragon, winged, serpentine, two-legged, four-legged, and the like, it is rather quaint to find that Pliny feels that there is a point after all where one must draw the line. He says that "in Ethiopia there are produced as great dragons as in India, being twenty cubits long. But I chiefly wonder at one thing: why Juba should think they were crested." This suggestion of the crass ignorance of Juba was certainly a little hard on him, as when so very much was believed a crest was a very little extra item to credit, besides as a matter of fact dragons as such, Ethiopian or otherwise, were often described by ancient authorities as having this feature. It really seems like accepting the sheeted spectre of the country churchyard, and then growing sceptical because its hollowed turnip head was still crowned with a little of the foliage that rustic haste or indifference to the verities had failed to cut away.

Aldrovandus, in his "History of Serpents and Dragons," published in 1640, goes very thoroughly indeed into the subject.* The work is in folio size, and the portion devoted to the dragon extends from pages 312 to 360. It must be duly noted that Aldrovandus entirely accepts the dragon as a reality; that this is so is obvious from his dealing with it in this volume instead of placing it in his "Historia Monstrorum." The book is written in Latin, and amongst the various sections concerning the dragon we find Differentiæ, Forma et Descriptio, Mores, Locus, Antipathia (unlike most other creatures treated by the old author, his vindictive savagery forbids

* On its noble title-page we see on either side of the title of the book a powerful dragon, beneath one is inscribed Dominium, and below the other Vigilantia. At the base a third dragon supports two shields. On one is represented the serpent twining round a staff, the well-known symbol of Æsculapius, inscribed Salus, and on the other the equally familiar symbol of eternity, the serpent with its tail in its mouth, inscribed Immortalitatis.

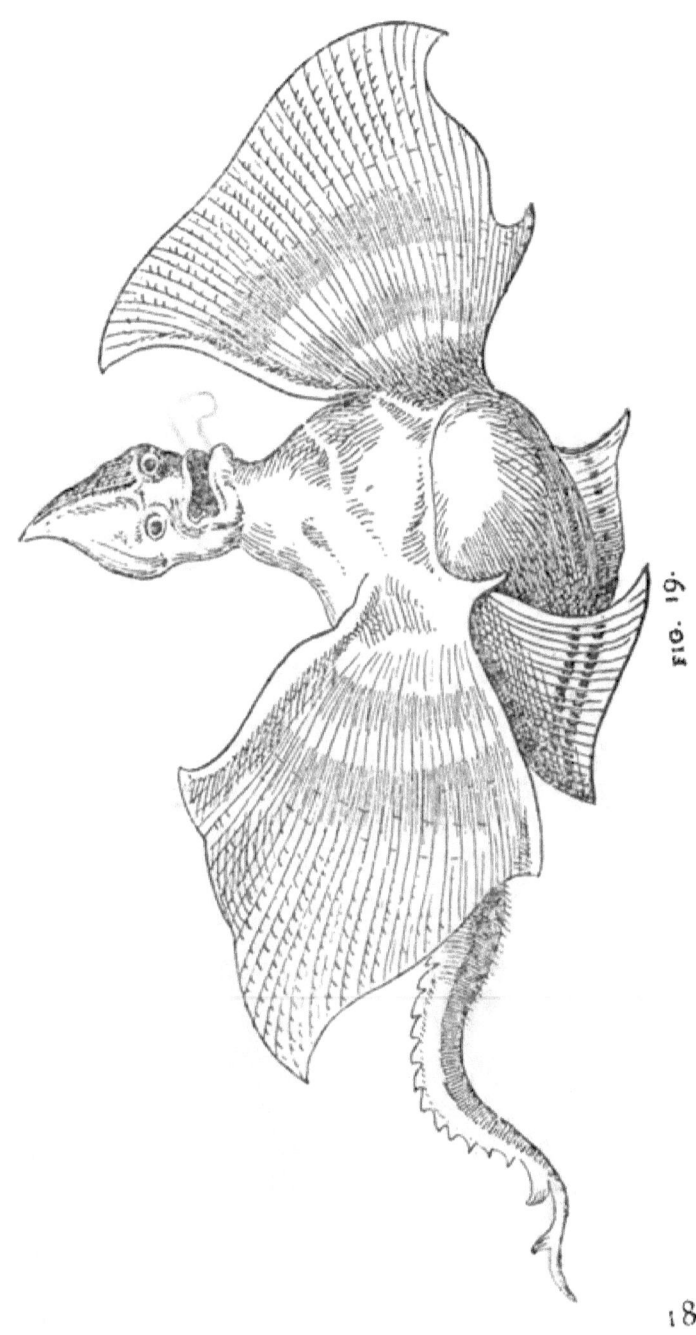

FIG. 16.

the usual chapter on Sympathia), and Usus in Medicina. Fig. 19 is one of the draconic forms illustrated in the book; the varieties given are very numerous, and of widely differing nature.

Our ancestors used always to prescribe divers kinds of herb-teas to be drunk in the Springtime, and it is a curious example of instinct in a reptile that the dragon likewise, whom he feels at this season of the year a certain loathing of meat, physics himself into rude health again with the juice of the wild lettuce. Many animals have, or at all events had, if we may credit the wisdom of our forefathers, considerable faith in the medicinal value of herbs. Thus pigeons and blackbirds when suffering from loss of appetite eat bay leaves as a tonic. The bay leaf, too, was a most valuable thing for internal application against the poison of the chameleon, though the elephant when he had inadvertently swallowed one of these creatures, a mistake that seems to have not unfrequently happened, probably from the resemblance in colour of the reptile to the foliage amongst which he was ensconced, pinned his faith in the wild olive leaf.

As the toad, ugly and venomous, bore yet in popular belief a precious jewel in its head, so we find in the writings of various authorities a belief that the still uglier and more venomous dragon bore in like manner the lustrous carbuncle. Jordanus tells us, for example, that in India the dragons that there abound are thus gifted, a fact that the natives turn to their advantage. "These dragons," he declares, "grow exceeding big, and cast forth from the mouth a most infectious breath, like the thickest smoke rising from fire. These animals come together at the destined time, develop wings, and begin to raise themselves in the air, and then, by the judgment of God, being too heavy, they drop into a certain river which issues from Paradise, and perish there. But all the regions round about watch for the time of the dragons, and when they see that one has fallen they wait for seventy days, and then go down and find the bare bones of the dragon, and take the carbuncle which is rooted in the top of his head."

Even the dragon, however, may not be quite so black as he is painted, for we read in one old author of a child in Arcadia that had a dragon for its playmate. There was much affection between them, but presently a considerable dread of the dragon's powers gained possession of the boy, and he compassed the brilliant idea of beguiling his companion well out into the desert and then slipping away. In the very consummation of this plan a new danger arose, as the stripling found himself in an ambush of robbers, whereupon he was only too thankful to call out to his discarded playmate, who immediately came to the rescue and very effectually scattered his despoilers. At this point the history unfortunately stops, but we may perhaps conclude that it follows on the lines of most stories of the affections, and that "they lived happy ever after." However this may be, it is a charming narrative, and opens out quite a new trait of dragon disposition.

Amongst the many strange creatures that were held to inhabit Ethiopia, the griffins were perhaps the most conspicuous amidst the weird fauna of that marvellous land. "Some men seyn," and Maundevile in his quaint book of travels fully endorses the idea, "that Griffounes han the Body upward as an Egle and benethe as a Lyoun and treuly thei ben of that schapp. But a Griffoun hathe the body more gret and is more strong thanne eight Lyouns and more gret and stronger than an hundred Egles such as we han amonge us. For a Griffoun ther wil bere, fleynge to his Nest, a gret Hors or two Oxen yoked togidere as thei gon at the Plowghe."

Chaucer, in the "Canterbury Tales," says of one of his characters :—

> "Blake was his berd, and manly was his face,
> The cercles of his eyen in his hed
> They gloweden betwixten yelwe and red,
> And like a griffon loked he about."

Ctesias describes the griffin in all sober earnestness as a bird with four feet of the size of a wolf, and having the legs and claws of a lion, their feathers being red upon the breast and black on the rest of the body. Glanvil says of it : "the claws of a griffin are so large and ample that he can seize an armed man as easily by the body as a hawk a little bird." The griffin is often met with in heraldry past and present, either as a crest, charge, or supporter of the arms. A very familiar example of its employment in the latter service may be seen in the arms of the City of London, or exalted on lofty pedestal, where, in lieu of Temple Bar, it marks the westward civic boundary. Shakespeare, Milton, and others of our poets and writers, refer to the griffin.

Anyone reading the herbals of Gerard, Parkinson, and others, or the various medical books of the Middle Ages, will scarcely have failed to notice how frequently reference is made to the scorpion. In these later days a man might well journey from John o' Groats to the Land's End, and run no peril of an encounter, but in the earlier times we have referred to, the sting of the scorpion was a very present dread, and numerous remedies for it were devised. The beautiful blue forget-me-not of our streams is in all herbals and floras till the beginning of this century called the scorpion-grass,* from its supposed virtue as a cure, a remedy that was supposed to be sufficiently indicated from its head of flowers and buds being rolled round into some more or less satisfactory resemblance to a scorpion's tail. Cogan, in his " Haven of Health," tells how " a certaine Italian, by often smelling the Basill, had a scorpion bred in his braine, and after vehement and long paines he died therof."

In the " Newe Iewell of Health, gathered out of the best and most approved Authors by that

---

* Thus Lyte tells us that in his day, 1578, it had " none other knowen name than this."

excellent Doctor Gesnerus,"* we find some extraordinary preparations. Most of these are of a botanical nature, but we also have "Oyle holy† prepared out of dead men's bones, Oyle or distilled lycour gotten out of the Gray, Oyle marveylous gotten out of the Beuer, Oyle of frogges ryght profitable to such as are payned of ye gout, Oyle of antes egges," and many other strange remedies for the ills that the flesh is heir to. Among them, a forerunner of the ideas of Hahnemann, and the notion of like curing like, we find "Oyle of Scorpion's distilled against Poysons." Apropos of the oil from dead men's bones, we may point out the special charm that our ancestors seemed to find in anything associated with the charnel house—thus one favourite remedy was the moss that grew on a dead man's skull, another was a pill compounded from the brains of a man that had been hanged; powder of mummy in like manner was in high repute, and to those who found pill or powder too nauseous a draught of spring water from the skull of a murdered man was at once refreshing and health-

---

* "Wherein is contained the most excellent Secretes of Phisicke and Philosophie deuided into fower Bookes. In the which are the best approued remedies for the diseases as well inwarde as outwarde, of all the partes of Man's bodie: treating very amplie of all Dystillacions of Waters, of Oyles, Balmes, Quintessences, with the vse and preparation of Antimonie and Potable Gold."

† The "holy" has, of course, no reference to the sacred character of the mess in question: it is merely the free and easy mediæval way of spelling the word wholly.

giving. The following recipe* for the cure of a wound seems to show that our forefathers had no great fear of blood poisoning : " Take of the moss of the skull of a strangled man two ounces, of the mumia of man's blood one ounce and a halfe, of earth wormes washed in water or wine and dryed, one ounce and a halfe, of the fatte of a Boare two drams, of oyle of Turpintine two drams : pound them and keepe them in a longe narrow pott, and dippe into the oyntment the yron or wood, or some sallowe sticke made wet with blood in opening the wound." The medicine and surgery of the Middle Ages must have been a powerful influence in checking redundance of population.

Toads were in great repute in sickness. " In time of common contagion," writes Sir Kenelm Digby in 1660, " men use to carry about with them the powder of a toad, and sometimes a living toad or spider† shut up in a box, which draws the contagious air, which otherwise would infect the party," and many other illustrations of their employment as preventives or remedies

* Extracted from the "Arcana Fairfaxiana," a facsimile reproduction of a manuscript book of recipes some three hundred years old, found in an old lumber room at the ancestral seat of the Fairfax family.

† Our readers will remember the use that Longfellow makes of this fancy in his " Evangeline : "—

"Only beware of the fever, my friends! Beware of the fever!
For it is not like that of our cold Acadian climate,
Cured by wearing a spider hung round one's neck in a nutshell."

In the diary of Elias Ashmole we find that on May 11th,

might be given. The spider and the toad seem to have been each regarded as most venomous creatures, and in many of the old remedies one or other of them at will are recommended, either alternative being regarded as equally efficacious; thus for whooping cough, if one cannot find a toad to thrust up the chimney, two spiders in a walnut shell will serve equally well.

There was held to be mortal antipathy between the toad and the spider, and the result of a meeting between them was a conflict fatal to one or both of the antagonists. The *Aster Tripolium*, a well-known English wild plant, was originally called the toad-wort. "When a spider stings a toad, and the toad is becoming vanquished, and the spider stings it thickly and frequently, and the toad cannot avenge itself, it bursts assunder," at least, the author of the "Ortus Sanitatis" says it does, but whether this arises from venom or from vexation he does not explain. "If such a burst toad be near the toad-wort, it chews it and becomes sound again; but if it happens that the wounded toad cannot get to the plant, another toad fetches it and gives it to the wounded one." Topsell, in his "Natural History," vouches for this having been actually witnessed.

1651, he was suffering from ague. He writes: "I took early in the morning a good dose of elixir, and hung three spiders about my neck, ague away, Deo Gratias!" Sometimes a pill made up of spider web is taken, and in some parts of the south of England a favourite remedy for jaundice was the living spider itself rolled up with butter into a pill.

That the skin of the toad gives forth an acrid secretion which serves the creature as a defence is established beyond doubt, but its hurtful properties have been greatly exaggerated. Dryden refers to the lady "who squeezed a toad into her husband's wine," the inference being she was in heart murderous. Spenser makes Envy ride upon a wolf and chew "between his cankred teeth a venomous tode," while Diodorus declares that toads were generated by the heat of the sun from the dead bodies of ducks putrefying in mud.*

Lily, in his "Euphues," declares that "the foule toade hath a faire stone in his head," an idea that Shakespeare has immortalized in the beautiful lines that remind us how :—

> "Sweet are the uses of adversity,
> Which, like the toad, ugly and venomous,
> Yet wears a precious jewel in its head."

The crapaudine, or toad-stone, is of a dull brown colour. It was believed to possess sovereign virtue against poison from its changing colour when in the presence of any noxious thing : hence it was often worn as a protection in finger rings. Figs. 20 and 21 are good examples of this use. They are both from rings in the Londesborough collection. The belief in the virtues of the toad-stone was not only popular in England, but was one of the fallacies accepted throughout Europe. Though the stone is well-

---

* Another of these ancient authorities affirmed that mud engendered frogs that lack feet. In other words, he made acquaintance with tadpoles!

known to geologists as a variety of trap-rock, the accepted belief was that it was found only in the head of the toad. Fenton, writing in 1569, affirms that "there is found in the heads of old and great toads a stone which they call borax or stelon, and Lupton, some fifty years afterwards, writes : "the crepaudia or toad-stone is very valuable, touching any part envenomed by the bite of a rat, wasp, spider, or other poisonous beast it ceases the pain and swelling thereof." Ben Jonson also refers to it in his play of "The Fox." Albertus Magnus, writing about 1275, adds the great wonder that this stone when taken out of the creature's head has the figure of a toad upon

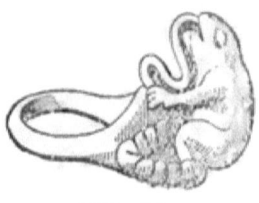

FIG. 20.

FIG. 21.

it, while others declare that the stone itself is of the form of a toad. It is a treasure not easily to be procured, for the toad "envieth much that man should haue that stone," declares Lupton, the author of "A Thousand Notable Things," hence it was very necessary to beware of useless counterfeits, and this old writer gives us a ready means of detecting them. "To know," says he, "whether the toad-stone called crepaudia be the righte and perfect stone or not, holde the stone before a toad so that he may see it, and if it be a

How to procure the Toad-stone.

right and true stone the toad will leap towards it, and make as though he would snatch it from you," a proceeding that must have required a considerable amount of nerve on the part of anyone duly impressed with the fear of the deadly venom of the creature.

The same ancient authority on the subject very obligingly gives "a rare good way to get the stone out of the toad." It suffices to "put a great or overgrown toad, first bruised in divers places, into an earthen pot : put the same into an ant's hillocke, and cover the same with earth, which toad at length the ants will eat, so that the bones of the toad and stone will be left in the pot." This certainly seems simplicity itself, but, unfortunately, most authorities agree in saying that the stone, to have any real virtue, should be obtained while the creature is yet alive. Porta has his doubts on the whole matter, nevertheless he gives some hints that might be of value to those of greater faith. "There is a stone," he says, "called Chelonites—the French name it Crapodina, which they report to be found in the head of a great old Toad ; and if it can be gotten from him while he is alive, it is soveraign against poyson. They say it is taken from living toads in a red cloth, in which colour they are much delighted ; for while they sport themselves upon the scarlet the stone droppeth out of their head and falleth through a hole made in the middle into a box set under for the purpose, else they will suck it up again. But I never met with a faithfull person who said that he had found it :

nor could I ever find one, though I have cut up many. Nevertheless, I will affirm this for truth that those stones which are pretended to be taken out of Toads are minerals. But the value is certain : if any swallow it down with poyson it will preserve him from the malignity of it, for it runneth about with the poyson and asswageth the power of it that it becometh vain and of no force." Boethius tells us how he watched throughout a whole night an old toad that he had placed on a piece of scarlet cloth, but is obliged to confess that nothing occurred to "gratify the great pangs of his whole night's restlessness," as the toad entirely declined to be lured into any frivolities that might cause him the loss of his precious jewel.

Browne, in his exposure of the various popular errors current in his time, presently arrives at this belief, but finds himself unable to express any very definite opinion, and takes refuge in compromise. "As for the stone," quoth he, "commonly called a Toadstone, which is presumed to be found in the head of that animall, we first conceive it not a thing impossible, nor is there any substantiall reason why in a Toad there may not be found such hard and lapideous concretions ; for the like we daily observe in the heads of Fishes, as Codds, Carps, and Pearches. Though it be not impossible, yet it is surely very rare, as we are induced to believe from inquiry of our own; from the triall of many who have been deceived and the frustrated search of Porta, who, upon the explorement of many, could scarce finde one.* Nor is it only of rarity, but may be doubted whether it be of existency, or really any such stone in the head of a Toad at all. For though Lapidaries and questonary enquires affirm it, yet the writers of Mineralls and natural speculators are of another belief, conceiving the stones which bear this name to be a Minerall concretion, not to be found in animalls but in fields. What therefore best reconcileth these divided determinations may be a middle opinion ; that of these stones some are minerall and to be found in the earth ; some animall, to be met with in Toads, at least by the induration of their cranies. The first are many and manifold, to be found in Germany† and other parts, the last are fewer in number, and in substance not unlike the stones in Carps' heads. This is agreeable unto the determination of Aldrovandus, and is also the judgment of the learned Spigelius in his Epistle unto Pignorius." If only a toad with an indurated cranium could be discovered, everything would fall into its right place !

Through the Middle Ages men believed that the toad exercised the power of fascination not only upon its insect prey, but upon all other

* It will be noted on turning back to our quotation from Porta, that this "scarce one" is altogether too favourable to the belief in the jewelled cranium of the toad. Porta, it will be seen, says, " nor could I finde one," an entirely different state of things.

† It will be seen from this that the state of things involved in the too familiar legend, " Made in Germany," is of ancient date.

creatures, including man himself, and even so far back as the days of the classical writers it was a fully accepted belief that whosoever had the misfortune to be looked squarely in the eyes by a toad would find that, basilisk-like, the gaze to him meant death.

The belief that the crocodile shed tears over his prey is a very ancient one; various motives have been assigned for this grief, but the generally accepted belief is that the whole proceeding is a fraud, perpetrated with the idea of attracting sympathetic passers-by within reach of his formidable jaws; hence he has been accepted as a symbol of dissimulation. We get an excellent illustration of this in Shakespeare's King Henry VIII., where Henry is said by Queen Margaret to be—

> "Too full of foolish pity; and Gloster's show
> Beguiles him, as the mournful crocodile
> With sorrow snares relenting passengers."*

Spenser, in the Faerie Queene,† deals equally clearly and explicitly with the same fancy in the lines—

> "As when a wearie traveiler, that strayes
> By muddy shore of broad seven-mouthed Nile,
> Unweeting of the perillous wandring wayes,
> Doth meete a cruell craftie Crocodile,
> Which in false grefe hyding his harmefull guile,
> Doth weepe full sore, and sheddeth tender teares;
> The foolish man, that pities all this while
> His mournful plight, is swallowed up unawares,
> Forgetfull of his owne that mindes an other's cares."

"Thereupon," ungallantly adds an old writer,

* Act iii., sc. 9.   † Book I., Canto V.

"came this proverb that is applied unto women when they weep. Lachrymæ Crocodili, the meaning whereof is, that as the Crocodile when he crieth goeth about most to deceive, so doth a woman most commonly when she weepeth." Thus Othello misanthropically exclaims—

> "If that the earth could teem with woman's tears,
> Each drop she falls would prove a crocodile."

In the same spirit Barnfield, in his "Cassandra," written in the year 1595, has the following passage :—

> "He, noble lord, fearlesse of hidden treason,
> Sweetely salutes this weeping Crocodile;
> Excusing every cause with instant reason
> They kept him from her sight so long a while;
> She faintly pardons him; smiling by art,
> For life was in her lookes, death in her hart."

The author of the "Speculum Mundi," who is ever seeking a moral* or an opportunity of improving the occasion, declares that "the crocodile when he hath devoured a man and eaten all up but the head, will sit and weep

---

* A very good illustration of this treatment may be seen in the statement that "the dogs in Egypt use to lap their water running when they come to Nilus, for fear of the crocodiles there, which cannot but be a fit pattern for us in the use of pleasures; for true it is, we may not stand to take a heartie draught, for then delights be dangerous, howbeit we may refresh ourselves with them as we go on our way, and may take them, but may not be taken by them; for when they detain us, and cause us to stand still, then their sweet waters have fierce Crocodiles; or if not so, they have strange Tarantulas, whose sting causeth to die laughing."

over it* as if he expressed a great portion of sorrow for his cruel feast, but it is nothing so, for when he weeps it is because his hungrie paunch wants such another prey. And from hence the proverb took beginning, viz. Crocodiles' tears; which is then verified when one weeps cunningly without sorrow, dissembling heaviness out of craftinesse; like unto many rich men's heirs who mourn in their gowns when they laugh in their sleeves; or like to other dissemblers of the like nature who have sorrow in their eyes, but joy and craftiness in their hearts." However this may be, the supposititious tears of the crocodile have been turned to abundant literary and moral account. The tears of the crocodile were supposed, according to some who were great authorities in their day and generation, to crystallize into gems, but as supposititious tears could only produce supposititious gems the actual value would be but small.

In an early Bestiary it states that "if a crocodile comes across a man it kills him, but it remains inconsolable the rest of its life;" but why it suffers this life-long remorse we are not told. This old writer also tells us of the hydra, "a very wise animal who understands well how

---

* We meet a like precision of statement in Cockeram's Dictionary, a quaint old volume, wherein "all such as desire to know the plenty of the English" will find some very strange illustrations of it. He says, edition of 1623, that "the crocodile having eaten the body of a man, will, in fine, weep over the head."

to injure the crocodile." The *modus operandi* is very simple, and the injury inflicted seems beyond question:—"When the hydra sees the crocodile go to sleep it covers itself over with slimy mud, and wriggles itself into the crocodile's mouth, penetrates into its stomach, and then tears it assunder." The dolphin appears to be another foe to be by no means despised. Pliny tells us that when these desire to pass up the Nile the crocodiles, who regard the river as their peculiar preserve, greatly resent their presence, and endeavour to drive them back. As the dolphins fully realize that they are no match for their foes in fair fight, they take refuge in their superior activity and craft, and having a dorsal fin as sharp edged as a knife, they swim swiftly beneath the crocodiles, and as the under portion of these creatures is unprotected by the armour that is so conspicuous on the upper parts of their bodies, with one sharp gash they rip the crocodile completely open.

It was a Greek superstition that beneath the visible exterior of the seal was concealed a woman, and that when a swimmer ventured too far he ran great risk of being seized by a seal and strangled. The creature then carried the lifeless body to some desert shore and wept over it, from which arose the popular saying that when a woman shed false tears she cried like a seal. As the desert shore implies absence of spectators, it seems difficult to tell what authority there is for the statement as to what went on there, and even when this initial difficulty is overcome it seems equally impossible to suggest any satisfactory reason for the gruesome proceedings of this weird woman-seal or seal-woman, either in the preliminary murderous attack or the subsequent lamentation. Whatever strange idea may have originally started the story, it is a curious parallel to that of the weeping crocodile.

The salamander received its full mythical development in mediæval days, though the older writers refer to it occasionally, and we note in the writings of such men as Pliny the first steps taken towards the erection of that fabric of fancy and superstition that later on became so conspicuous. The ancients asserted that the salamander was never seen in bright weather, but only made its appearance during heavy rain, and that it was of so frigid a nature that if it did but touch fire it quenched it as completely as if ice were piled thereon. It was, moreover, declared to be so venomous that the mere climbing of a tree by the animal is amply sufficient to poison all the fruit, so that those who afterwards eat thereof perished without remedy, and that if it entered a river the stream was so effectually poisoned that all who drank thereof must die. Glanvil, an English writer in the thirteenth century, roundly declares as historic fact that four thousand men and two thousand horses of the army of Alexander the Great were killed by drinking from a stream that had been thus infected.

It was in the Middle Ages an article of faith that the salamander was bred and nourished in fire,* hence when the creature is represented it is always placed in the midst of flames. Our illustration, fig. 22, from Porta, is a fair typical example. How the creature should be nourished in the flames, while its mere contact with them suffices to extinguish them, seems a practical difficulty, but the contradiction of ideas does not seem to have troubled our forefathers, and the two mutually destructive statements rest side by side equally unquestioned in the writings of all the authorities. Pliny, having his doubts, thrust a salamander into the fire, and the unfortunate victim of science was quickly shrivelled up and consumed.† One would have thought that this crucial test of actual experiment would have settled the whole matter, and reduced the fire-extinguishing theory to oblivion, but it takes much more than that to kill an old and well-established belief, as we may see even in our own day where many superstitions still flourish in spite of common sense, education, and experience arrayed against them.

---

* Readers of Shakespeare will recall how Falstaff rails at Bardolph, calling him the "Knight of the Burning Lamp," and other sarcasms inspired by the effects of strong liquor on his rubicund countenance. "Thou hast saved me a thousand marks in links and torches, walking with thee in the night. I have maintained that Salamander of yours with fire any time this two-and-thirty years."

† Galen, in one of his prescriptions, includes the ashes of a salamander, an ingredient impossible to obtain if fire had no power to destroy the creature.

292 *Natural History Lore and Legend.*

De Thaun in his "Bestiary" declares that "the Salamander is of such a nature that if it come by chance where there shall be burning

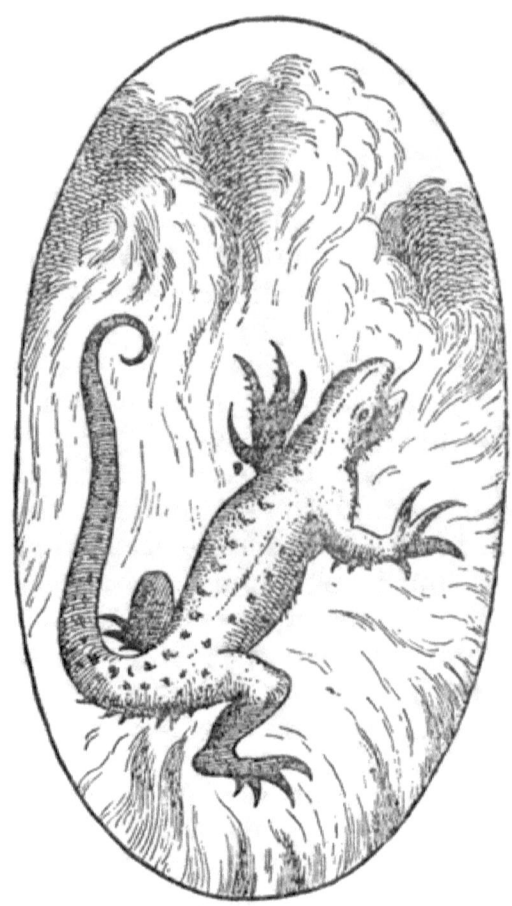

FIG. 22.

fire it shall at once extinguish it. The beast is so cold and of such a quality that fire will not be able to burn where it shall enter, nor will trouble happen where it shall be." This latter statement is entirely at variance with the general belief in its deadliness, but all these statements are dwelt on, exaggerated, or suppressed, as occasion and the moral to be deduced requires. As in this particular case the pious writer desired to see in the creature an emblem of Azarias, Ananias and Misael praising God without hurt in the fiery furnace, any reference to its noxious properties was clearly out of place, and on the strength of this association it even receives a somewhat negative form of commendation on its virtues as a peace-producer. This we are bound to say is the only good word we have ever seen ascribed by any of the writers of the past to this unfortunate creature, and it beyond doubt only receives even this solitary commendation because the exigencies of what the old writers thought the greater truth appeared to call for it.

Asbestos was, from its incombustible property, long held to be the wool of the salamander. In the Middle Ages popular imagination was greatly exercised over a mysterious Ruler in the East known as Prester John. He was held to be a Christian, and to bear sway in Asia over a widely-extended empire, but the stories of returning travellers showed that the idea had no foundation in fact, and the scene of the monarchy was then shifted to Abyssinia. The first reference to this sovereign would appear to be in the Chronicle of one Otto of Freisingin, who wrote about the middle of the twelfth century, and afterwards allusions to this mysterious monarch frequently recur. In the Chronicle of Albericus, about a hundred years later than that of Otto, we read that "Presbyter Joannes sent his wonderful letter to various Christian princes, and especially to Manuel of Constantinople, and Frederic, the Roman Emperor." In this letter, a very lengthy one, he claims to be Lord of Lords, and to receive the tribute and homage of seventy-two kings. "In the three Indies," saith he, "our Magnificence rules, and our land extends beyond India: it reaches toward the sunrise over the wastes, and it trends towards deserted Babylon, near the Tower of Babel." Whatever of credence, much or little, we may give to this letter, it is at least interesting to us as showing the set of opinion on, amongst other matters, things zoological, and therefore comes within the scope of our book. He gives many details as to the plants, the gold, and precious stones, and so forth, and also states that "our land is the home of elephants, dromedaries, camels, crocodiles, metacollinarum, cammetennus, tensevetes, white and red lions, white bears, crickets, griffins, lamias, wild horses, wild men, men with horns, one-eyed, men with eyes before and behind, centaurs, fauns, satyrs, and pygmies; it is the home, too, of the phœnix, and of nearly all living animals. In one of our lands, hight Zone, are worms called in our tongue salamanders. These worms can only live in fire, and they build cocoons like silkworms, which are unwound by the ladies of our palace and spun into cloth and dresses, which are worn by our Exaltedness. These dresses, when we would wash them and clean, are cast into flames." Browne, in his exposure of vulgar errors, gravely denies the existence of wool on a salamander at all, truly pointing out that "it is a kinde of Lizard, a quadruped corticated and depilous, that is, without woolle, furre, or haire," an altogether hopeless animal to shear.

Porta mentions that some peculiar creatures called "Pyragones be generated in the fire: certain little flying beasts so called because they live and are nourished in the fire, and yet they fly up and down in the air. This is strange; but that is more strange, that as soon as ever they come out of the fire into any cold air presently they die." Porta of course uses the word presently in the older sense of at this present moment, so that it really is, as he says, a wonder that these creatures are able to fly about in the air, when its effect upon them is immediate death. We have ourselves been gravely told that if the fires at the great iron-works in the Midland Counties were not occasionally extinguished an uncertain but fearful something would be generated in them, and it seems only natural that after the imagination has peopled earth and sea with strange monsters, and placed in the upper regions of the air the paradise-birds and other creatures that derived all needful sustenance from that element alone, that the remaining element, fire, should also have its peculiar inhabitants and monsters.

The chamæleon was for centuries supposed to live only on air, while its property of changing colour under the influence of its surroundings was greatly exaggerated.

Shakespeare, the great storehouse of mediæval folk-lore, makes Speed, in the Two Gentlemen of Verona, exclaim :—

> "Tho' the chamæleon Love can live on the air,
> I'm one that am nourish'd by my victuals,"

while Gloster, in King Henry VI., boasts that he could "add colours to the chamæleon."

Gower, in like manner, asserts that vain-glory is

> "Lich unto the Camelion
> Whiche upon every sondry hewe
> That he beholt he mote newe
> His colour."

Hence, again, other moralists declare that men and women inconstant and fickle are like unto chamæleons.

It has been asserted by Avicenna that a decoction of chamæleon put into a bath will make him green-coloured that stayeth long therein, but that by degrees this verdant hue will pass away, and the man recover his natural colour, while Porta declares that "with the Gall of a Chamæleon cut into water Wheezles will be called together." Why anyone should want to call a wheezle together he does not explain, so that the receipt, simple as it is, seems to be of no great practical value.

It has been rather a disgusting belief that if a man will lick a lizard all over he will not only be safe from the personal inconvenience of having a lizard go down his throat some day when he might be sleeping in the fields, but that he will have the power henceforward of healing any sore to which he applies his tongue.

Our ancestors held many strange beliefs respecting serpents and snakes—one of these was they were created from hair, "women's hairs especially"—as one old writer is careful to emphasize—"because they are naturally longer than men's." One old authority, our oft-quoted Porta, hesitates not to say that "we have experienced also that the hairs of a horse's mane laid in the waters become serpents, and our friends have tried the same," and he goes on to mention as a truism to be almost apologized for from its self-evident character, that "no man denies but that serpents are easily gendred of man's flesh, specially of his marrow." Ælianus in like manner declares that a dead man's marrow, being putrified, becomes a serpent. Florentinus affirms that basil chewed and laid in the sun will engender serpents.*

Another strange idea was that serpents conferred the power of invisibility. Thus John Aubrey, an antiquary and author, and one of the earliest Fellows of the Royal Society, gives in full faith the following recipe : "Take on Midsummer night at xii, when all the planets are above the earth, a serpent, and kill him, and skinne him, and dry him in the shade, and bring

* A parallel idea is that if the body of a crab be laid in the sunshine while the sun is in Cancer it will generate scorpions.

it to a powder. Hold it in your hand, and you will be invisible." His book entitled "Remaines of Gentilisme and Judaisme" is a perfect storehouse of old-world superstitions, an inexhaustible mine of quaint imaginings.

The "pretious stone" theory that we have already encountered in one or two other cases, the toad being the most notable, is in full force again amongst the various strange notions concerning serpents. The recipe for its possession, given by Jacobus Hollerius, is simplicity itself, as it is merely necessary that the "snake be tyed by the tayle with a corde, and hanged up, and a vessell full of water set below; after a certayne time he will avoyde out of his mouth a stone." The stone is of great medicinal value; for instance, "it fullye and wholelye helpes the partye that hath the dropsye," by merely being attached to the body of the sufferer, and in divers other ways that we need not stay to particularize, proves itself a stone of price. Jordanus, amongst his other Indian experiences, came across serpents with horns, evidently the cerastes or horned viper, and others with precious stones. Tennant tells us that the Cingalese believe that the stomach of the cobra contains a stone of inestimable value, and this belief, absurd as we deem it, is really hardly more far-fetched than such a story as pearls being found in oyster-shells would appear to a man who heard it for the first time.

Snakes and serpents, like most other repulsive things, have found their way into the pharmacopœia and the menu. Galen tells us that the

Egyptians used to eat vipers as other people did eels, and it is a very old-world superstition that viper's flesh is an antidote to the viper's poison. In classic and mediæval days a famous remedy, originally known as mithridate or theriaca, and later on as Venice treacle, was held to owe much of its virtue as a vermifuge and antidote to all kinds of poison to the vipers that formed one of its ingredients. It was retained in the London Pharmacopœia until about a hundred years ago. Its constituent parts changed somewhat from time to time; at one period we see it contained seventy-three ingredients. The vipers were added to the horrible mess by Andromachus, the physician to the Emperor Nero,* and became a leading element in the prescription. The name treacle was at one time applied to any confection or syrup, and it is only in these latter days that the name has become associated exclusively with the syrup of molasses : it is derived from the Greek Therion, a name given to the viper, so that the schoolboys' lunch of bread and treacle is the direct etymological outcome of the abominable adder's broth of the Roman emperor.†

* " Andromachus a voulu changer le nom de Mithridate en celuy de Theriaque, à cause des vipères, auxquelles il a attribué le nom, et lesquelles il a ajouté pour la base principale de cette composition." (Chares, " l'histoire des Animaux etc. qui entrent dans la Theriaque," Paris, 1868.) See also Heberden's " Antitheriaca."

† A viper drowned in a bowl of wine gave the draught great healing virtues for leprosy. This happy discovery, like many others of still greater value, was the result of accident. Some mowers found on going to their provisions that a viper had got

One often sees in these ancient remedies a foreshadowing of the homœopathic notion of like to like; thus Porta prescribes "a present remedy" for the poison of the viper, declaring that "the viper itself, if you slay her, and strip off her skin, cut off her head and tail, cast away all her entrails, boil her like an Eele, and give her to one that she hath bitten, it will cure him," but in another place he says "for serpent's bites I have found nothing more excellent than the earth which is brought from the isle of Malta, for the least dust of it put into their mouths kills them presently." There is evidently here some sort of connection endeavoured to be established between the escape of St. Paul while in Malta from the evil effects of the poison of a viper and this present prescription, and it no doubt arose from the old legend that, like St. Patrick in Ireland, St. Paul, after his experience of them, banished all snakes from the island. Once granted that a serpent cannot live on the soil of Malta, it follows almost as a matter of course that a little of this same soil administered to

> into the wine, so they, very naturally, "contented themselves with water; but when they had finished their day's work, and were to go out of the field, as it were out of pity they gave a leprous man the wine wherein the viper was drowned, supposing it better for him to die than to live on in that misery, but he, when he had drank it, was miraculously cured," at least, so we read in the "Miracles of Art and Nature," Galen being referred to as the original authority for the story. The first essential in many of these ancient remedies appeared to be that they should be most improbable and unreasonable, and, secondly, that they should be as repulsive as possible.

it anywhere the wide world over will prove fatal to it. The recipe is, nevertheless, a little vague, as it deals exclusively with the destruction of the serpent, which is not at all the same thing as the restoration to health of the sufferer from its poison fangs.

Prevention being better than cure, the hint that Cogan gives in his "Haven of Health" should prove of value. "The setting of Lauender within the house in floure pots must needes be very wholesome, for it driueth away venemous wormes, both by strawing and by the sauour of it," and he adds that "being drunke in wine it is a remedie against poyson." Tusser, in his book on Husbandry, gives a long list of "strowing herbes," their fragrance and remedial value being held in high esteem by our forefathers :—

 "No daintie flowre or herbe that growes on grownd,
   No arborett with painted blossoms drest,
 And smelling sweete, but there it might be fownd
   To bud out faire, and throwe her sweet smels al around."*

The bunches of flowers that are still presented to the Judges on the opening of the Law Courts are the graceful and now happily needless developments of the bunches of herbs that were once placed on their desks to avert the dangers of the gaol fever, that with its noxious breath slew not the hapless prisoners alone, but the judges on the bench, and administered wild justice on all alike for the contempt of sanitary

* Spenser.

laws, and for the brutality that was rampant and supreme.*

Fennel was, according to our forefathers, held in esteem by the serpents themselves, and one scarcely wonders that this should be so, if it be true that "so soone as they taste of it they become young again, and with the juice thereof repair their sight." How this juice is applied externally by the serpent is not explained, but it very naturally suggested the idea to the medical men of the Middle Ages that what was so good for serpents might prove equally valuable to suffering humanity, hence "to repair a man's sight that is dim" nothing better than fennel could be found, though they hesitated to promise also to the human subject rejuvenescence.

The Syrians, according to one venerable authority, had a most singular defence for their country, the land being full of snakes that would do no harm to the natives even if they trod upon them, but which eagerly assailed the people of any other nation and destroyed them. Naturally therefore the Syrians cherished such a valuable protection, though such a state of things would hardly accord with modern notions of free trade and the intercourse of nations. The discovery of one wonder frequently leads to knowledge of others, and Aristotle has a companion story in his "History of Animals," of scorpions that in Caria

* In "the Ceremonies to be observed at the Coronation of His most Excellent Majesty King George IV.," the order of the procession is given, the first item of all being "the King's Herbwoman with her six maids, strewing the way with Herbs."

sting to death the natives of the country, but do no harm to strangers. In like manner, according to Maundevile, in the island called Silha, where-ever that may be, "the men of that yle seen comonely that the Serpentes and the wilde Bestes of that Countree nee will not don non harm, ne touchen with evylle, no strange man that entreth into that Contree, but only to men that ben born of the same Countree." This differential treatment seems distinctly hard on the aborigines.*

"It is observable," quoth the author of the "Miracles of Art and Nature," that "in Crete there is bred no Serpents or Venomous Beasts or Worms, Ravenous or hurtful Creatures, so their Sheep graze very securely without any Shepheard; yet if a Woman happen to bite a Man anything hard he will hardly be cured of it," a statement which brings forth the very natural conclusion that "if this be true, then the last part of the Priviledge foregoing (of breeding no hurtful Creature) must needs be false."

Amongst various familiar country beliefs lasting even to the present day is the one summed up in the well-known expression, "deaf as an adder." It has for centuries been an accepted belief that the adder lays one ear upon the ground, and closes the other with its tail, and it doubtless has its origin in that passage in the psalms of David where it states that "the deaf

---

* In this mysterious isle also "there ben wylde gees that han two Hedes, and ther ben Lyouns all white and als grete as oxen, and many othere dyverse Bestes."

adder stoppeth her ears, and will not heed the voice of the charmer, charm he never so wisely," and we meet with this idea over and over again in our own literature. Thus Shakespeare writes in King Henry VI.—

> "What! art thou, like the adder, waxen deaf?
> Be poisonous too."

And, again, in his Troilus and Cressida we find the passage—

> "Pleasure and revenge have ears more deaf than adders."

In Orlando Furioso, too, we find an interesting reference to the old fancy :—

> "He flies me now, nor more attends my pain
> Than the deaf adder heeds the charmer's strain."

Many varieties of serpents were known to the ancients, and some of them, as the Cerastes, are quite recognizable from the descriptions given, but of others we have no means of identification. The two-headed Amphisbæna, for example, that was credited with such venomous malignity that nothing but twice the normal power of offence sufficed for its deadly attack. The Amphisbæna was an article of faith with Nicander, who was the first to introduce it to the scientific world of his name, and it is referred to by Galen, Pliny, Ælian, and many other ancient writers, who gravely describe this especially objectionable reptile, "a small kind of serpent which moveth backward and forward, and hath two heads, one at either extreme." The creature is now entirely lost to science.

Aldrovandus, in his history of serpents, gives an illustration of the basilisk, a serpentine form, but having eight legs, and on its head a crown. Another of his figures shows us a serpentine form again, this time with two legs, the moderation in this direction being fully compensated by the gift of seven heads of human form, while another has the serpent-like body, but to this are added two legs and feet like those of a cock, and the creature has six cocks' heads. All these creatures are put forth and described in all seriousness, so it is evident that the author must either himself have been excessively credulous, or that he must have expected to find his readers so. It

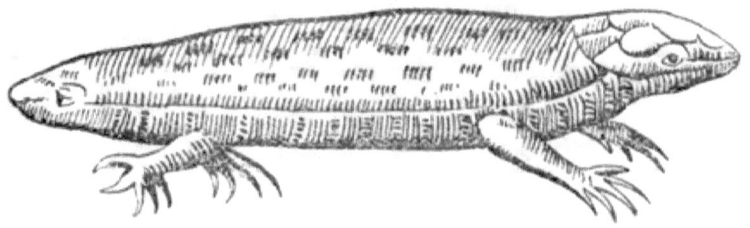

FIG. 23.

is manifest that such inventions are of the lamest possible type. Nothing could be easier or more fatuous than to fill a folio volume with serpents having three cats' heads, five lions' heads, seven bisons' heads, or twenty rats' heads, and distribute legs in the same liberal and senseless manner. His drawing, fig. 23, of a two-headed lizard is the nearest approach we can give our readers to the Amphisbæna.

Burton tells us that in Samogitia, a small

province in Poland, the people nourish amongst them "a kind of four-footed serpents, above three handfuls in length, which they worship as their household gods, and if mischance do happen to any of their family, it is imputed presently to some want of due observations of these ugly creatures." Some old writers tell us of hairy serpents, and depict a thing something like the well-known larva of the tiger-moth, the caterpillar popularly known as the "woolly bear," and familiar enough to all dwellers in the country,

FIG. 24.

the only difference, though that a very serious one, being that the woolly bear is barely three inches long, while the hairy serpents are stretched to any number of feet that the credulity of the narrator will permit.

Fig. 24 is a facsimile from one of the illustrations in Munster's "de Africæ regionibus," and represents the sort of thing that he would have us believe was to be found in his days in Africa, that great home of the weird and mysterious. The perspective effect of the coils of the upper creature, as they recede in the distance towards the horizon, suggests a terrific length, something far exceeding any of the possibilities of the present day, but this may be only a slip of draughtmanship, or a polite desire on the part of the two-headed reptile not to crowd up its three-headed companion.

The asp, from being freely found in Egypt and other parts of North Africa, was well known to the naturalists of Greece and Rome, and its deadly nature fully understood, though the facts are perhaps rather against them when they assert that they are such affectionate creatures that they are always found in pairs and cannot live without their mates. We are told that should one of the pair be killed, this sweet connubial bliss is exchanged for deadly ferocity and instant revenge. The unhappy man is closely pursued and relentlessly tracked, and finds no safety amongst his fellows, as the avenger knows him from all others, and will not be turned aside. Distance is no object, and difficulties no hindrance, and all that the luckless individual can do is to take to his heels with all celerity, and at the earliest opportunity embark in a boat or swim a river, and thus shake off his relentless pursuer.

Democritus tells us that if we mingle the blood of certain birds together a serpent will be engendered. Whoso eateth of this serpent shall know the language of birds, and be able to join in the conversation of any or all of the great feathered host, singing with the lark, cawing with the rook, hooting with the owl, and being thoroughly conversant with all that passes between them.

Maundevile tells us, in his wonderful "Voiage and Travaile," of an island where one finds "a kynde of Snayles that ben so grete that many persones may loggen hem in hur Schelles, as men woulde done in a lityll Hous"—a sufficiently striking feature in the landscape of that now unknown land.

Snails entered largely into the rustic Materia Medica, and not only indeed into rural practice but into the most courtly and exclusive circles, for we find Sir John Floyer, the physician to Charles II., prescribing thus for dulness of hearing: "Take a grey snaile, pricke him, and putt ye water which comes from him into ye eare and stop it with black woole, and it will cure." He left behind him a folio volume of such-like valuable recipes, and the manuscript may yet be seen in the Cathedral Library at Lichfield. He was a native of that city.

Spiders were also deemed of great remedial value. When a child has whooping cough, one of the parents should catch a spider and hold it over the head of the patient, repeating three times, "Spider, as you waste away, whooping cough no longer stay." The spider must then be hung up in a bag over the mantelpiece, and when it has dried up the cough will have disappeared."*

* There is a notion in Cheshire that this complaint can be cured by holding a toad or frog for a few minutes within the child's mouth, at the imminent risk, one would imagine, of

Burton, the author of the "Anatomy of Melancholy," writes: "Being in the country in the vacation time, not many years ago, at Lindley in Leicestershire, my father's house, I first observed this amulet of a spider in a nutshell wrapped in silk, so applied for an ague by my mother. This methought was most absurd and ridiculous. I could see no warrant for it, till at length, rambling amongst authors, as I often do, I found this very medicine in Dioscorides, approved by Matthiolus, and I began to have a better opinion of it, and to give more credit to amulets when I saw it in some parties answer to experience." Gerarde, in his "Historie of Plants," found that such a remedy, however good in theory, however supported by ancient authority, would not bear the strain of actual use. He shall however speak for himself in his own refreshingly quaint way. "It is needlesse," he writes, "here to alledge those things that are added touching the little wormes or magots, found in the heades of the Teasell,* which are to be hanged about the necke, for they are nothing else but most vaine and trifling toies, as my selfe haue proved a little before, hauing a most grieuous ague, and of long continuance: notwithstanding physicke charmes,

choking the patient. In Norfolk, they had greater faith in giving the child milk to drink that a ferret had previously lapped at.

* "The knops or heads are holow within, and for the most part hauing wormes in them, the which you shall find in cleaning the heads. The small wormes that are founde within the knops of teasels do cure and heale the quartaine ague, to be worne or tied about the necke or arme."—*Lyte's translation of Dodœns*, A.D. 1586.

these wormes hanged about my necke, spiders put into a nutshell and divers such foolish toies that I was constrained to take by phantasticke people's procurement: notwithstanding, I say, my helpe came from God himselfe, for these medicines, and all other such things, did me no good at all." It is passing strange that such so-called remedies, so easily proved valueless, should have held their ground for centuries, and are doubtless even now in the byways of our land as firmly believed in as they were nigh two thousand years ago. When one of our own family was ailing, a woman in the little Wiltshire village where we were then staying strongly advised us to drop some peas down the well as an infallible means of restoration to health!

Bees were held to be bred out of putrefying carcases, an idea that doubtless arose in very early times, as we find it referred to by Virgil and other ancient authors, and the Biblical story of the swarm of bees found by Sampson in the carcase of the lion that he slew would be held as confirmation, though anyone reading the story* carefully would see that no such inference could be drawn from it. Many weeks had elapsed between the slaying of the lion and the discovery of the honey, ample time for the birds and beasts of prey to have cleared away the flesh, and for the heat of the sun to have dried up all putrefaction and rendered the skeleton a sufficiently cleanly and suitable place for the wild bees to form their combs within. Herodotus tells us

* Judges, chap. xiv.

that when the Amathusians revenged themselves on Onesilus, by whom they had been besieged, by cutting off his head and hanging it over one of their city gates, the skull presently alone remained, and in this hollow chamber a swarm of bees settled and filled it with honeycomb.

The fourth Georgic of Virgil, which is devoted to the subject of bees, gives account of a simple method whereby the race of bees, if diminished or lost, might be replenished. He speaks of it as an art practised in Egypt, and it is easy to see that it originated in accounts of bees swarming in the dead bodies of animals. The process was to kill a young bullock by stopping up his nostrils, so that the skin should be unbroken by any wound, and then leaving it for nine days in a position where it would be undisturbed, when:—

> " Behold a prodigy, for from within
> The broken bowels and the bloated skin,
> A buzzing sound of bees the ear alarms:
> Straight issuing through the sides assembling swarms.
> Dark as a cloud they make a wheeling flight,
> Then on a neighbouring tree descending, light.
> Like a large cluster of black grapes they show,
> And make a large dependence from the bough."*

In this account we see clearly enough that the belief in the generation of the bees from the putrefying body is frankly accepted. The author of the "Speculum Mundi," hundreds of years after the Georgics were written, declares that a dead horse breeds wasps, that from the body of an ass proceed humble bees, while a mule produces hornets. Those who would have bees must seek

* Dryden's Translation.

them in a dead calf, though he adds the curious limitation, "if the west winde blow." He goes on to say "whether the bees in Samson's dead lion were bred anywhere else no man knoweth." As an Englishman, more familiar with the possibilities of a dead calf than with those of a dead lion, he declines to commit himself to an opinion as to what is or is not possible in far distant lands over sea.*

The strange association of ideas that we have seen in many other instances may be well seen again in the notion that if one pounds up those luminous creatures of the night, glowworms, the result will be an ink that will render any writing performed by its aid visible in the dark. Winstanley, in his "Pathway to Knowledge," gives a simple receipt for the manufacture of this useful ink, and other writers are content to copy him, or each other, in the laudable desire to spread abroad the knowledge of this luminous fluid. One can easily realize that such a preparation might at times be really very useful.

Turning, in conclusion, our attention to the creatures of sea and stream, we at once encounter the favourite mediæval theory that all creatures of the land had their marine counterparts. "There is nothing," says the comparatively

* This old writer, not being aware of the various stages of egg, larva, pupa, and imago through which butterflies and moths pass, is much perplexed over the silkworm, "whether I may name it a worme or a flie," he says, "I cannot tell. For sometimes it is a worm, sometimes a flie, and sometimes neither worm nor flie, but a little seed which the dying flies leave behinde them."

modern writer, Camden, "bred in any part of Nature, but the same is in the sea;" while Olaus Magnus affirms that "there be fishes like to dogs, cows, calves, horses, eagles, dragons, and what not." These mysterious denizens of the deep were an unfailing resource in the romances and poems of the Middle Ages, and an article of faith with the writers on natural history. On the Assyrian slabs we see the monster "upward man and downward fish," while the mermaid we all recognize as a most familiar instance of the presence of creatures at least semi-human in the broad and mysterious expanse of ocean. Bœwulf, the Saxon poet, writes of "the sea-wolf of the abyss, the mighty sea-woman." The quotation is not altogether complimentary in its sentiment: no lady of one's acquaintance would feel flattered on being addressed as a sea-wolf. But while a certain halo of romance has in these later days gathered round the idea of the mermaid, those who really believed in her gave her credit for deeds considerably more heinous than combing her flowing hair in the sunlight, since her beauty was a snare and destruction to all who came within its fatal influence.

Sir Thomas Browne, in his merciless dissection of the vulgar beliefs of his day, writes, with his accustomed quaintness and equally accustomed sound common sense, "that all Animals of the Land are in their kinde in the Sea, although received as a Principle, is a tenet very questionable and that will admit of restraint. For some in the Sea are not to be matcht by any enquiry at Land

and hold those shapes which terrestrious formes approach not, as may be observed in the Moon-fish and the severall sorts of Raias, Torpedos, Oysters, and many more, and some there are in the Land which were never mentioned to be in Sea, as Panthers, Hyænas, Cammells, Molls, and others, which carry no name in Ichthology, nor are to be found in the exact descriptions of Rondoletius, Gesner, and Aldrovandus. Again, though many there be which make out their nominations, as the Sea-serpents and others, yet there are also very many that bear the names of Animalls at Land, which hold no resemblance in corporall configuration, wherein while some are called the Fox, the Dog, or Frog-fish, and are known by common names with those at Land, as their describers attest, they receive not these appellations from a totall similitude in figure, but any concurrence in common accidents, in colour, condition, or single conformation. As for Sea-Horses, which much confirm this assertion in their common descriptions, they are but Grotesco delineations which fill up empty spaces in Maps, and meer pictoriall inventions, not any Physicall shapes. That which the Ancients named Hippocampus is a little animall about six inches long, and not preferred beyond the classis of Insects. That they termed Hippopotamus, an amphibious animall about the River Nile, so little resembleth an horse that, except the feet, it better makes out a swine. Although it be not denied that some in the water doe carry a justifiable resemblance to some at Land, yet are the

The wondrous Sea-Bishop.

major part which bear their names unlike, nor doe they otherwise resemble the creatures on

FIG. 25.

earth than they on earth the constellations which passe under Animall names in heaven: nor the

Dogfish at Sea much more make out the Dog of the Land than that his cognominall or namesake in the heavens." He then goes on to show that this belief restrains Omnipotence and abridges the variety of creation, making the creatures of one element but a counterpart of the other.

This belief in sea-monsters of all kinds was naturally not a chance that a man like Aldrovandus could miss. He gives his imagination full scope, or perhaps we should rather say his credulity, as he introduces these creatures to us as things as real as a rabbit; his sea-monk, for instance, with tonsured human head, arms replaced by fins, and legs by fishy tail, being as matter of fact as one's vicar. Fig. 25 is given by him in all good faith as the true presentment of a sea-bishop, though not at all our notion of a bishop in his see. The right hand, it will be seen, is giving the benediction. The dragon of the deep, shown in fig. 26, aims at being terrible, but merely succeeds in being feeble. We cannot but feel that the draughtsman here failed to reach our ideal; for one has certainly seen many representations of landdragons far more fear-inspiring than this bloated monster with ears like a King Charles spaniel, and tail like a rat. This illustration is from another source, the work of Ambrosinus on the same subject, published "permissu superiorum" in the year 1642. While the book is as quaint and grotesque as any of its rivals, the skill of the artist has in divers cases not paralleled the gifts of description of the author.

The "monstrosus sus marinus," or terrible

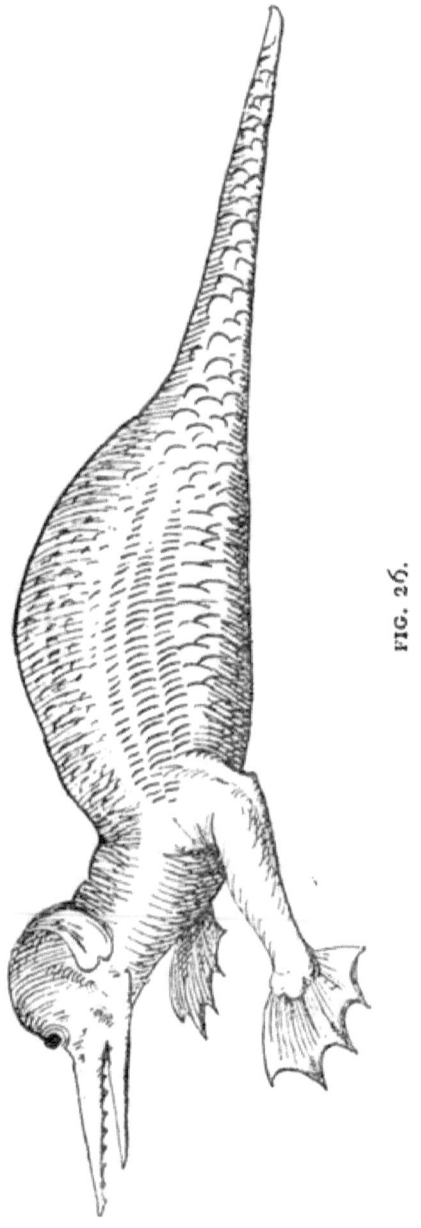

FIG. 26.

sow of the sea, or more especially perhaps of Aldrovandus (fig. 27), will surely fully come up to everyone's expectation of what a marine pig should be like. Catching a weasel asleep should be a comparatively easy task to circumventing sus marinus; it seems such a peculiarly wide-awake animal. Possibly in the struggle for existence in the watery depths its toothsome flesh may place it in jeopardy, and Nature may have bestowed upon it these numerous eyes to enable it to evade dragons and other foes having a penchant for pork; a rather unexpected addition to the various better-known examples of that comfortable doctrine for the well-to-do, the survival of the fittest.

Purchas tells us of a fish called the Angulo or Hog-fish. "It hath," he says, "as it were two hands, and a tail like a target, which eateth like pork, and whereof they make lard, and it hath not the savour or taste of fish. It feedeth on the grasse that groweth on the banks of the river and never goeth out; it hath a mouthe like the mozell of an ox, and there be of them that weigh five hundred pound a piece." This is found, he tells us, in the River Congo.

Another of the strange creatures of ocean is shown in fig. 28. It is somewhat startling to reflect that our ancestors had at least the expectation that such a monster might at any moment rise alongside their vessel and address them in the peremptory tones that the figure suggests: and it must be borne in mind that these illustrations are not a tithe of the strange imaginings that even this one old book sets forth, though it is needless to multiply examples from it. We have carefully drawn our figures in facsimile from the originals, and have naught extenuated, nor set down aught in malice. They are fairly typical examples of the sort of thing that is encountered on page after page.*

In the excellent book of Rondeletius (doctoris medici et medicinæ in schola monspeliensi

FIG. 27.

professoris regii), published in the year 1554, on the subject of marine fishes, the illustrations are full of spirit and life. Amongst these fish of

* Apart from these various monsters, and the hundreds of others that bear them company, Aldrovandus seems to have been always accessible to anyone who would bring him one wonder the more; hence he also figures a bunch of grapes terminating in a long beard; representations of cloud-warriors in conflict in the sky; comets like blazing swords, and many other wonderful things that set our ancestors wondering in fear and amazement as to what such portents should signify.

the ocean we find the sea-bishop, sea-monk, &c., all over again, and such creatures as the sea-lion, fig. 29; this latter, except for his scaly hide, has nothing very suggestively aquatic about him. The book, in addition to such impossibilities, contains very good and life-like representations of the sun-fish, sturgeon, hammer-headed shark, ray, and many others.

The author of the "Speculum Mundi" confirms all these wonders, and adds his quota to the general store. He affirms that, "In the year 1526 there was taken in Norway, neare to a seaport called Elpoch, a certain fish resembling a mitred bishop, who was kept alive six days after his taking, and there was, as the author of Du Bartas his summarie reporteth, one Ferdinand Alvares, Secretarie to the store-house of the Indians, who faithfully witnesseth that he had seene not farre off from the Promontorie of the Moon, a young Sea-man coming out of the Waters, who stole fishes from the fishermen and ate them raw. Neither is Olaus Magnus silent on these things, for he also saith there be monsters in the sea, as it were imitating the shape of a man, having a dolefull kinde of sounde or singing. There be also sea-men of an absolute proportion in their whole body; these are sometimes seene to climbe up the ships in the night times, and suddenly to depresse that part upon which they sit; and if they abide long the whole ship sinketh. Yea (saithe he), this I adde from the faithfull assertions of the Norway fishers, that when such are taken, if they be not presently let

How Sudden Tempests arise.

go again, there ariseth such a fierce tempest, with an horrid noise of those kinde of creatures and other sea-monsters there assembled, that a man would think the verie heaven were falling, and the vaulted roofe of the world running to ruine, insomuch that the fishermen have much ado to escape with their lives; whereupon they con-

FIG. 28.

firmed it as a law amongst them that if any chanced to hang such a fish upon his hook he should suddenly cut the line and let him go on. But these sudden tempests are very strange, and how they arise with such violent speed exceeds the bounds of ordinary admiration. Whereupon it is again supposed that these monsters are verie devils, and by their power such strange storms are raised. Howbeit for my part I think otherwise, and do much rather affirm that these storms, in my judgment, are thus raised, namely, by the thickening and breaking of the aire; which the snortling, rushing, and howling of these beasts, assembled in an innumerable companie, causeth. For it is certain that sounds will break and alter the aire (as I have heard it of a citie freed from the plague by the thundering noise of cannons), and also I suppose that the violent rushing of these beasts causeth much water to flie up and thicken the aire, and by their howling and snortling under the waters they do blow up, and as it were attenuate the waves, and make them arise in a thinner substance than at other times; so that Nature, having all these helps, in an instant worketh to the amazement of the mariners, and often to the danger of their lives. Besides, shall we think that spirits use to feed, and will be so foolish as to go and hang themselves on an hook for a bait? They may have occult properties (as the loadstone hath) to work strange feats, and yet be neither spirits nor devils; for experience likewise teacheth that they die sooner or later after their taking, neither can a spirit have flesh and bones as they have."

The monsters of the deep are best seen at the times of the equinox, "for then," says Pliny, "by the whirlwinds, rains and tempests which rush with violence from the rugged mountains, the seas are turned up from the very bottom, and thus the billows roll and raise these beasts out of the deep parts of the ocean." It certainly seems a much more reasonable theory that the storms produce the beasts than that the beasts produce the storms.

On an antique seal we remember to have seen a sea-elephant, a creature having the forelegs, tusks, trunk, and great flapping ears of the

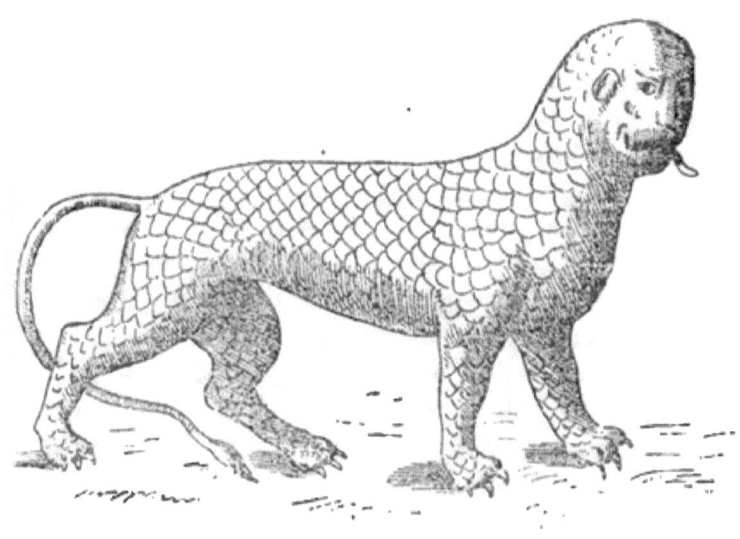

FIG. 29.

African elephant, yet terminating in the body of a fish, and duly furnished with piscine tail and fins. This outrageous combination would seem to indicate the limit possible to absurdity in this direction. When the ancient writers would desire to people the vast unknown of air and sea, their thoughts naturally turned to those creatures

21 *

of the land with which they were more familiar. Hence, the denizens of the air or ocean are not really creations at all, but adaptations, wings or fins being added to horses, lions and the like, according to the new element in which they were to figure. Of these the sea-horses that drew the chariot of Neptune through the waves, or the winged steed Pegasus, are examples that at once occur to one's mind.

The sea-horse according to some authorities is found floating on the ice between Britain and Norway, and is taken by the whalers for the oil he contains. He is described as having a head like a horse, and as sometimes neighing, but his hoofs are said to be cloven like those of a cow, while his hinder parts are those of a fish. This creature would appear to be now quite lost to science. The sea-horse naturally suggests the idea of the sea-unicorn, depicted as of equine form, but having the hinder parts piscine in character. The horn of the sea-unicorn occasionally brought home by merchants and mariners was probably the "sword" of the swordfish or the tusk of the narwhal, as it is often mentioned that it was able to penetrate the ribs of ships, and later experience has proved that an encounter beween swordfish or narwhal and ships has occasionally taken place. The tusk of the narwhal is a spiral tapering rod of ivory, sometimes attaining to the length of eight or ten feet. Purchas mentions a horn of a sea-unicorn that was presented by Frobisher to his sovereign, and preserved at Windsor, and the name of this great arctic voyager naturally suggests that this horn was the tusk of a narwhal, a creature of the northern seas. One old writer speaks of the horn as a "wreathy spire," a description which admirably accords with the narwhal tusk. The fact once established that there were creatures in the sea with horns like unicorns, it was at once assumed that they had the horse-like form assigned to the land-unicorn, and in some of the old authors the sea-unicorn is represented as of purely equine form, plus the horn.*

In a book published in 1639, entitled "A Helpe to Memorie and Discourse," we find this question asked, " Whether doth a dead body in a shippe cause the shippe to sail slower, and if it doe, what is thought to be the reason thereof?" The answer to the query is that "the shippe is as insensible of the living as the dead, and as the living make it goe the faster, so the dead make it not goe the slower ; for the dead are no Rhemoras to alter the course of her passage, though some there be that thinke so, and that by

---

* "To be shewn at the Royal Infirmary of this city, price sixpence, the largest and most beautiful lion that was ever seen in this country. Also an Egyptian mummy, lately sent as a present to the Infirmary by Alexander Drummond, Esq., Consul of the Turkey Company at Aleppo. Likewise a very large horn of a sea unicorn, which all connoisseurs acknowledge to be a remarkable curiosity.

"N.B.—As the money collected on this occasion is to be applied solely for the relief of the Indigent Sick in the said Hospital, therefore if persons of Substance and Distinction shall give more, it will be thankfully accepted on behalf of the distressed Patients."—*Edinburgh Chronicle*, 1758.

a kind of mournful sympathy."* The potent influence of the remora or sucking-fish to arrest the progress of a ship by merely adhering to its keel is a curious fancy that has been handed on for centuries. Pliny and many other ancient writers had full belief in this foe to the mariner, and references to it in much more recent authors are by no means uncommon. Thus Ben Jonson alludes to it in the lines—

> "I say a remora,
> For it will stay a ship that's under sail."

While Spenser in his "Visions of the World's Vanity," writes—

> "Looking far forth into the ocean wide,
>   A goodly ship, with banners bravely dight,
> And flag in her top-gallant I espied,
>   Through the main sea making her merry flight:
> Fair blew the wind into her bosom right,
>   And th' Heavens looked lovely all the while
> That she did seem to dance, as in delight,
>   And at her own felicity did smile:
> All suddenly there clove unto her keel
>   A little fish that we call remora,
> Which stopt her course, and held her by the heel,
>   That wind nor tide could move her thence away."

We may indeed be thankful that this mysterious power, worse even than the more prosaic barnacles and other sea impedimenta that plague the modern shipowner by fouling

---

* In the travels of Boullaye le Gouz, published in 1657, we find a reference to this notion. He says, "I had among my baggage the hand of a Syren, or fisherwoman, which I threw, on the sly, into the sea, because the captain, seeing that we could not make way, asked me if I had not got some mummy

the bottom of his good ship, and so retarding her course, seems to be no longer exercised. The merchantman speeding home with perishable cargo, the yachtsman burning to carry off the challenge cup, the great record-breaking Atlantic liner, carrying under heavy penalty for delay Her Majesty's mails, would all be terribly hampered in their several ambitions in presence of so potent yet so apparently insignificant a foe. Well might Spenser add—

"Strange thing meseemeth that so small a thing
Should able be so great an one to wring."

One old writer feeling the impossibility of giving a satisfactory explanation of the marvel is content to say "of which there can be no more reason given than of the loadstone drawing iron; neither is it possible to shew the cause of all secrets in Nature," a statement as true to-day as the day it was written, though this particular secret of Nature has in the interval been disestablished.

That the dolphin was the swiftest of all living creatures, more rapid than a bird, swifter than an arrow shot from a bow, will probably be an entirely new idea to most of our readers, yet such was the ancient belief. The dolphin occurs

or other in my bags which hindered our progress, in which case we must return to Egypt to carry it back again. Most of the Provençals have the opinion that the vessels which transport the mummies from Egypt have great difficulty in arriving safe at port: so that I feared, lest coming to search my goods, they might take the hand of this fish for a mummy's hand, and insult me on account of it."

very freely in blazonry, on ancient coinage, and in classic and renaissance decoration, and it is almost always represented either as "embowed," that is to say, bent round like a bow, such being the significance of the heraldic term, or else it is introduced with its lithe body coiled gracefully round an anchor or trident. In either case the representation suggests an easy-going and leisurely state of affairs that is very different to the picture conjured up by the arrowy rush of the creature through the waves, as Pliny paints it for us.*

It is a very old belief that the dolphin has an especial fondness for man. "Of a man he is nothing afraid, neither avoideth from him as a stranger: but of himselfe meeteth their ships, plaieth and disporteth himselfe, and fetcheth a thousand friskes, and gambols before them. He will swimme along by the mariners, as it were for a wager, who should make way most speedily, and alwaies outgoeth them, saile they with never so good a forewind." The representation of the

* "That dolphins are crooked is not only affirmed by the hand of the painter, but commonly conceived their naturall or proper figure, which is not only the opinion of our times, but seems the belief of older times before us: for besides the expressions of Ovid and Pliny, their Portraicts in ancient Coynes are framed in this figure, as will appear in some thereof in Gesner, others in Goltzius, and Lævinus Hulsius in his description of Coynes. Notwithstanding, to speak strictly, in their naturall Figure they are streight, nor have they their spine convexed or more considerably embowed than Sharkes, Porposes, or Whales, and therefore what is delivered of their incurvity must either be taken Emphatically, that is, not really, but in appearance; which happeneth when they leap above

dolphin with the anchor is not simply a type of maritime supremacy, but is a distinct illustration of this belief in the dolphin's kindly regard for man. Thus Camerarius asserts that "when tempests arise, and seamen cast their anchor, the dolphin, from its love to man, twines itself round it, and directs it, so that it may more safely lay hold of the ground."

The works of the ancient writers abound with illustrations of the friendly regard of the dolphin for mankind. Thus in one wonderful story we have a schoolboy, the son of a poor man, who had to travel each day from Baianum to Puteoli, who used at the water's edge to call a dolphin to his aid. The dolphin would at once respond to the call, and the boy used to mount upon his back and be taken across the sea, and be brought back again at night. This went on for some years, and at last, when the boy fell sick and died, his constitution probably not being able to stand the constant wetting and exposure, the dolphin was inconsolable, and promptly died

water or suddenly shoot down again : which is a fallacy of vision, whereby streight bodies in a sudden motion protruded obliquely downward appear to the eye crooked, and this is the construction of Bellonius: or, if it be taken really, it must not be universally and perpetually, that is, not when they swimme and remaine in their proper figures, but only when they leape or impetuously whirle their bodies anyway : and this is the opinion of Gesnerus. Or, lastly, it must be taken neither really nor emphatically, but only emblematically; for being the Hieroglyphic of Celerity, and swifter than other animails, men best expressed their velocity by incurvity, and under some figure of a bowe, and in this sense probably do Heralds also receive it."—*Browne.*

of a broken heart. In another story, equally veracious, the rider was so unfortunate as to pierce himself with one of the sharp spines of the dorsal fin, and an artery being severed, he bled to death. The dolphin, seeing the water stained with blood, and finding that his rider did not sit on his back in the light and active way that had been his wont, concluded that some catastrophe had happened, and when he realized the full truth, resolved not to outlive him whom he had affectionately loved, and therefore ran himself with all his might upon the shore, and so perished. Pliny, Mecænas, Fabianus, Flavius Alfius, Ælian, Aulus Gellius, Apion, Egesidemus, Theophrastus, and many other old writers, all give equally surprising illustrations of this wonderful love of the dolphin for mankind.

The dolphin is also a great lover of music, and equally wonderful stories are told in illustration of this taste also. Another well-known belief in connection with it is the imaginary brilliancy of its changeful colours when dying. The idea has been a favourite one with poets in all ages: an example from Byron's "Childe Harold's Pilgrimage" will suffice as an illustration :—

> " Parting day
> Dies like the dolphin, whom each pang imbues
> With a new colour as it gasps away ;
> The last still loveliest, till 'tis gone, and all is gray."

Another strange fish believed in by our forefathers was the Acipenser, "a fish of an unnatural making and quality," as an old writer terms him ;

and indeed he may very well do so, as we are told that "his scales are all turned towards his head." We are not therefore much surprised to learn that "he ever swimmeth against the stream," though we might well be more astonished if we ever found him swimming at all.

The amiable dolphin stands not alone in its friendship with man. The ray too, if we may believe a mediæval authority, is "a loving fish to man: for swimming in the waters, and being greedily pursued by the devouring Sea-dogs, the Ray defends him, and will not leave him untill he be out of danger." Sometimes the friendship is with some other creature; thus Porta gives an unfailing recipe for catching a sargon, whatever that may be, by taking advantage of this kindly trait in its character. "The Sargi," he declares, "love Goats unmeasurably: and they are so mad after them that when so much as the shadow of a Goat that feeds neer the shore shall appear neer unto them they presently leap for joy and swim to it in haste, and they imitate the goats, though they are not fit to leap, and thus they delight to come unto them. They are, therefore, catcht by those things that they so much desire. Whereupon the Fisher, putting on a Goat's skin with the horns, lies in wait for them, having the Sunne behind his back and paste made wet with the decoction of Goat's flesh: this he casts into the Sea where the Sargi are to come: and they, as if they were charmed, run to it, and are much delighted with the sight of the Goat's skin and feed on the paste. Thus the Fishermen catcheth abundance of them." Porta gives no suggestion that this affection is reciprocal.

Another mediæval writer has a still more extraordinary story of the kind, and in this case it is pleasant to know that the loving feeling is mutual. "Amongst the severall sort of shell fishes," saith he, "the glistering Pearl-fish deserves remembrance, not only in respect of herself but also in regard of the Prawn, another fish and her companion: for between these two there is a most firm league of friendship, much kindnesse, and such familiaritie as cannot but breed admiration in the reader. They have a subtill kinde of hunting, which being ended, they divide their prey in loving manner: for seeing they one help the other in the getting of it, they likewise joyn in the equall sharing. And, in few words, thus it is—when the Pearl-fish gapeth wide, she hath a curious glistering within her shell, by which she allureth her small fry to come swimming unto her: which when her companion the Prawn perceiveth, he gives her a secret touch with one of his prickles, wherupon she shuts her gaping shell, and so incloseth her wished prey: then (as I said) they equally share them out and feed themselves. And thus, day by day, they get their livings, like a combined knot of cheaters, who have no other trade than the cunning deceit of quaint consenage: hooking in the simpler sort with such subtill tricks, that be their purses stuft with either more or less, they know a way to sound the bottome and send them lighter home: lighter in purse, though heavier in heart." The moral seems perhaps needlessly severe, and we trust that henceforth our readers, after reading this romance of the deep, will have a kindlier feeling for these faithful friends, the artful oyster and the watchful prawn. The only drawback to the sentiment of the thing seems to be that this loving alliance has a somewhat low motive as its basis. One at least of the partners is capable of a more tender passion, as we have the authority of Sheridan for saying that an oyster may be crossed in love.

Olaus Magnus gives an awful example of voracity in the swam-fish, one of the most greedy cravens of the denizens of the sea, and cites many stories of it that amply justify the bad character bestowed on it. Another old writer affirms that when danger threatens "he will so winde up himselfe and cover his head with the skinne and substance of his own body that he is then bent like unto a piece of dead fish, and nothing like himself. The plan however appears to have its drawbacks, as the venerable and veracious author goes on to say that this feat "he seldome doth without hurt or damage, for still fearing that there be those about him who will prey upon him and devoure him, he is compelled for lack of meat to feed upon the substance of his own body, choosing rather to be devoured in part than to be consumed by other more strong and powerful fishes"—at best a most painful alternative.

In the account of the Creation the forming of the whale is specially dwelt upon: "And God created great whales and every living creature that moveth, which the **waters** brought forth abundantly after their kind." Luther, commenting on this, says that the creation of whales is specified by name, lest affrighted with their greatness we should believe them to be only visions or fancies. Though later commentators have decided that the leviathan of the Bible is the crocodile, it was long held to be the whale. Milton, in the first book of the "Paradise Lost," **writes of** that **sea beast—**

> "Leviathan, which God of all his works
> Created hugest that swim the ocean stream,"

and the Jews had a legend that the first whales were so immense in bulk, so formidable in attack, so voracious, that there was considerable risk of their overtoppling the rest of creation; so while as yet there were but two of them in existence, one was destroyed in order that the race might not be continued and the general balance of Nature upset.

Our ancestors found apt moral against the scornful in the reason assigned for the mouth **of the** flounder being on one side. It appears that at one time the flounder's mouth was as fair to see as any other, but that it lost all its beauty through contemptuous flouting of the herring, and it has borne this evil mark of its jealousy ever since, and will probably so bear it to the end of **time.** At **the** vague date known **as once** upon a time we are told that all the fishes of the sea assembled to choose a king, and that the herring was elected to this dignified position. The flounder, on account of his red spots and other features that were evidently more appreciated by himself than by the main body of electors, had strong hope that he should himself be chosen, and the unlovely grimace with which he saluted his sovereign was, as a judgment upon him, made a fixture for all time as a punishment to himself and a warning to others.

The tench was commonly called the physician, for it was believed by our forefathers that when the other fish were in any way hurt and required the aid of surgeon or physician, they healed themselves by rubbing against the tench, finding the slime of his body to be a "soveraigne salve" for their needs. For the sufferings of humanity the beasts, birds, and plants appear to have supplied a sufficient materia medica, and the less accessible creatures of the waters were but rarely pressed into the mediæval pharmacopœia. The blood of the eel was rubbed upon unwelcome warts, and a cruel remedy for bad eyes, the cruelty being, as we have seen over and over again in those old remedies, by no means an exceptional feature, was to capture a crab alive, cut out its eyes and then let it go.*
The eyes were then bound upon the neck of the man, woman, or child, and a satisfactory result was speedily anticipated, though very possibly not so speedily forthcoming.

The Cuttle fish is scarcely one's ideal of beauty, yet it is by its vanity and belief in its personal

* In Sussex no better remedy could be found for toothache than the application of a paw cut from a living mole.

attractions that it is most readily captured. **Porta** tells us that pieces of looking glass are let down by the fishermen into the waters, and that the Cuttle seeing his image reflected, clasps the glass around, and while he is still enamoured with the reflection of his charms is drawn to the surface by the wily fishermen. In the "Pathway to Knowledge," published in the year 1685, we are told that if we take the juice of Nettles and Houseleek, and anoint our hands therewith, the fish will gather round and "you may take them out at your pleasure." This seems almost as simple a method as the catching of birds by placing a pinch of salt on their tails.

If we may credit Maundevile, and the "if" is a most important point, in one favoured land instead of the people going for the fish, the fish come to the people. In a certain isle, or we may perhaps more truthfully say an uncertain isle, called Calonak, many wonderful things were to be seen, but one of these he especially, and very justly, calls "a gret Marvayle," and when he goes on to add that "it is more to speke of than in ony partie of the World," one is loath to gainsay his opinion. He tells us that "alle manere of Fissches that ther ben in the See abouten hem, comen ones in the Yeer, eche manere of dyverse Fissches, one maner of kynde aftre another; and thei casten hem selfe to the See Banke of that Yle in so gret plentee and multitude that no man may see but Fissche, and ther thei abyden thre dayes, and euerie man of the Countree takethe of hem als many as him lykethe, and that maner of Fissche aftre the thridde day departeth and gothe in to the See. And aftre hem comen another multitude of Fissches of anothre kynde and don in the same maner as the firste diden othre three dayes. And aftre hem another, tille alle the dyverse maner of Fissches have ben there, and that men have taken of hem that hem lykethe. And no man knowethe the cause wherfore it may ben. But thei of the Contree seyn that it is for to do reverence to here Kyng, that is the most worthi Kyng that is in the World, as thei seyn." The reason assigned for the king's special worthiness is a somewhat peculiar one, and though it is duly set forth at full length by the old author, other times have brought other manners and ideas, and one can scarcely insert in a book of the present day many things, and this amongst them, that were set forth in the greatest simplicity and directness of language in books of earlier date.

At all events this "most worthie Kyng" was so far under the special care of Providence that "God sendethe him so the Fissches of dyverse kyndes, of all that ben in the See, to be taken at his wille, for him and alle his peple. And therfore all the Fissches of the See comen to make him homage as the most noble and excellent Kyng of the World, and that is best beloved of God as thei seyn." Well may Maundevile say, as he realized the idea of the various finny tribes of Ocean thus sacrificing themselves in so orderly a sequence, that "this me semethe is the most

22

merveylle that evere I saughe. For this mervaylle is agenst kynde, that the Fissches that have fredom to environe all the Costes of the See at here owne list comen of hire owne wille to profren hem to the dethe with outen constreynynge of man." It must have been an immense convenience to have known thus readily what was in season, and even if in this Hobson's choice of diet one did not happen to be very partial to plaice or conger, there was always the happy knowledge that next Tuesday or possibly Thursday week, soles or turbot would be "in." We may conclude that a fresh series of herrings, mackerel, or whatever they might be, would come ashore on each one of the three days that they were due, or by the termination of that period they would certainly all be smelt.

After this great marvel the cruel pontarf that beguiled children away to sport with them and finally to eat them, the silurus that at the rising of the dog-star is struck insensible, the dead crabs that turn to scorpions, the eels that rub themselves against stones, and, in so doing, scrape off fragments that come to life, and are the only cause and means of their increase, the fish that swim in the boiling water of some tropical stream that is now unknown, all sink as wonders into insignificance.

The whole world has now been so ransacked that there is little room in these times for the imagination to play; but in mediæval days travellers brought back such wonderful stories, some of them true, and others, perhaps, a little wanting in that respect, of the things that they had seen, that almost anything seemed a possibility. Of this our present pages may be considered some little indication, though it will be abundantly evident that we have not used up one hundredth part of the great store of folk-lore and ancient and mediæval science that is open to investigation.

INDEX.

"Accedence of Armorie," 52, 121, 232
Acipenser, 330
Acosta, "travels in the Indies," 44
Acrid secretion in skin of toad, 281
"Actes of English votaries," 69
"Adam in Eden," 48
Adder, 173. Adder eaters, 77
Ælianus, works of, 95
Agriophagi, 72
Ague, specifics for, 172, 186, 309
Ainos of Japan, 61
Albert Nyanza in old maps, 13
Albertus Magnus, 160, 282
Alciatus, Book of Emblems, 84
Aldrovandus, 63, 272, 305, 316
Alectorius, 235, 247
All creation a moral text book, 51, 125
Ambrosinus, 316
Amphisbœna, 304
"Anatomy of Melancholy," 309
Anchor and Dolphin, 329
André on theory of Creation, 125
Andrew Marvel's "Loyal Scot," 69
Andromachus, physician to Nero, 299
Angulo or Hog-fish, 318
Animals in art and fable, 175
"Annals of Winchester," 269
Anthropophagi, 11, 72
Antipathies, animal, 94, 153, 182, 187, 230, 232, 280, 289
Antipathy and sympathy, 153
Ant's eggs, oil of, 278
Ants of India, 196

Ape, 122, 153
Apollo and Raven, 241
"Arcana Fairfaxiana," 279
Arena, lions in the, 123
"Areopagitica," 225
Ariosto, 207, 224
Aristotle, 30, 31, 55, 302
"Armonye of Byrdes," 239
Armories, Natural History in, 32, 51, 119, 120, 121
Arms of the City of London, 277
Art, animals in, 175
"Art of simpling," 188
Asbestos, its supposed nature, 293
Ashmole, diary of, 279
Askham on hare, 165
Asp, 51, 307
"As Pliny saith," 4, 20
Assyrian seals, 131
Astrological influences, 11
"As you like it," 206
Aubrey, extract from, 165, 179, 184, 238, 297
Augustine on higher and lower truths, 49
Authors consulted by Pliny, 26
Avicenna on chamæleon, 296
Azores in old map, 39

Bacci on unicorn, 131
Bacon's "Natural History," 166
Badge, panther, of King Henry VI., 151
Badger, 198
Bale on scandalous reports, 69
Ballasting of cranes and bees, 260

Index.

Bandicoot, 196
Barbary, lions of, 127
Barnacle goose, 214
Barnfield, "Cassandra," 287
Barrow, "Travels in Africa," 131
Bartholinus on unicorn, 131
Basilisk, 265, 286, 305
Bay-leaf as medicine, 274
Bearded grapes, 319
Bear, 161, 167, 182
Beaumont and Fletcher, 162, 176
Beaver, oil from the, 278
Bee, 260, 310
Beef, the praise of, 46
Beehives attacked by bears, 163
"Belvedere" of Bodenham, 170
Berens on unicorn, 131
"Bestiare Divin" of Guillaume, 48
Bestiaries of Middle Ages, 31, 50
Blackbird, Sagacity of, 177
Black Swan, 230
"Blazon of Gentrie," 119, 224
Blood of lion black, 116
Boar, 175
Bœwulf on Mermaid, 80
Boiling river, 43
"Bonduca," extract from, 162
"Book of Emblems," 84
"Book of Knowledge," Winstanley, 183, 248
Boorde's "Dyetary," 46
Bosjesmen, ancient Troglodytes, 3, 61
Bossewell's "Armorie," 52, 169, 194
Bostock on Pliny, 29
Browne on Vulgar Errors, 56, 92, 106, 157, 162, 178, 205, 255, 267, 284, 313, 328
Buffon on Pliny, 21
Burton, "Miracles of Art and Nature," 18, 19, 127, 131, 305
Bussy d'Amboise on Unicorn, 130
Butler, Hudibras, extract from, 214
Byron, extract from, 229, 330

Cabbage, the praise of, 47
Camel, 182, 198, 294
Camelopardilis, 124

Camerarius on dolphin, 329
Camillus, mirror of stones," 247
Cammetennus, 294
Camoens, extract from, 181
Camphor-tree, 152
Cancer, specific for, 189
Canibali, home of the, 37
"Canterbury Tales," 276
Capture of elephant, 145
Carbuncle borne by dragon, 274
Carew, extract from, 164
Carlyle on books, 33
Carrier pigeons, 16
Cartazonos, 130
"Cassandra," extract from, 287
"Castle of Memory," 166
Cat, 168, 189
Catelan on Unicorn, 131
Cathay, palace at, 151
Catoblepas, 197
Centaur, 79, 294
Cerastes or horned viper, 298, 304
Ceylon, mermaids of, 88
"Ceylon, Natural History of," 196
Chameleon, 136, 178, 274, 296
Chanticleer, 239
Chares on Theriaca, 299
Chaucer, extract from, 11, 30
Chelidonius, 247
Chelonites of Porta, 283
Chester's "Love's Martyr," 170
"Childe Harold's Pilgrimage," 330
Chinese referred to by Pliny, 28
Churchyard grass, remedial virtues of, 189
Cinirius, 124
Cinnabar, how produced, 137
Coats, extract from, 120, 194
Cobbe on the creation of monsters, 145
Cobra stone, 298
Coca plant, properties of, 18
Cock, 154, 232, 238
Cock-ale, 234
Cockatrice, 236, 267
Cockeram's Dictionary, 288
Cockle, 196
Cogan, "Haven of Health," 45, 167, 231, 277, 301
Coleridge on Nightingale, 252

Cole's "Adam in Eden," 48. "Art of simpling," 188
Colours of dying dolphin, 330
Comets like blazing swords, 319
Composition of Venice Treacle, 229
Coney-fish, 209
Convulsions, remedy for, 167, 186
Coolness of blood of elephant, 149
Cornishmen tailed, 68
Corvia, 247
Cos, dragon of, 110
"Cosmography," Munster's, 34, 97, 127, 130, 139, 149, 220
Crabs' eyes a remedy, 235, 335
Crabs generating scorpions, 297
Crane, 56, 260
Crapaudine, or toad stone, 281
Creatures of the fire, 295
Crippled feet of Chinese ladies, 15
Crocodile, 286, 294
Crocuta, 124
Cross on donkey's back, 184, 186
Crow, sagacity of, 177
Cruelty in preparation of recipes, 48, 248, 335
Ctesias on griffin, 276; on unicorn, 130
Cubs of bear a shapeless mass, 161
Cuckoo broth, 235
Culverwort, 16
"Curiosities of Heraldry," 237
"Cursor Mundi," extract from, 242
Cuttlefish, 335
Cuvier on phœnix, 204; on Pliny, 21
"Cymbeline," extract from, 208
Cynamolgi, 72

Dagon, the fish god, 93
Daily Post, advertisement from, 90
Dallaway on unicorn, 133
Dead animals generating other creatures, 311
Dead men's bones, oil from, 278
Deaf as an adder, 303
"De Animalibus" of Aristotle, 31
Death song of the swan, 229
Death-dealing cocatrice, 237

Decker on unicorn's horn, 134
Deer, 173, 270
"De Humana Physiognomica," 78
"De Miraculis," story from, 108
Democritus on serpent generation, 307
Derceto, 97
De Thaun, "Bestiary" of, 50, 124, 132, 185, 204, 292
Devil's-bird, 241
"De Virtutibus Herbarum," 160
Diamond dissolving, 178
Differences in aim in zoological study, 4
Digby, "The Closet Open," 234
"Dirge," extract from Gay's, 241
Dioscorides, writings of, 95
"Discoverie of witchcraft," 113
"Display of Heraldrie," Guillim, 52, 120
Divining rod in use, 37
Doctrine of Signatures, 251
Dodœns, extract from, 309
Dog, 8, 119, 187, 189, 270, 316
Dog-headed men, 11, 42, 72
Dog-king, 73
Dolphin, 83, 289, 327
Donkey, 184, 188
Double-bodied animals, 65
Dove, 177, 240
Draconites, 247
Dragon, 268, 274
Dragon-maiden, 110
Dragon and elephant, feud between, 136, 147
Drayton, extract from, 250, 253, 259
Dropsy, remedy for, 298
Drunkenness, to avert, 249
Dryden, extract from, 161, 165, 224, 227, 259, 281
Du Bartas on barnacle-goose, 218
Du Chaillu on gorilla, 3; on pygmies, 60
Dulness of hearing, remedy for, 308
Dust of Malta a remedy, 300
"Dyetary" of Boorde, 46

Eagle, 108, 223, 240, 276

Index.

Eale of Ethiopia, 197
Earless animals, 74
Earthworms in medicine, 279
Eastern love of the wonderful, 213
Eastern Travels of John of Hesse, 81
Eel's blood for warts, 335
Eels from hairs, 182
Effects of climate on human tail growth, 71
Egyptians and the ass, 185
Einhorn, 130
El Dorado of Raleigh, 44
Elephant, 36, 107, 135, 177, 182, 213, 274, 294, 323
Elephant-headed boy, 64
Elizabeth, portrait of Queen, 176
Ellison, "Trip to Benwell," 165
"Emblemes and Epigrames," 210
"Emblems" of Witney, 136
England, first elephant seen in, 142
Epilepsy, cure for, 173, 190
Ermine, the spotless, 176
Ethiopia, land of marvels, 73, 146, 276
"Euphues," extract from, 262, 281
"Evangeline," extract from, 247, 279
Evil spirit in donkey, 185
Eye-bright for the sight, 48, 298

Fable, animals in, 175
"Fairie Queen," extract from, 80, 113, 129
Fakirs of India mentioned by Pliny, 28
Famous horses of antiquity, 181
Fascination, power of, 285
Fennel, value of, 47
Fenton on toad stone, 282
Ferne, "Blazon of Gentrie," 119, 224
Ferret, 173, 309
Feuds, animal, 129, 136
Filial love of storks, 259
Fishes choosing a king, 334
Fletcher on phœnix, 207
Flounder the wry-mouthed, 334

Fondness of dolphin for man, 328
Forget-me-not, 251, 277
Formosa men with tails, 70, 71
Four-eyed men, 74
Four-footed ducks and pigeons, 65
Four-legged serpents, 306
Fox, 167
Foxglove, 251
Freckles, cure for, 166
Frenzel on Unicorn, 131
Frog, 189, 278, 281, 308
Fulgentius on note of Raven, 242
Fuller, extracts from, 117

Galen, prescription of, 291
"Garden of the Muses," extract from, 170
Garnier, the loup-garou, 108
Gay, extract from, 184, 241
Geliot's "Indice Armorial," 120
Gentleman's Magazine, extract from, 93
Geranites, 247
Gerarde, extract from, 214, 309
Gesner's "History of Animals," 129
Giants, 75
Gift of eloquence, To acquire, 249
Gift of invisibility, 235
Gilbert White's "Selborne," 180
Glanvil, assertions of, 113, 276, 290
Glow-worm, 257
Goat, 177, 234, 331
"Golden Gem for Geometricians," 262
Gonzale on monstrous men, 79
Gorilla mentioned by Hanno, 3, 67
Gosse, "Romance of Natural History," 86
Gout, remedy for, 244, 246, 278
Gray, oil from the, 278
Great-lipped men, 76
Green lizards in mediæval recipe, 8
Grimalkin, 192
Guiana of Sir W. Raleigh, 44
Guillaume, "Bestiare Divin" of, 48

Guillim's "Display of Heraldrie,"
  52, 120, 132, 176, 243
Gujerat, lions of, 124

Hairy men, 67. Hairy serpents, 306
Hakluyt's "Voyages," 44
Halcyone, myth of, 258
Halle on knowledge for Chirurgeons, 12
"Hamlet," extract from, 228
Hanno's pursuit of gorilla, 3, 67, 68
Hare, 8, 164, 165, 184
Harpy, 64, 146
Hartebeest, 124
"Haven of Health," Cogan's, 45, 167, 231, 277, 301
Hawkweed, 248
Headless men, 34, 65, 75
Heberden's "Antitheriaca," 299
Hedgehog, 168, 256
Hentzner on horn of unicorn, 134
Heraldic animals, 83, 127, 276, 328
Herbert's book of travels, 39, 176
Herb-tea in the Spring, 274
Herodotus, writings of, 30
Herring, the king of fishes, 334
Herschell on love of books, 32
Heylin, travels of, 42
Heywood on stork, 259
"Hind and Panther," extract from, 161, 165
Hippeau on theological treatment, 6, 49
Hippocampus, 314
Hippopotamus, 118, 143, 149, 314
"Histoire des Anomalies" of St. Hilaire, 62
"Historia Naturalis" of Jonston, 130
"Historie of Plants," Gerarde, 214
"History of America," Robertson, 79
"History of Animals," Gesner, 129
"History of Serpents and Dragons," Aldrovandus, 272
Hog-fish, 209, 318
Holland, English version of Pliny, 29

Hollerius on snake stone, 298
Homer on eagle, 225; on pygmies, 55
Hoopoe, stone from, 247
Horned men, 76, 294
Horned viper, 298
Hornets from dead mule, 311
Horn of unicorn, 133, 324
Horse, 181, 189, 236, 270, 276, 294, 297
Horse-shoe, 184
Hound's-tongue, value of, 188
Howling of dogs an evil omen, 188
How serpents are developed, 297
How tempests may arise, 321
How the raven became black, 241
How to procure toad-stone, 283
Hudibras, quotation from, 162, 214
Hudson on mermaids, 85
Humble bees from dead ass, 311
Hyæna, 152, 156; Men turned into, 104
Hydrophobia, treatment of, 189, 234
"Hymn on the Nativity," Milton, 258

Iliad, extract from, 225
Incubators mentioned by Jordanus, 15
Indian customs mentioned by Pliny, 28
"Indice Armorial," 120
Indifference to animal suffering, 48, 167, 248, 335
Inhabitants of the sea-depths, 313
Insomnia, specific for, 177
Instances of sagacity in birds, 177
Invisibility, gift of, 245, 297
Ipotayne, half-man, half-horse, 79
Izaak Walton, extract from, 209

Jaguars, men turned to, 104
Jaundice, specific for, 189
Java, home of the pygmies, 58
Jewel-bearing toad, 281
Job on the eagle, 224

John of Hesse, travels of, 81
Jonson's "Historia Naturalis," 130
Jordanus, extract from, 13, 58, 73, 196, 213, 274
Juggernaut, 15
"Julius Cæsar," extract from, 130
Jumar, 124

Keen sight of eagle, 225
Kentish men tailed, 68, 69
Kingfisher, 255
"King Henry IV.," extract from, 166, 254
"King Henry VI.," extract from, 161, 208, 224, 246, 266, 296, 304
"King Henry VIII.," extract from, 286
"King Lear," extract from, 254
King of beasts; 116, of birds, 232; of fishes, 334; of serpents, 266
Kite, sagacity of, 177
"Knight of Malta," extract from, 176

Lady loup-garou, 109
Lalla Rookh, extract from, 210
Lamia, 294
Lamb-tree, 223
Land of the pygmies, 57
Landseer's animal painting, 175
Language of beasts, to learn, 42
Lapwing, 177
Lark, sagacity of, 177
Larva of tiger-moth, 306
Laterrade on the unicorn, 131
Lavender as a remedy, 301
Legend of the robin, 250
Legh, "Accidence of Armorie," 52, 121, 144, 178, 187, 242
Leo, "History of Africa," 158, 271
Leontophonos, 128
Leopards, men turned to, 104
Leviathan, 334
Licking little bears into shape, 161
Lightning, protection against, 258
Like to like, 300
Lily, "Euphues" of, 281
Lion, 116, 232, 270, 276, 294, 303, 310

Lipless men, 73
"Livre des Creatures" of De Thaun, 50, 124
Lizard, 8, 296
Lomie, 197
Long-eared men, 42, 77
Long-headed men, 78
Longfellow, extract from, 247, 279
Loup-garou, 108
Love of the marvellous, 10
"Love's Martyr" of Chester, 170
"Loyal Scot" of Andrew Marvel, 69
Luminous ink, 312
Lupton, extract from, 282
"Lusiad" of Camoens, 181
Luther on whale, 334
Lycanthropy, 101

"Macbeth," extract from, 192
Macaulay on books, 32
"Maccabees," extract from, 145
Macer on fennel, 47
Mad as a March hare, 165, 166
Mad dog, 9
"Magick of Kirani," 251, 270
Maneless lions, 123
Manticora, 156, 197
Manufacture of mermaids, 91; of pygmies, 58
Maori traditions, 61
"Mappæ Clavicula," extract from, 182
Marcellus, cure of blindness, 248
Marco Polo, travels of, 40, 144, 211
Marlowe, extract from, 241, 255
Marmalade for students, 46
Martin's "Philosophical Grammar, 132
Marvellous Isle of Dondum, 75
Matthew Prior, drawing of elephant, 143
Maundevile, extract from, 15, 16, 110, 138, 147, 151, 195, 202, 244, 276, 308, 336
Mauritius veal, 89
Medical zoology, 4, 45
Mediæval theory of creation, 125
Melancholia, its cause, 166

Men who lived on odours, 58, 75
Mendez Pinto the marvellous, 41
Mermaid, 79, 80, 313
Matacollinarum, 294
"Merchant of Venice," extract from, 54, 192, 229
"Metamorphoses," Ovid, 101
Metempsychosis, 107
Mewing nuns, 105
"Midsummer night's dream," extract from, 83
Milton, extract from, 226, 253, 258, 334
"Miracles of Art and Nature," extract from, 18, 19
"Mirror for Mathematics," 262
Mirror of stones, 247
Mithridate, 299
Mole, 168, 172, 335
Monoceros, 130
"Monstrorum Historia" of Aldrovandus, 63
Moon-worshipping elephants, 139
Moore, Extract of, 210
Moral-pointing treatment of zoology, 4, 6, 173, 244, 287, 293
Moss from dead man's skull, 278
Moufflon in Munster's book, 35
Mouse, 137, 167, 194
Mouthless men, 75, 76
Munster's "Cosmography," 34, 97, 127, 130, 139, 149, 220, 306
Music, dolphins love of, 330
Musinus, 129
Mussel, 196
Mutianus on monkeys, 139

Narwhal tusk, 324
"Natural History," Bacon's, 166
"Natural History of Norway," 87
"Natural History of Selborne," 180
"Natural Magick," 154
"New Jewell of Health," 277
Nightingale, 251
Nile represented in old maps, 13, 36
Noah and the raven, 242
Noseless men, 73

Oannes the fish-god, 96
Odin's wolf, 157
Oil of swallows, 249
Oils of medicinal repute, 278
Olaus Magnus, writings of, 106, 320, 333
Omens from animals, 164
One-legged men, 42, 294
"Orlando Furioso," extract from, 207, 304
"Ortus Sanitatis," extract from, 280
Oryges, 197
Ostrich devouring iron, 231
"Othello," Extract from, 241, 287
Ovid, the "Metamorphoses" of, 101
Owl, 246
Oxford life in the year 1636, 46
Oyster, the susceptible, 196

Panther, 149, 232
"Paradise lost," extract from, 334
Parkinson, on barnacle goose, 219
Parrot-fish, 209
Parsee funeral customs, 13
"Pathway to Knowledge," extract from, 312, 336
Peacock, 240, 254
Pearl-fish, 332
Pegasus, 324
Pelican, 227, 240
Percy Society Publications, 240
Performing elephants, 138
"Periplus" of Hanno, 67
Philomela, 252
"Philosophical Grammar," Martin, 132
Philostratus on pygmies, 55
Phisiologus on the mermaid, 80
Phœnix, 200, 240, 294
Physician-tench, 335
Pietro del Porco, 176
Pillars of Hercules, 36
Pinto, liar of first magnitude, 41
Plagiarism, 45
Playmate, dragon as a, 275
Pliny's "Natural History," 21, 95, 123, 150, 246

Plutarch, quotation from, 37
Poison fish, 209
Polypus and the significance thereof, 4, 5
Pomphagi, 72
Pontarf, 338
Pontoppidan, writings of, 87
"Poor Robin's Almanack," extract from, 170
Pope on learned blockheads, 33
Porta, extract from, 78, 122, 124, 152, 154, 160, 172, 182, 233, 283, 295, 300
Potter's " Booke of Phisicke," 45
Powdered mummy, 278
Praise of method, 53
Prawn, 332
Prester John, kingdom of, 293
" Pseudodoxia Epidemica," 92
" Purchas his Pilgrimage," 44, 318
Pygmies, 54, 294
Pyragones, 295

"Quentin Durward," extract from, 157

Rabbit, 119
Raleigh, Sir Walter, on Guiana, 44
Ram, 198. Ram-headed man, 64
Rat, 194, 196, 282
Raven, 177, 241. Raven-stone, 244
Ray, its love for man, 331
Reginald Scot, " Discoverie of Witchcraft," 113
Rejuvenescence of the eagle, 226
Relentless asp, 307
" Remaines of Gentilisme and Judaisme," 165, 298
Remedies for hydrophobia, 189
Remora, 326
Rheumatism, remedy for, 167
" Rich Jew of Malta," extract from, 241
Rings bearing toad-stone, 281
Robbers checkmated, 9
Robertson, " History of America," 79
Robin, 249

Rochester rudeness to A Becket, 68, 69
Roc or Rukh, 211
" Romance of Natural History," Gosse, 86
Roman mosaic at Brading, 98
" Romeo and Juliet," extract from, 192
Rondoletius, book of, 319
Roulet, the loup-garou, 109

Sachs on unicorn, 131
"Saducismus Triumphatus," 113
Sagacity of the crane, 261
Salamander, 154, 209, 290
Sargon, 331
"Savage Africa," Winwood Reade, 61
Sciatica, specific for, 182
Scoresby on mermaids, 84
Scorpion, 9, 277, 278, 302, 338
Scorpion-grass, 251, 277
Scots Magazine, extract from, 87
Screech-owl, 108
Sea elephant, 323
Sea horse, 314
Seal, Greek superstition respecting, 289
Serpent, 173, 178, 236, 267
Serpentine monstrosities, 305
Shakespeare, extract from, 11, 32, 54, 55, 130, 173, 180, 192, 208, 228, 229, 241, 246, 253, 254, 255, 266, 277, 291, 296, 304
Shakespeare on learning, 33
Sheep as great as oxen, 76
Shelley on nightingale, 253
" Ship of Fools," 39
Shoney, the storm-dog, 191
Shrew-ash, 180
Shrew-mouse, 179, 234
Silkworm, 312
Silurus, 338
Single-footed men, 20
Sir Emerson Tennant on travellers' tales, 2
" Six Pastorals," extract from, 250
Skelton's poem on birds, 240
Sleeplessness, to cause, 251
Snail-shells as houses, 308

Snake charmers mentioned by Pliny, 29
Song of the nightingale, 252
Southey, extract from, 232
"**Speculum** Mundi," extract from, 5, 81, 88, 131, 133, 144, 180, **194**, 227, 229, 252, 265, 266, 287, 320
"Speculum Regale," 86
Speechless men, 73
Spenser, quotation from, 80, 113, 129, 150, 226, 240, 281, 286; 301, 326, 327
Sphinx, 146
Spider, 279, 282, 308
Squirrel, 174
Stag-wolf, 160
Stanley rediscovering pygmies, 3, **60**
Stellion, 154
Stolbergh on unicorn, 131
Stone in lapwing's nest, 8
Stones of magic virtue, 247
Stork, 259
Storm-raisers, **191**
Strabo on the pygmies, 55
Strewing herbs, 302
Struy's voyages and travels, 44, 70
Subjects dealt with by Pliny, 22
Sucking fish or remora, 326
"Survey of Cornwall," extract from, 164
Sus Marinus, 317
Suttee an ancient usage, **14**
Swallow, 8, 240, 247, 260
Swallow-wort, 248
Swam-fish, 333
Swan-song, 228
Swift, quotation from, **37**
Symbol of resurrection, 203
Sympathy and antipathy, **153**
Syrens, 82

Tacitus on phœnix, 201
Tailed men, 43, 68, 69
"Tale of a Tub," Swift, **37**
"Taming of the Shrew," **extract** from, 180
Tavernier on bird of paradise, 210

Tears of the crocodile, 286
Teasel-heads, 309
"Tempest," extract from, 79, **209**
Tench, the physician fish, 335
Tennant on works of ancient travellers, 2
Tensevetes, 294
Ten-tailed lizard, **63**
"Theater of plants," 219
Theocritus on halycon calm, **258**
Theologians, a study of zoology, **4**
Theriaca, 299
Thoes, 124
"Thousand notable things," 282
Three-eyed men, 74
Three-headed monster, 65
Thynne's "Book of Emblems," 210
Tiger, 118, 198. Tiger-men, 104
"Timon of Athens," extract from, 130
Titian, device of, 161
Title-pages full of interest, old, **6, 34, 272**
Titles of old books, 12
Toad, 236, 274, 279, 308
Toad-stone, 281
Toad-wort, 280, 298
To catch Sargi, 331
Tooth-ache, remedy for, 335
Topsell, **extract** from, 165, **168**, 171, 179, **280**
Torpedo, 257
Tortoise, sagacity of, 178
Tradescant's museum, 209
Transfer of valuable animal properties to man, 8
Travellers' tales, 3, 338
"Travels in Africa," Barrow, 131
Travels of Le Gouz, 326
Treachery of the shrew mouse, **179**
"**Trip to** Benwell," extract from, 165
Troglodytes mentioned by Pliny and others, 3
"**Troilus** and Cressida," extract from, 304
Tusser's "Husbandry," **301**

"Two Gentlemen of Verona," extract from, 296
Two-headed animals, 65

Unchangeableness of old customs, 13, 28
Urcheon, urchin, or hedgehog, 169
Use of elephant in war, 137

Value of personal observation, 199
"Varia Historia," extract from, 95
Venice treacle, 9, 299
Venomous men, 43
Versipillis, the skin-turner, 106
Vervain in recipe, 8
Victoria Nyanza in old maps, 13
Viper in medicine, 298, 299
Virgil on bees, 261, 311
"Voiage and Travaile" of Maundevile, 15, 16, 110, 138, 202, 308

Warder, Dr., on bees, 261
Wart, to cure, 182, 190
Wasps from dead horse, 311

Waters of Lethe, 99
Weasel, 119, 188, 296, 318
Weather prognostics, 82, 170
Weeping of deer, 173
Wehr-wolves, 99, 104
Whales pacified with tubs, 37, 39
When venison should be avoided, 173
Whitney's "Emblems," 136
Whooping cough, remedy for, 163, 186, 188, 308
Why bears attack bee-hives, 163
Winstanley's "Book of Knowledge," 183, 248, 312
Wolf, 8, 118, 154, 157, 182
Wolf-headed man, 79
Wondrous beasts of mediæval fancy, 197
Woolly bear, 306
Wren, 249
Wright's translation of De Thaun, 50

Xenophon on boar, 175

Ylio of De Thaun, 51
Yule's translation of Jordanus, 14

G. NORMAN AND SON, PRINTERS, FLORAL STREET, COVENT GARDEN.

May, 1895.

Valuable Books on Sale

BY

BERNARD QUARITCH,

15 *Piccadilly, London, W.*

MR. WILLIAM MORRIS'S PRODUCTIONS
of the KELMSCOTT PRESS.

THE GOLDEN LEGEND. Translated by
WILLIAM CAXTON. 3 vols. large 4to., *printed with the type specially cut from Mr. Morris's patterns, with ornamental letters and borders designed by William Morris, and* 2 *full-page woodcuts from designs by* E. BURNE-JONES, bds., £5. 5s   1892

THE RECUYELL OF THE HISTORIES
of TROYE. Translated by WILLIAM CAXTON. A new Edition of the First Book printed in English, black letter, 2 vols. sm. folio, *in black and red, vellum*, £7. 7s   1893

THE HISTORYE OF REYNARD THE
FOXE. Translated from the Dutch by WILLIAM CAXTON. Reprinted from the edition of 1481, sm. folio, 4to., black letter, *vellum*, £4. 4s   1893

—— the above three works, of which but few copies remain, if bought in one transaction, £15.

THE BOOK OF WISDOM AND LIES.
Translated by Oliver Wardrop from the original of Sulkhan-Saba Orbeliani. 8vo., 250 *printed in black and red, vellum,* £2. 2s   1894

A BOOK OF TRADITIONAL STORIES from GEORGIA, *in Asia.*

THE SAGA LIBRARY. By William Morris,
Author of "The Earthly Paradise," with the assistance of EIRIKR
MAGNUSSON, crown 8vo. *Roxburghe* 1890-93

> Each Volume, 7s 6d; or LARGE PAPER, royal 8vo., *hf. bd. morocco*, £1. 11s 6d
>
> Vol. I.: 1. STORY OF HOWARD THE HALT; 2. STORY OF THE BANDED MEN; 3. THE STORY OF HEN THORIR, 7s 6d   1891
>
> Vol. II: THE EYRBIGGIA SAGA, or, The Story of the Ere Dwellers, with the Story of the Heath-Slayings, with notes and three Indexes, 7s 6d   1892
>
> Vol. III.: THE HEIMSKRINGLA, or, The Stories of the Kings of Norway, called the Round World (Heimskringla), done into English out of the Icelandic, Vol. I, *with a large map of Norway*, 7s 6d   1893
>
> Vol. IV.: THE HEIMSKRINGLA, Vol. II, 7s 6d   1894
>
> The Purchaser of the Large Paper issue binds himself to take the entire Series.
> The Large Paper issue consists of 125 numbered copies, printed by **hand-press**, on Whatman Paper, at Whittingham's Chiswick Press.

BEWICK (Thomas) WORKS:
The Memorial Edition of the Works of THOMAS BEWICK, in five vols, royal 8vo., *cloth, uncut*, £5. 5s   1885-87

> Vols. I, II. History of British Birds; Land Birds and Water Birds, with the woodcuts of the Supplements incorporated, 2 vols.
>
> Vol. III. History of Quadrupeds, 1 vol.
>
> Vol. IV. Æsop's Fables, 1 vol.
>
> Vol. V. Memoir of Thomas Bewick, written by himself, with numerous woodcuts prepared for a projected History of British Fishes, 1 vol.

BLAKE (William) WORKS: Poetic, Symbolic, and Critical. Edited, with Lithographs of the Illustrated "Prophetic Books" and a Memoir, by EDWIN JOHN ELLIS, *Author of* "*Fate in Arcadia,*" *etc*, and WILLIAM BUTLER YEATS, *Author of the* "*Wandering of Oisin,*" "*The Countess Kathleen,*" *etc.*, 3 vols. large 8vo., with *portraits and* 290 *Facsimiles of Blake's privately-printed and coloured works, symbolical cloth binding,* £3. 3s   1893

────── The same, Large Paper, 3 vols. 4to.
half bound morocco, gilt top, £4. 14s 6d   1893

www.ingramcontent.com/pod-product-compliance
Lightning Source LLC
Chambersburg PA
CBHW031426230426
43668CB00007B/446